Contents

Preface

Once upon a time, a bit more than 30 years ago—I stood in the same position as you—the first termer. I had no idea what the Army was about, and, outside a few wise old sergeants who thought to give me the time of day, the only way I could learn about the Army was to experience it. And yes, over a career spanning 30 years there were ups and downs, with the ups far outweighing the downs. However, I will admit that at every reenlistment or extension I thought of voting with my feet. Something changed over time and I stayed on. The camaraderie, the different duty assignments and countries. After a while it was not The Army, it was my Army. This book is dedicated to the first termer from one of those hopefully wise old sergeants.

I edited the *Enlisted Soldier's Guide* to provide information that I wanted to know when I was a first termer and what I wanted *my* soldiers to know when I was a sergeant major. As a reference tool, the guide can help soldiers better understand the Army and their roles in it. It includes information about promotion to noncommissioned officer (NCO) rank, uniformed service standards and systems, programs and services, policies and opportunities, soldiers' rights and military law, and other topics soldiers must understand, relate to, and effectively deal with each duty day.

This edition of *Enlisted Soldier's Guide* is directly aligned with an associated Stackpole Books publication, *NCO Guide, 7th Edition.* All chapters of this guide relate to chapters in *NCO Guide.* I mention the relationship between *Enlisted Soldier's Guide* and *NCO Guide* because of the natural relationship between junior soldiers and NCOs. A noncommissioned officer's primary duty is to train junior soldiers to take their place, and a junior soldier's duty is to learn what it takes to measure up to earn sergeant's stripes.

Soldiers must handle progressively more authority and responsibility as they work toward becoming leaders and supervisors in the NCO corps. This edition of *Enlisted Soldier's Guide* is an educational resource and ready reference to key Army subjects that will assist soldiers in their initial years. It draws from education, experience, training, and hundreds of sources. The guide begins with discussion of how and why the Army continues to change and ends a ready reference guide. *Enlisted Soldier's Guide* serves the reader when fellow soldiers have questions about pay, benefits, entitlements, personal appearance, uniforms, and insignia. It also contains aids that quickly lead soldiers to official or other publications that may contain updates. This edition of *Enlisted Soldier's Guide* has reformed content and improved relevancy. All new material was tightly composed and edited to contain less mundane detail, flow more logically, and be more readable and indispensable.

The sixth edition contains new or updated information about how to be a better soldier: how to improve marksmanship and PT scores, as well as obtain promotion points for military and civilian education. It also addresses sensitive contemporary Army issues, such as professional ethics, fraternization, AIDS, discrimination, sexual harassment, and homosexuality, and includes a professional reading and multimedia list. Readers will also find sections on promotions, assignments, uniforms, the military justice system, as well as how to make the most of a transition from service to civilian life.

As our Army continues to change to counter evolving regional threats, as our federal government makes service attractive by offering education and other incentives, as soldiers aim for professional goals, as uniformed traditions remain intact, and as hard career decisions continue to be made, *Enlisted Soldier's Guide* will continue to do its duty. Much of the information in this guide is timeless; that which is not was current at the time of publication. Policies, procedures, regulations, systems, and other aspects of service life change regularly. Remember that nothing is sacred, to include this book, and ensure that when in doubt check the regulation.

This book is what I needed thirty years ago when I was a young soldier. I sincerely hope it serves you in good stead.

Deeds, Not Words

Robert S. Rush
CSM, USA (Ret.)

Acknowledgments

Hallelujah for the Internet! By using the many sites available to all soldiers, I was able to ensure that the latest information is included in this update. Many sites contributed to this revision, including the following: Department of the Army; Department of Veterans Affairs; Defense Activity for Nontraditional Education Support; Army Family Advocacy Program; Army Community Services; Civilian Health and Medical Program of the Uniformed Services; American Forces Information Service; Total Army Personnel Command; Enlisted Records and Evaluation Center; Army Career and Alumni Program; Training and Doctrine Command; Army and Air Force Exchange Service; Army Training Support Center; Association of the United States Army; Office of the Chief of Public Affairs; Defense Finance and Accounting Service; and Department of Education.

The following organizations also contributed: Noncommissioned Officers Association; U.S. Army Fitness School; Army News Service; *SOLDIERS* magazine; *NCO Journal;* Army Continuing Education Services; Army Safety Center; Army Family Liaison Office; Judge Advocate General's Corps; DOD Still Media Records Center; the Center of Military History; and the Army Community and Family Support Center.

I am indebted to my Stackpole editors for their professional support and guidance during production of the *Enlisted Soldier's Guide, 6th Edition.* I also want to thank all those old sergeants and officers who had faith and much forbearance with a soldier who spoke his mind perhaps a bit too often. Lastly, I thank my wife, Edith, for everything she has done and the support she has shown not only toward this project, but to the many years she put up with a ragged old ranger who was seldom home. Without her, I would have failed before I had even started.

Code of Conduct

For Members of the Armed Forces of the United States

Serving our country as a member of the armed forces is the noblest public service a citizen of the United States can perform. Since 1955, American soldiers have memorized this Code, which defines the essence of military service and the high standards required of men and women in the military service.

I.

I am an American, fighting in the forces which guard my country and our way of life. I am prepared to give my life in their defense.

II.

I will never surrender of my own free will. If in command, I will never surrender my men while they still have the means to resist.

III.

If I am captured, I will continue to resist by all means available. I will make every effort to escape and aid others to escape. I will accept neither parole nor special favors from the enemy.

IV.

If I become a prisoner of war, I will keep faith with my fellow prisoners. I will give no information or take part in any action which might be harmful to my comrades. If I am senior, I will take command. If not, I will obey the lawful orders of those appointed over me and will back them up in every way.

V.

When questioned, should I become a prisoner of war, I am required to give name, rank, service number, and date of birth. I will evade answering further questions to the utmost of my ability. I will make no oral or written statements disloyal to my country and its allies or harmful to their cause.

VI.

I will never forget that I am an American, fighting for freedom, responsible for my actions, and dedicated to the principles which made my country free. I will trust in my God and in the United States of America.

PART I

The Army

1

The Army of
the Twenty-first Century

Serving in today's all-volunteer Army is one of the finest forms of public service an American citizen can do. Today's Army has 480,000 men and women on active duty, another 357,000 in the National Guard, and still another 206,000 in the Army Reserve. In all, about 1 million soldiers wear the Army uniform either full-time or part-time.

Since the Spanish-American War at the end of the nineteenth century, over 41 million Americans have served in the armed forces at home and abroad. There are nearly 26 million veterans alive today. Throughout our history, 24 of our 42 presidents have had military service, and of that number, 17 served in the Army, 10 of whom were generals. Within the last half century, only one president did not serve in the military.

To be a soldier is to be a member of a highly respected profession. Public opinion polls have repeatedly shown that the armed forces have the highest trust and confidence of the American people. The country knows military service is tough duty, with high risk and many hardships, and that our soldiers are dedicated to getting the job done—a job that amounts to nothing less than being the defenders of our nation's highest and most important interests.

ARMY HISTORY

The Army's high reputation is due to the professionalism of the soldiers who served in it from the days of its creation over 225 years ago. The American Army was created on June 14, 1775, when the Continental Congress first authorized the muster of troops to serve under its authority. Those soldiers came from the provincial forces of the colonies, which were at that time laying siege to Boston. From its birth, the American Army has relied on the citizen-soldier, exemplified by the militia and the Minutemen who fought the British at Lexington and Concord. Commanded by General George Washington and supported by our French allies, the Continental Army defeated the British at Yorktown and secured the freedoms so eloquently stated in the Declaration of Independence. Thus, the birth of the Army preceded and guaranteed the birth of the nation.

The Army on Parade—Yesterday and Today

The Army's fundamental purpose is to fight and win the nation's wars by establishing conditions for lasting peace through land force dominance. This dominance is established through integration of the complementary capabilities of all the services. With this fundamental purpose in mind, the framers of the Constitution intended that armies be raised to "provide for the common defense" and, together with the Navy, to "repel invasion." The Army raised for the nation's defense incorporates two uniquely American ideas: civilian control of the armed forces, and reliance on the citizen-soldier. Over the years, the organization and structure of the Army have adapted to each challenge the nation has faced, but these basic ideas have remained unchanged. Throughout the formative years of the nation, the Army responded—on the frontiers, in the War of 1812, in the war with Mexico—in fulfillment of this role. During the Civil War, the Army was called upon to support another clause of the Constitution, to "suppress insurrection." As the nation became a colonial power following the Spanish-American War, the Army was called upon to secure and administer the new territories.

When the United States became a world power in the twentieth century, the Army was called upon to defend our national interests and rights on a wider scale, which drew us into alliances in regions far removed from our shores. In the combat operations of the World Wars, in Korea, Vietnam, Panama, the Persian Gulf, and today in Iraq and Afghanistan, the Army has responded to the call to duty and performed that duty well. In the 40-odd years of Cold War, in many locations around the world, the Army performed a deterrent role as part of the containment strategy. In other places, at other times, the Army fulfilled the nation's expectations in operations too small to be called "wars," although no less dangerous. The Army's deployment is the surest sign of America's commitment to accomplishing any mission that occurs on land. To the soldiers on the ground, operations in Grenada (1983), Panama (1989), Kuwait and Iraq (1991), Afghanistan (2002), and Iraq (2003) are indistinguishable from the combat operations of their forefathers. Operations in Somalia, Haiti, Bosnia, and Kosovo, although peace operations, also have been or may prove to be dangerous. However, like those who went before them, American soldiers responded readily in fulfilling the unlimited-liability aspect of their contract. Knowing that simply joining the Army demands a willingness to place one's life at risk, many have joined and made the ultimate sacrifice.

At the time of publication, the United States is at war with terrorism, with soldiers serving in far-flung corners of the globe. The global Al Qaeda terrorist network remains the most immediate and serious threat to the United States. Since 1998, Bin Ladin has declared all U.S. citizens legitimate targets of attack. Terrorists are capable of planning multiple attacks with little or no warning, as shown by the bombing of our embassies in Africa in 1998, the Millennium plots in 1999, and the World Trade Center and Pentagon attacks in 2001.

Although terrorism is our most important challenge today, President Bush has named Iraq, Iran, and North Korea as states that are threats to the United States. The 2003 war in Iraq showed clearly that America's Army—all its armed forces—were well trained and well led. This highly skilled, agile, and flexible force, in relatively small numbers, was able to defeat a well-armed enemy in a country the size of France in a mere thirty days of combat.

There also remains uncertainty about the future of Russia and China—two major powers undergoing great change—plus other issues, such as the potential new threat on the Korean peninsula; the prospects for lasting peace or continuing conflict in the Middle East; genocidal, ethnic, religious, and tribal conflict in Africa; the global impact of the proliferation of military technology; and an array of upcoming leadership changes in many already unstable countries.

THE ARMY MISSION

Protecting the nation's highest and most important interests is the Army's and the other services' mission. The Army's national mission is well stated in Title 10 of the Code of Laws of the United States. When it passed this law, Congress intended to provide an Army that, in conjunction with the other armed forces, would:

- Preserve the peace and security, and provide for the defense of the United States, its territories, its commonwealths and possessions, and any areas occupied by the United States.
- Support U.S. national policies.
- Implement U.S. national objectives.
- Overcome (i.e., *win a war against*) any nations responsible for aggressive acts that endanger the peace and security of the United States.

Today, the Army mission boils down to three major tasks:

- *Deterrence:* to be so competent and powerful that no enemy will risk attacking us, and if he does, to fight and win any resulting engagement, conflict, or war.
- *Power projection:* to be able to move combat forces anywhere in the world and support them on a sustained basis until victory is achieved or peace restored.
- *Military operations other than war (MOOTW):* to support those national and international peacekeeping, humanitarian assistance, disaster assistance, counterinsurgency, counterdrug, counterterrorist, and other related operations that the government determines are in the U.S. national interest.

This is serious business. National security, national defense, and the willingness and ability to fight for those vital interests are what the Army is all about. For the Army to accomplish these tasks, however, it needs the right strategies, tactics, techniques, and procedures; the right organizations; the right equipment; and, above all, trained soldiers. The Army's command structure and its organization exist to see that we have an efficient and effective Army and that it is well led and well trained.

COMMAND OF THE ARMY

Because the Army operates in response to America's most important interests, the U.S. Constitution designates the President as commander in chief. He is assisted by the Secretary of Defense and the Chairman of the Joint Chiefs of Staff, who are in the chain of command for all military operations.

The Army Chief of Staff is a member of the Joint Chiefs of Staff. He and the Secretary of the Army direct the Army to ensure that it is capable of performing the mission and tasks described above. They are the Army's principal advocates in the annual competition for national resources when the Army budget is negotiated within the government. They ensure that the Army is properly organized and equipped, and they make the regulations that govern all aspects of the Army from soldier recruitment through retirement.

ARMY ORGANIZATION

Active Army

For combat, the active Army includes five army-level headquarters deployed for overseas operations as part of the all-service unified commands; four corps that command the Army's ten active-duty divisions; eight National Guard divisions; and several separate combat arms brigades, groups, and regiments for artillery, air defense, aviation, special forces, and other fighting functions.

A variety of other commands, brigades, and groups provide engineer, chemical, civil affairs, intelligence, communications, medical, transportation, supply, maintenance, military police, and other support services essential to the conduct of combat operations.

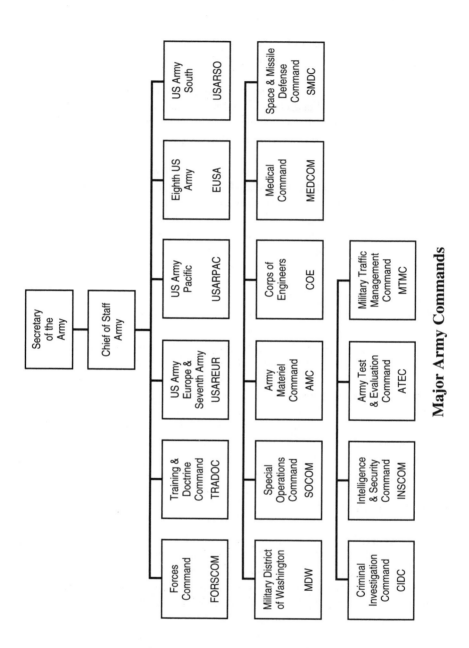

Major Army Commands

In addition to the tactical organizations, there is a supporting structure of units that perform a wide range of Army activities, such as command and control, logistics, training, military education, recruiting, research and development, procurement, and engineering and base support activities.

Army National Guard
The Army National Guard has some of the oldest units in the country, whose lineage extends to the years before the United States became independent. The Guard today provides a great amount of potent combat and combat support power to the Army. It contains 8 divisions and 15 "enhanced readiness" combat brigades. Eighty percent of the Army's field artillery is in the National Guard. The National Guard can be called to duty by the governor of a state for a state mission. It can also be called to active federal duty by the President to support a military operation that is beyond the capability of the active Army.

Army Reserve
The Army Reserve was first formed in 1908. It includes both units and individuals who join units when mobilized. The Army Reserve forces are essential to the accomplishment of the Army's mission. These forces provide the bulk of the Army's backup combat support and combat service support, without which many operations could not be carried out. For instance, the Army Reserve contains 100 percent of the Army's railway units, military police enemy prisoner of war brigades, and chemical brigades; 97 percent of all civil affairs units; 85 percent of the psychological operations units; 80 percent of the transportation groups; and 69 percent of the petroleum supply battalions.
    Most soldiers will not complete an enlistment without working with units or individuals in the Army Reserve.

Deployed Army
As of spring 2003, 225,000 soldiers are stationed in Iraq, Afghanistan, Bosnia, Kosovo, Korea, Japan, Germany, the Middle East, and elsewhere. Several thousand soldiers support counterdrug operations in Central and South America, and thousands of Special Operations Forces members operate in dozens of countries. Many thousands more are busy providing security assistance to foreign allies, training for combat, doing medical research, providing disaster relief, and meeting other needs. Most Army forces deployed overseas fall under one of the Army's major overseas commands, which are:
    U.S. Army Europe, headquartered in Germany
    U.S. Army Pacific, headquartered in Hawaii
    Eighth U.S. Army, headquartered in Korea
    U.S. Army South, headquartered in Miami, Florida
    Third U.S. Army, headquartered in Atlanta but which controls Army units
        in Southwest Asia

Rapid deployment task forces stationed in the continental United States remain ready to deploy to trouble spots in less than one day. Units on Division Ready Force (DRF)-One status must be prepared to stage for deployment on Air Force aircraft in less time than it takes to view a feature film about combat. Follow-on units that are on DRF-Two and DRF-Three status deploy sequentially behind the DRF-One force. Other rapid-deploying units operate likewise and can quickly begin to "flesh out" an area of operations in about 24 hours. Interim Brigade Combat Teams—built to fill the operational gap between quickly deployable but vulnerable light forces and more survivable but slower to deploy heavy forces—would next follow. If necessary, further "legacy" heavy forces in divisions would ship to the threatened area.

TACTICAL ORGANIZATION OF THE ARMY

The division is the Army's largest tactical organization that trains and fights as a combined arms team. It is a self-sustaining force capable of independent operations. The division is composed of varying numbers and types of combat, combat support, and combat service support units. The mix and types of combat units determine whether a division is armored, infantry, light infantry, airborne, or air assault.

Army Corps

When two or more divisions are required to conduct a military operation, they are commanded by an Army corps headquarters. The United States currently has four active Army corps headquarters and affiliated corps-level combat, combat support, and combat service support units. U.S. Army corps are:

I Corps, with headquarters at Fort Lewis, Washington

III Corps, headquartered at Fort Hood, Texas

V Corps, headquartered at Heidelberg, Germany

XVIII Airborne Corps, located at Fort Bragg, North Carolina

Army Active Divisions

The Army's 10 active divisions are located across the United States and overseas. Not all division headquarters and subordinate combat brigades are located at the same installations. The active division headquarters and subordinate combat brigade locations are:

1st Infantry Division (Mechanized), headquarters and two brigades in Germany, one brigade at Fort Riley, Kansas

1st Armored Division, headquarters and two brigades in Germany, one brigade at Fort Riley, Kansas

1st Cavalry Division, headquarters and three brigades at Fort Hood, Texas

2nd Infantry Division, headquarters and two brigades in Korea, one brigade at Fort Lewis, Washington

3rd Infantry Division (Mechanized), headquarters and two brigades at Fort Stewart, Georgia, one brigade at Fort Benning, Georgia

4th Infantry Division (Mechanized), headquarters and two brigades at Fort Hood, Texas, one brigade at Fort Carson, Colorado

10th Mountain Division (Light Infantry), headquarters and two brigades at Fort Drum, New York, and the 1st Brigade, 6th Infantry Division (Light) at Fort Richardson, Alaska

25th Infantry Division (Light), headquarters and two brigades at Schofield Barracks, Hawaii, and one brigade at Fort Lewis, Washington

82nd Airborne Division, headquarters and three brigades at Fort Bragg, North Carolina

101st Airborne Division (Air Assault), headquarters and three brigades at Fort Campbell, Kentucky

Army National Guard Divisions

Until they are federalized by order of the President, Army National Guard divisions are under the authority of their respective state governors and are available for missions within their states. State missions usually include disaster assistance, protection of key assets or facilities during periods of civil unrest, and similar tasks. In recent years, more and more units from the reserve components have been deployed overseas to support national missions. In all cases, however, National Guard divisions have the same combat function as active Army divisions when called to federal duty in time of crisis or war. These divisions are:

28th Infantry Division, Harrisburg, Pennsylvania

29th Infantry Division, Fort Belvoir, Virginia

34th Infantry Division, St. Paul, Minnesota

35th Infantry Division, Fort Leavenworth, Kansas

38th Infantry Division, Indianapolis, Indiana

40th Infantry Division, Los Alamitos, California

42nd Infantry Division, Troy, New York

49th Armored Division, Austin, Texas

Nondivisional Organizations

Soldiers assigned to combat service support and combat support organizations can serve in divisional or "nondivisional" units. Nondivisional units are also tactical formations, but their organization varies, depending on type. The most common types of nondivisional units are commands, brigades, and groups; these formations usually command battalions, which are in turn composed of companies. Nearly all soldiers are assigned to a company of one type or another. For instance, there are engineer, air defense artillery, and signal brigades; transportation commands and groups; signal commands and signal brigades; and military intelligence and special forces groups.

BRANCHES OF THE ARMY

The Army has 24 active-duty branches organized into four major categories: combat, combat support (CS), combat service support (CSS), and special branches (SB).

Combat Arms

Infantry. Infantry is the oldest of the combat arms. Its mission is "to close with the enemy by fire and maneuver to destroy or capture him, and to repel his assault by fire, close combat, and counterattack." Today's infantryman can move by land, sea, or air. The modern infantryman may fight on foot or go into action by parachute, helicopter, assault boat, or Bradley fighting vehicle. The infantry can operate at night, under any climatic conditions, and it can overcome natural and manmade obstacles that would stop other forces.

Light infantry units are rapidly deployable and are especially useful in missions conducted in complex and urban terrain due to their streamlined nature and lack of dependence on masses of heavy equipment for transportation. Air assault infantry units are more heavily equipped and, although fully capable of dismounted operations, typically incorporate the large numbers of helicopters available in the air assault division's aviation groups. Airborne infantry units are uniquely qualified and equipped for arrival in combat by parachute but are fully capable of dismounted or air assault operations as well. Mechanized infantry are the most heavily armed and protected infantry, riding into battle in Bradley infantry fighting vehicles (IFVs), which are armed with 25mm automatic cannon, antitank missiles, and machine guns. The new interim brigade is equipped with the wheeled Stryker series vehicle, which provides mobility and protection to the infantrymen riding within.

Ranger infantry are trained to go into battle by parachute, special operations helicopter, small boat, or dismounted. Although trained as infantry, ranger infantry units are increasingly being used as special operations forces.

Armor. Armor branch includes both armor and armored cavalry and is the modern successor to the horse cavalry. Armor operates in a combined arms team with infantry, artillery, and the other combat and combat support branches. Armor tactics emphasize mobility, firepower, and shock action to overcome and destroy enemy forces in rapid actions. Armored cavalry units exist in Army division and at corps level to conduct the reconnaissance and other security missions. The M1 series tank is armor's principal weapon system; it is a world-class tank. Like the Bradley IFV, the Bradley cavalry fighting vehicle in the armored cavalry units furnishes great speed and mobility, as well as maximum firepower and armored protection for use on the forward edge of the battle area.

Field Artillery. A historic branch of the Army, the field artillery mission is more challenging than ever before—to destroy, neutralize, or suppress the enemy by cannon, rocket, and missile fire and to integrate all supporting fires into the combined arms operation. Howitzers, rockets, and missiles are the muscle of the field artillery. Currently, towed field artillery systems include the M102 and M119A1 105mm howitzers and the M198 155mm howitzer. Self-propelled artillery systems include the M109-series 155mm howitzer and the Multiple Launched Rocket System (MLRS). The artillery's current ground-to-ground missile system is the Army Tactical Missile System (ATACMS), which is fired from the MLRS launcher and provides long-range fires against personnel and material targets. Artillery units provide fire support teams (FISTs) that plan and coordinate artillery fire in support of infantry and armor combat teams and call for and adjust artillery fires on enemy targets. The FIST uses many tools, including the ground/vehicular laser locator designator to determine ranges to targets and the designation of targets for laser-guided munitions, such as the tank-killing Copperhead round or the Hellfire missile. When the tactical situation warrants, the FIST may employ naval gunfire and joint close air support, as well.

Air Defense Artillery. The mission of the air defense artillery (ADA) is to protect the force and selected geographical assets from attack by enemy aircraft and missiles and to conduct antiaircraft surveillance. With its multicapable, phased-array radar and long-range, high-altitude missiles, the Patriot battery is the most formidable air defense system in the world today. It has the capability to intercept incoming tactical ballistic missiles, a role it performed with success in the Gulf War. While the Patriot provides long-range protection, the Avenger missile system, mounted on a high-mobility multipurpose wheeled vehicle (HMMWV) and found in divisions and corps, is a formidable weapon against low-flying aircraft and unmanned aerial vehicles.

Combat Engineers. Today's combat engineers provide the battlefield commander with mobility, countermobility, and survivability support. Combat engineer units are located primarily in divisions and corps. They provide bridging, mine laying, mine clearing, obstacle construction and removal, electric power, topographic support (terrain analysis), and a variety of combat construction and land-clearing tasks for combat units before, during, and after an attack, defense, or retrograde operation. As a secondary mission, combat engineers are trained to fight as infantry.

Aviation. Aviation branch provides combat and combat service support aviation to the combined arms Army maneuver unit from aviation brigades located at division, corps, and higher echelons. Combat missions include attack, air assault, reconnaissance, show of force, intelligence, and logistical (air delivery) support. Its principal equipment is the UH-1 and UH-60 (Black Hawk) utility and troop transport helicopter, the AH-64 (Apache) and AH-1 (Cobra) attack helicopters, the CH-47D (Chinook) cargo and transport helicopter, and the OH-58D small observation helicopter.

Special Forces. Special Forces (SF) is the Army's newest separate branch. As the name indicates, SF provides the Army with special tactics and techniques to accomplish very special missions, which range from special reconnaissance, direct action, foreign internal defense, unconventional warfare, and counterterrorism. SF mobile training teams travel all over the world to assist allied armies with modern training. Soldiers destined to SF units require considerable extra training and are specially selected. In addition to their traditional roles, SF branch includes units dedicated to civil affairs and military government and psychological operations.

Combat Support Branches

Chemical Corps. The Chemical Corps provides expertise in the area of nuclear, biological, and chemical (NBC) operations and defense. This includes use of nuclear and chemical weapons during war, training units on NBC defense, reconnaissance of the NBC battlefield, and decontamination of units and equipment contaminated by NBC hazards. The Chemical Corps is also responsible for providing large-area smoke and obscurants on the battlefield and for the use of field flame weapons and techniques against enemy forces.

Military Intelligence. Military Intelligence (MI) branch is responsible for providing a large number of critical intelligence support services to the battlefield commander. These include intelligence and information collection, counterintelligence support, cryptologic and signals intelligence, electronic warfare, operations security, enemy order of battle analysis, interrogation of enemy prisoners of war (EPWs), aerial surveillance, imagery (aerial and other photography) analysis, and related work.

Military Police. Military Police (MP) provide combat operations against opposing forces in U.S. rear areas of a battlefield. They provide traffic control to expedite movement of critical combat resources to the front. They process EPWs and evacuate them from the battle area. MPs provide security for critical facilities such as command posts and special ammunition sites, and they conduct law-enforcement operations much along the lines of the order given by General Washington in 1776 to the Army's first provost martial to "apprehend deserters, marauders, drunkards, rioters, and stragglers."

Signal Corps. As one of the Army's high-technology branches, the Signal Corps performs a broad range of communications-related tasks in support of the Army mission. These range from procuring, installing, operating, maintaining, and reconfiguring communications networks from the battlefield level to the Pentagon. It leads the Army's digitization effort for information management on the battlefield.

Combat Service Support Branches

Adjutant General Corps. One of the oldest branches in the Army, the Adjutant General (AG) Corps operates the military personnel system from a soldier's accession at a military processing station to his or her retirement or departure from the service. AG units are found at all levels from division on up. AG soldiers are also responsible for band operations and for operation of the military postal system.

Finance Corps. One of the Army's smallest branches, the Finance Corps is responsible not only for soldier pay matters, but also for the payment and auditing of accounts of the various vendors and contractors who sell items to the Army. One of the Finance Corps' most time-sensitive functions is the funding of contingency contracts usually needed in overseas areas to purchase supplies and services for deploying forces.

Ordnance Corps. Ordnance soldiers perform one of the Army's most important missions: repair and maintenance of equipment and materiel, supply and maintenance of ammunition, and explosive ordnance disposal (EOD). Given the extensive array of high-technology weapon systems, other sophisticated equipment, missiles, and munitions in the Army, and the need to maintain these items in the highest state of readiness, the Ordnance Corps is staffed with a variety of units at all echelons of service.

Quartermaster Corps. Along with the Ordnance and Transportation Corps, the Quartermaster (QM) Corps forms the basis of Army logistics. QM soldiers supply the Army. This includes all aspects of supply—procurement, cataloging, inventory, storage, distribution, salvage, and disposal of material. This includes the vital commodities of food, fuel, and water and the battlefield distribution networks that get these commodities to the fighting forces. The QM Corps pioneered the technology of aerial delivery, including air-drop and parachute delivery of personnel and supplies. It provides the Army's parachute riggers. The QM Corps also provides the Army with essential field services such as laundry, bath and shower facilities, clothing exchange, and mortuary support.

Transportation Corps. As the name implies, the Transportation Corps (TC) provides motor, air, rail, and water transport in support of Army operations worldwide. It operates the Army's line-haul truck fleets, ocean ports, railroads, and watercraft and coordinates logistic air operations. It operates motor transport depots and trailer transfer points. It also provides movement control units that schedule transportation assets in and through the battle area. Transportation companies and battalions are found at all echelons in the Army.

Special Branches

Chaplain Corps. Chaplains provide religious support to soldiers and their families. Chaplains of most major faiths and chaplain's assistants are found on most Army posts in the United States and overseas to provide regular religious services, military community services, and personal counseling.

Judge Advocate General Corps. The JAG Corps is primarily a branch of trained officer-attorneys and enlisted paralegal specialists who serve in the Army as judges, trial attorneys, defense attorneys, and legal counsel to commanders, soldiers, and families.

Medical Corps. Part of the Army Medical Department (AMD), and working under the Army Surgeon General, the Medical Corps is the part of the department that provides the medical doctors who staff Army hospitals and clinics throughout the world and provides the surgeons for the Army's field and battlefield hospitals in combat areas.

Dental Corps. Also part of the AMD, the Dental Corps provides the Army with dentists and dental technicians.

Veterinary Corps. The Army uses veterinary medicine doctors for care of Army animals, for meat inspection, and for preventive veterinary medicine support to Army communities.

Medical Service Corps. The MSC provides allied medical scientist support to the Army. This includes medical supply, ambulance support, pharmacists, optometrists, biochemists, physiologists, podiatrists, audiologists, entomologists, epidemiologists, and sanitary engineering and environmental health support.

Army Nurse Corps. The ANC was the first of the branches of the Army to admit women. As its name indicates, it provides commissioned and noncommissioned nursing services of all types to the Army mission at home stations and on battlegrounds around the world.

Army Medical Specialist Corps. Therapists, dieticians, and physician assistants constitute the members of this professional medical branch that supports soldiers as part of the AMD.

TYPES OF UNITS

Enlisted soldiers are trained for and serve in each of the above branches. All enlisted soldiers progress through Basic Combat Training (BCT) and Advanced Individual Training (AIT) for their military specialty. Officers are commissioned through the U.S. Military Academy at West Point, the Reserve Officers' Training Corps (ROTC), or the Officer Candidate School (OCS) and attend a basic course for their branch. Once initial training is completed, all soldiers—enlisted and officer—are assigned to units within the Army, and all work together to accomplish the Army's missions.

Even though there are many different types of units, the size and designation of units is fairly standard.

Designation	Symbol	Size	Usually Led By
Fire team	•(-)	About 5	Sergeant
Squad	•	10–15	Staff sergeant
Section	••	10–15	Staff sergeant
Platoon	•••	About 40	Lieutenant
Battery, company, troop			100–200	Captain
Battalion, squadron	||	400–800	Lieutenant colonel
Group, regiment	|||	3–5 battalions	Colonel
Brigade	X	3–5 battalions	Colonel
Division	XX	4–6 brigades	Major general
Corps	XXX	Several divisions	Lieutenant general
Army	XXXX	Several corps	General

For every officer leading an organization, there is a noncommissioned officer to assist him or her.

- A sergeant first class (SFC) platoon sergeant assists the platoon leader.
- A first sergeant (1SG) assists the commander of a company.
- A command sergeant major (CSM) assists commanders at all levels at battalion and above.

Today, the Army sits at the crossroads at the beginning of the new millennium. Computerization, modernization, and digitization on the battlefield—from target acquisition to logistical support—are leading to an increased reliance on small-unit leaders and soldiers and on a smaller yet more capable force. Operations are devolving to smaller, more capable, self-sustaining units digitally linked to artificial intelligence, analysis, combat support, and combat service support nodes that provide real-time information on the battlefield, whether it be a battlefield in a traditional sense or a peacekeeping operation.

To operate all the digitized high-technology equipment, as well as fight in the mud, the Army—as in the past—will continue to require trained, disciplined, and cohesive soldier teams. To attain this goal, the Army's enlisted training system operates for the purpose of producing the kind of soldiers needed on the modern battlefield.

2

The Enlisted Training System

While you are on active duty, your opportunity for military training is extensive. The Enlisted Training System (ETS) is a subsystem of the Enlisted Personnel Management System (EPMS). It is characterized by progressively
higher levels of performance capability, experience, and rank. Five "skill levels"
of training have been established to support the ETS. They are administered in
two distinct but closely related phases: Initial Entry Training (IET) and the
Noncommissioned Officer Education System (NCOES).

IET provides a foundation of professional and technical knowledge needed
to perform at the first duty station; combined with subsequent individual training in the unit, the soldier qualifies at skill level one (SL-1) in one of the
Army's military occupational specialties (MOSs). The next four skill levels are
taught through the NCOES.

CAREER MANAGEMENT FIELDS

The MOSs of all enlisted soldiers from private to sergeant major are grouped
into career management fields (CMFs). A CMF is a grouping of related MOSs.
MOSs are grouped so that soldiers in one specialty have abilities and aptitudes
appropriate for training and assignments in other specialties within that CMF.
This flexibility means that a soldier can move laterally within a CMF as well.
Training leads to progression and promotions. Each soldier has a career path
mapped out for him or her, identifying appropriate schooling, assignments, and
opportunities.

As soldiers climb the promotion ladder within a CMF, new recruits fill in
the lower rungs of the ladder, preparing themselves for upward mobility as
well. The Army has established career paths for each CMF so soldiers can be
counseled on the training and education they will need.

Within each CMF, the EPMS has identified the skills necessary for successfully functioning at each rank. Soldiers seeking promotions need to con-
stantly prepare themselves for the next higher skill level. SL-1 includes skills,
proficiencies, and abilities typically needed to perform efficiently up through
the rank of specialist. SL-2 relates to sergeant; SL-3 to staff sergeant; SL-4 to
sergeant first class; and SL-5 to master sergeant through command sergeant

major. Because MOSs are grouped into CMFs, the skills necessary for SL-2 in one CMF will not necessarily be the same skills required at that level in a different CMF. Included among the CMFs for enlisted soldiers are the following:

11 Infantry
13 Field Artillery
14 Air Defense Artillery
15 Aviation
18 Special Forces
19 Armor
21 Engineer
25 Communications and
   Information Systems
   Operations
27 Paralegal
31 Military Police
33 Electronic Warfare/Intercept
   Systems Maintenance
37 Psychological Operations
38 Civil Affairs

42 Adjutant General
44 Financial Management
46 Public Affairs
56 Religious Support
63 Mechanical Maintenance
74 Chemical
79 Recruiting and Retention
88 Transportation
89 Ammunition
91 Medical
92 Supply and Services
94 Electronic Maintenance and
   Calibration
96 Military Intelligence
98 Signals Intelligence/Electronic
   Warfare Operations

The CMFs are organized into three branches: combat arms, combat support, and combat service support. The ETS recognizes the distinction necessary among branches, but leadership training is required to some degree in all three branches.

INITIAL ENTRY TRAINING
Every soldier in the Army has gone through Initial Entry Training (IET). The two phases of IET are Basic Training (BT) and Advanced Individual Training (AIT), which is MOS training.

Generally, soldiers entering the combat arms branch or the military police receive One-Station Unit Training (OSUT); they remain in the same unit for their BT and AIT. Soldiers entering combat support or combat service support branches generally change duty assignments for their AIT, primarily because of the technical nature of many MOSs in these branches. The primary functions of IET are to prepare recruits for military life and to provide soldiers with basic combat skills and SL-1 technical training.

Drill sergeants are key figures in preparing recruits for the rigors of Army life. It is the responsibility of a drill sergeant to teach a new soldier about the Army and to help him or her appreciate how individuals contribute to the military structure. The drill sergeant instills self-confidence, self-respect, and self-discipline in young soldiers so they can perform their duties as soldiers. Equally important, the drill sergeant must ensure that soldiers are physically fit.

It is essential that each soldier be proficient in the combat basics regardless of the branch in which he or she will serve. Marksmanship, field fortifications, first aid, hand-to-hand combat, NBC defense, and small-unit teamwork are emphasized.

All soldiers are given additional training in basic combat skills during the AIT phase of IET. Field training exercises are used to combine specialized MOS training the soldier must receive with basic soldier skills that need to be reinforced. AIT highlights the specific skills soldiers will need to perform in their MOS at SL-1.

Upon completion of IET, soldiers go to their units with skills sufficient to effectively contribute to the team. Training, however, is by no means complete. Field units provide continuing on-the-job training to round out the soldier's initial training and to enhance the first-termer's potential.

UNIT AND INDIVIDUAL TRAINING

Upon assignment to a unit, the new soldier practices and refines the individual soldier skills learned in BT and AIT. The Individual Training and Evaluation Program (ITEP) provides a formal structure for the soldier's ongoing training. The ITEP focuses on Common Task Training and the Commander's Evaluation.

Common Task Training (CTT) emphasizes combat skills that *all* soldiers must perform. Tasks such as map reading, communications, and NBC defense are reinforced through performance-oriented, hands-on training. Each year, soldiers must pass a battery of common skills tests that evaluate their ability to perform basic skills.

The *Commander's Evaluation (CE)* is a hands-on test designed to help unit leaders determine the proficiency level each soldier has achieved in relationship to standards outlined in the soldier's job book and appropriate soldier's manual.

Although the focus of each soldier's training is on developing individual soldier skills, unit leaders are responsible for ensuring that the unit can perform collective tasks. At the unit level, the Army Training and Evaluation Program (ARTEP) is to assist commanders in identifying appropriate training standards for the accomplishment of collective unit tasks. Each commander evaluates his or her unit's wartime mission and assesses which tasks require emphasis in the unit's training plans. The commander uses ARTEP manuals to develop a unit training strategy and then develops, executes, and evaluates unit training.

NONCOMMISSIONED OFFICER EDUCATION SYSTEM

The second phase of the ETS is the Noncommissioned Officer Education System (NCOES), which has a single goal: to train NCOs to be trainers and leaders of soldiers who work under their supervision. The NCOES prepares soldiers to

Enlisted Training System

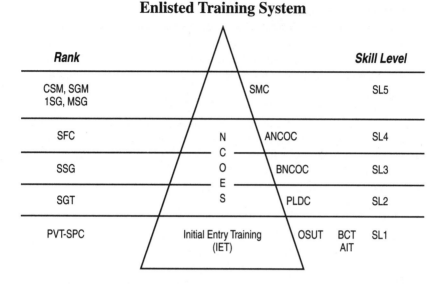

Rank		Skill Level
CSM, SGM 1SG, MSG	SMC	SL5
SFC	N C ANCOC	SL4
SSG	O E BNCOC	SL3
SGT	S PLDC	SL2
PVT-SPC	Initial Entry Training (IET) / OSUT BCT AIT	SL1

perform at the next higher skill level and combines leadership study with technical training. It provides an extensive network of courses at all levels of the NCO corps. It is conducted in service schools and NCO academies (NCOAs).

The four levels of the NCOES are the Primary Leadership Development Course (PLDC), the Basic NCO Course (BNCOC), the Advanced NCO Course (ANCOC), and the U.S. Army Sergeants Major Academy (USASMA).

The PLDC is a common leadership course that concentrates on how to lead and train and emphasizes the duties, responsibilities, and authority of the NCO. This four-week course is conducted at NCOAs and is open to soldiers in all MOSs.

The BNCOC, conducted at NCOAs, is designed to produce hard-hitting squad and section leaders who can lead and train soldiers in combat. The length of the course varies according to the MOS. Graduation from BNCOC is required for consideration of promotion to staff sergeant.

The ANCOC stresses MOS-related tasks, with emphasis on technical and common leader combat skills required to train and lead other soldiers at the platoon or comparable level. Courses are presented at NCOAs and vary in length according to MOS requirements. ANCOC is required for consideration of promotion to sergeant first class.

The USASMA prepares master sergeants and first sergeants for troop and staff assignments throughout the Army and the Department of Defense. Graduation from the U.S. Army Sergeants Major Course at the USASMA must precede promotion to sergeant major.

ACADEMIC EVALUATION FORM

All soldiers who attend NCOES schools are evaluated by course instructors on DA Form 1059, *Service School Academic Evaluation Report.* The form is forwarded for posting to soldiers' official records. Once entered on the official record, the report is available for review by members of Army promotion and selection boards.

Block 13, "Performance Summary," indicates a soldier's overall performance. Note that the "Exceeded Course Standards" block is limited to the top 20 percent of a class. Block 16 is completed by the service school instructor. Soldiers who remain physically fit and strive to develop written and oral communications skills and leadership skills, and who make a strong effort to support group work and do effective research, will have an advantage when attending PLDC.

OTHER MILITARY TRAINING OPPORTUNITIES

Military educational opportunities are not limited to NCOES courses. During basic training, soldiers whose native language is not English are tested and evaluated on their English comprehension. For those having difficulty with their second language (English), self-paced instruction is available through Army Education Centers (AECs). English as a second language (ESL) courses are presented to the basic trainee. In addition, refresher and sustaining courses are available at most installations. Once at the permanent duty station, the ESL graduate requests further training through the unit commander. The primary consideration is the soldier's willingness to learn and use English skills to enhance productivity and efficiency.

DISTANCE LEARNING

The Army is rapidly entering the digital age. Through digital and VTC links, soldiers can now attend military education courses presented by schools and instructors located at far off institutions. Soldiers attending courses, whether through a resident school, a Total Army Schools System (TASS) training battalion, or a digital learning facility, receive the same credit for successfully completing resident training, with documentation in the soldier's MPRJ reflecting identical codes for any of the types of training. All diplomas, certificates, or DA Form 1059 will be the same and will not reflect non-resident, distant learning, reserve component, or other similar remarks. Promotion and evaluation boards will not discriminate against soldiers who completed their professional military training through distant learning.

Soldiers may split their training phases with some occurring at the resident school and the remainder conducted through distant learning. One of the considerations for determining a training location is whether the costs of TASS or distant learning exceeds the costs of sending a soldier to the proponent school for the full resident course.

SERVICE SCHOOL ACADEMIC EVALUATION REPORT For use of this form, see AR 623-1; the proponent agency is MILPERCEN.		DATE		
1. LAST NAME - FIRST NAME - MIDDLE INITIAL	2. SSN	3. GRADE	4. BR	5. SPECIALTY/MOSC
6. COURSE TITLE	7. NAME OF SCHOOL			8. COMP

9. TYPE OF REPORT
☐ RESIDENT
☐ NONRESIDENT

10. PERIOD OF REPORT *(Year, month, day)*
From: Thru:

11. DURATION OF COURSE *(Year, month, day)*
☒ From: Thru:

12. EXPLANATION OF NONRATED PERIODS

13. PERFORMANCE SUMMARY

*a. ☐ EXCEEDED COURSE STANDARDS
(Limited to 20% of class enrollment)

b. ☐ ACHIEVED COURSE STANDARDS

*c. ☐ MARGINALLY ACHIEVED COURSE STANDARDS

*d. ☐ FAILED TO ACHIEVE COURSE STANDARDS

Rating must be supported by comments in ITEM 16.

14. DEMONSTRATED ABILITIES

a. WRITTEN COMMUNICATION
☐ NOT EVALUATED   ☐ UNSAT   ☐ SAT   ☐ SUPERIOR

b. ORAL COMMUNICATION
☐ NOT EVALUATED   ☐ UNSAT   ☐ SAT   ☐ SUPERIOR

c. LEADERSHIP SKILLS
☐ NOT EVALUATED   ☐ UNSAT   ☐ SAT   ☐ SUPERIOR

d. CONTRIBUTION TO GROUP WORK
☐ NOT EVALUATED   ☐ UNSAT   ☐ SAT   ☐ SUPERIOR

e. EVALUATION OF STUDENT'S RESEARCH ABILITY
☐ NOT EVALUATED   ☐ UNSAT   ☐ SAT   ☐ SUPERIOR

(SUPERIOR/UNSAT rating must be supported by comments in ITEM 16)

15. HAS THE STUDENT DEMONSTRATED THE ACADEMIC POTENTIAL FOR SELECTION TO HIGHER LEVEL SCHOOLING/TRAINING?
☐ YES   ☐ NO   ☐ N/A   *(A "NO" response must be supported by comments in ITEM 16)*

16. COMMENTS *(This item is intended to obtain a word picture of each student that will accurately and completely portray academic performance, intellectual qualities, and communication skills and abilities. The narrative should also discuss broader aspects of the student's potential; leadership capabilities, moral and overall professional qualities. In particular, comments should be made if the student failed to respond to recommendations for improving academic or personal affairs)*

17. AUTHENTICATION

a. TYPED NAME, GRADE, BRANCH, AND TITLE OF PREPARING OFFICER   SIGNATURE

b. TYPED NAME, GRADE, BRANCH, AND TITLE OF REVIEWING OFFICER   SIGNATURE

18. MILITARY PERSONNEL OFFICER

a. FORWARDING ADDRESS *(Rated student)*

b. DISTRIBUTION
☐ STUDENT   ☐ UNIT CDR *(P/B NCOES only)*
☐ STUDENT'S OFFICIAL MILITARY RECORDS

DA FORM **1059**
1 NOV 77

EDITION OF 1 JUL 73 IS OBSOLETE.   8-0478-003

Service School Academic Evaluation Report

SKILL RECOGNITION PROGRAM

The Skill Recognition Program provides ways to get recognition within the civilian sector for skills learned in service. This recognition can come in the following forms:

Army Apprenticeship. This program provides participants with documentation of apprentice skills acquired while in the Army that is understood by civilian industry. It improves the performance and motivation of soldiers, provides a recruiting incentive for MOSs that are related to skills with apprenticeships, and improves the supervisor-soldier relationship.

Occupations with apprenticeships are those that are learned through experience and on-the-job training and are supplemented by related technical instruction. They involve manual, mechanical, or technological skills and knowledge requiring a minimum of 2,000 hours of work experience plus related instruction. They do not fall into the categories of selling, management, clerical, or professional skills requiring advanced knowledge and academic degrees. These apprenticeship occupations are identified in Department of Labor pamphlets and appendix I, AR 621-5.

Enrollment is open to soldiers who perform satisfactorily on the job and possess an MOS (primary or secondary) that relates to the program and that has been registered with the Bureau of Apprenticeship Training. Also eligible are soldiers who possess a qualifying MOS in which they were initially registered but are no longer serving because of priorities and mission requirements.

Certification. Some Army MOSs correspond to civilian occupations that require licensing or certification as a prerequisite for employment in certain states or businesses. Certification requirements and agencies are listed in Army apprenticeship or industry recognition pamphlets in the AR 621 series.

Involvement in these programs is voluntary. Army training programs are not altered to meet civilian standards for skill recognition programs. However, as a prerequisite to registration, certification, or formal recognition, some civilian agencies might require additional nonmission-related training or experience before recognizing a soldier as fully qualified. When this is necessary, the soldier must acquire the additional training and experience through local trade or vocational schools, or by other means.

Programs stress individual initiative. An individual cannot be enrolled in more than one occupational skill area within an apprenticeship program at any one time. The soldier may, however, change to another occupational area or program as many times as desired, provided prerequisites are met.

FUNCTIONAL ACADEMIC SKILLS TRAINING

Functional Academic Skills Training (FAST), formerly called Basic Skills Education Program (BSEP), provides instruction in academic competencies necessary for job proficiency and preparation for advanced training. FAST, available at Army Learning Centers (ALCs), helps improve soldiers' job performance and helps them meet reenlistment eligibility and MOS classification requirements. Because this program is self-paced using instructional material (software at those ALCs that are computer-equipped), FAST is available during duty and off-duty hours. FAST covers reading, writing, arithmetic, and other subjects that soldiers must comprehend to excel in service.

NCO EVALUATION SYSTEM

Some first term soldiers will reach the rank of sergeant during their first enlistment, and will begin receiving written NCO Evaluation Reports (NCOER) from their immediate supervisors. The NCOER provides formal recognition of duty performance, a measurement of professional values and personal traits, and is the basis for performance counseling by rating officials. Subsequent school selection, promotion, assignment, MOS classification, and qualitative management are based largely on information found in the NCOER. The NCOER is designed to strengthen the NCO Corps' ability to meet the professional challenges of the future.

3

Service in Today's Army

In his most recent *Army Vision Statement*, the Chief of Staff of the Army stated: "The Army—is people. The [greatness of our achievements] as an Army will continue to be delivered by our people. They are the engine behind our capabilities, and the soldier remains the centerpiece of our formation. We will continue to attract, train, motivate, and retain the most competent and dedicated people in the Nation to fuel our ability to be persuasive in peace and invincible in war."

CHARACTERISTICS OF ARMY SERVICE

For over 225 years, the Army has employed its military doctrine, organization, procedures, and *ideals* of service to meet whatever challenge the nation has asked of it in the realm of national defense, military deterrence, and warfighting. Today, and for the foreseeable future, Army service will be characterized by a number of key attributes all soldiers need to understand.

Continuous Training

Training is the cornerstone of military life. The Army has an extensive program of *individual* and *unit* training that is virtually continuous. Individual training is the responsibility of the Army's enlisted NCOs. Unit training is the responsibility of the unit's leaders and commanders. Unit training is accomplished during recurring field training exercises (FTX) and other collective training events. Every FTX, whether it lasts one day or several weeks, measures how ready individual soldiers, their units, and larger collective organizations are to perform their respective missions in war. Soldiers find out how fit, tough, trained, and ready they are during an FTX, especially when they get cold, hot, tired, wet, hungry, or thirsty and encounter other unpleasant conditions or forces, such as the simulated "enemy" opposing force found at major training centers.

Professional Competence

The Army of the new millennium incorporates intellectual ingenuity, technological innovation, and a set of corporate values that have shaped America's Army throughout its more than 200-year history. Our Army will continue to need skilled, versatile, and highly motivated soldiers capable of accomplishing their mission in ever-changing environments. Today's soldiers will become the leaders of tomorrow's soldiers. They are the young men and women who will provide to America a corps of leaders who have an unmatched work ethic, who have a strong sense of values, who treat others with dignity and respect, who are accustomed to hard work, who are courageous, who thrive on responsibility, who know how to work as a team, and who are positive role models for all around them. Today's Army is manned with professionally competent soldiers and leaders. They know their jobs, and they do them well.

World-Class Missions

America's Army is the best land combat force in the world, serving the nation every day at home and abroad. It is often the commitment of our Army into trouble spots that makes the difference between success and failure of America's national security policy. When ground troops deploy, the world knows the United States means business. Land forces remain decisive and provide the most visible and sustained form of U.S. commitment. Our country has used the military 30 times in the years since 1989, with the Army shouldering almost 60 percent of the deployments. In the 40 years prior to 1989, there were only 10 major deployments.

Today, two-thirds of the active Army is located in the continental United States, with many soldiers assigned to contingency units that are able to deploy on short notice to the world's trouble spots. Hundreds of thousands of other soldiers are involved in highly important missions on a daily basis. Several thousand soldiers support counterdrug operations in Central and South America. More than 1,000 Special Operations Force members operate in dozens of countries, and 225,000 soldiers are stationed in Korea, Japan, Europe, the Middle East, and elsewhere. Many thousands more are busy providing security assistance to foreign allies, training for combat, doing medical research, providing disaster relief, and meeting other needs.

An Army of Values

Soldiers learn and draw strength from those soldiers and leaders who nurture and encourage the development of values as inalienable professional attributes. Soldiers are expected to live by and exemplify those values. Internalizing these values—living by them—is what builds professionalism in America's Army and character in our nation. Values and traditions are the soul of the Army.

The Army lives by seven bedrock values to which all soldiers must adhere. Army values follow the acronym LDRSHIP:

Loyalty	Being faithful to the country, the Army, your unit, and other soldiers in good times and bad.
Duty	Performing your military responsibilities and fulfilling your legal obligations faithfully and reliably under all conditions.

Respect	Treating all people with dignity and courtesy and as you would wish to be treated.
Selfless service	Putting the welfare of the nation, the Army, and your colleagues before your own welfare.
Honor	Having the personal integrity, courage, and honesty to know and support what is right without being forced to do so.
Integrity	Doing what's right, legally and morally, and not allowing yourself to be corrupted by that which is not. This includes taking responsibility for your actions.
Personal courage	Being brave and doing your duty in the face of fear, danger, or adversity.

Additionally, two personal characteristics go hand in hand with values. They are:

Teamwork	Working or performing duties in cooperation with others.
Discipline	Controlling your personal behavior to avoid doing wrong, and focusing your talents and skills on doing well what is required.

These values have served the Army well in peacetime and in war. Values, along with professional job competence, contribute directly to mission success. Soldiers who develop within themselves a sense of mental and moral strength—courage—will accomplish the mission when in combat. Understand also that commitment to the unit's mission takes priority over personal wishes, wants, pleasures, and, perhaps, needs. It means sincere involvement—doing something—to find solutions to problems and just not paying lip service to them.

Although soldierly values and character attributes are not new, there is a renewed interest in them. The Soldier's Code best encapsulates the compact among the soldier, the leader, and the Army.

An Army of Standards

Today's Army is also an army of standards. There are two types of standards: standards of *personal behavior* and standards of *duty performance.* The standards of personal behavior apply to all ranks. The standards of duty performance apply to all soldiers according to their military occupational specialties and the levels of responsibility and authority they hold.

Standards are those principles or rules by which behaviors and tasks are measured as successfully accomplished. When members of a squad, section, or platoon share and adhere to the Army values and to the standards that flow from them, they are a more cohesive organization. Soldiers will measure other soldiers by the standard as it gradually becomes a criterion for acceptance by the whole team.

Army Field Manual (FM) 1 [FM 100-1], titled simply *The Army,* capstones the Army's guiding beliefs, standards, and ideals succinctly in one word—*duty.* Duty means to fulfill your obligations. It is behavior required by moral obligation, demanded by custom, or enjoined by feelings of rightness. It requires the impartial administration of standards without regard to friendship, personality, rank, or other bias. It is one of the key Army values.

SOLDIER'S CODE

I. I am an American soldier, a protector of the greatest nation on earth—sworn to uphold the Constitution of the United States. *I will always perform my duties to the utmost of my abilities and will strive to exhibit the moral and physical courage expected of a soldier. Throughout my years as a soldier and after, I will put my obligations before self. My word is my bond.*

II. I will treat others with dignity and respect, and expect others to do the same. *I will not tolerate soldiers being treated differently because of race, color, sex, religion, or national origin. I will notify my chain of command if I observe instances which affect the good order and discipline of the organization.*

III. I will honor my Country, the Army, my unit and my fellow soldiers by living the Army values. *I will obey the lawful orders of my superiors and will uphold the standards established by the leadership.*

IV. No matter what situation I am in, I will never do anything for pleasure, profit, or personal safety which will disgrace my uniform, my unit, or my country.

V. I expect my leadership to discipline me when I do wrong and commend me when I exceed expectations. I rely on my leadership to establish an organizational climate where I can learn and grow as an individual.

VI. Lastly, I am proud of my country and its flag. *I want to look back on my time in the Army and say that I am proud to have served my country as a soldier.*

CURRENT TRENDS IN THE ARMY

Army Transformation: New Doctrines for New Missions

Assigned Army missions affect how the military is structured, trained, and employed. The Army's new regional focus, combined with major troop reductions overseas, puts enormous emphasis on strategic mobility. Airlift and sealift mobility improvements being made today will enable deployment of an Army light division and a heavy brigade to any crisis area in about two weeks, and two heavy divisions in about a month. The new brigade combat teams will be able to deploy in 96 hours.

As stated in chapter 1, rapid deployment task forces remain ready to deploy to trouble spots in less than one day. Units on Deployment Ready Force-One (DRF-1) status and other rapidly deploying units operate similarly and can begin to "flesh out" an area of operation in about 24 hours. The currently forming Interim Brigade Combat Teams, built to fill the operational gap between quickly deployable but vulnerable light forces and more survivable but slower to deploy heavy forces would next follow. If necessary, further heavy forces in divisions would ship to the threatened area. Regardless of how roles, missions, functions, and force structures change with the new post-Cold War era, soldiers will feel the impact and adjust. The effort is worth making, because the objective, as always, is to transform and improve combat readiness for 21st-century Army missions.

New Structures

The Army has begun the process of determining how to restructure many of its forces and units to meet the requirements of the types of operations the Army is expected to conduct in the coming years. The ultimate organization is the "objective force," which will be the Army's organization in 2015; the "legacy force," or the equipment and organization of the Cold War Army, modernized to meet the Army's near term needs; and the "interim force," which is the organizational bridge between the two.

Combat support, unit manning and logistics procedures are also undergoing major changes as the Army seeks to increase the speed of deployment and reduce the large burden of logistics support of rapidly deployed forces. Soldiers in all types of units and all career fields from the infantry (11) to the signals intelligence (98) will see significant and exciting changes in the next few years. The Army is seeking a structure that is:

- *Responsive:* Responsiveness means getting the right force at the right place in the shortest possible time. An American threat of the use of force, if it deters miscalculation by adversaries, provides a quality of responsiveness all its own. The Army will provide strategic responsiveness through forward-deployed forces, forward-positioned capabilities, engagement, and, when called for, force projection from the continental United States to any other location where it is needed.
- *Deployable:* The Army will continue to refine its capability to put combat force anywhere in the world in 96 hours after liftoff for both warfighting missions and MOOTW.

- *Agile:* Army units and leaders will attain the necessary agility in the force structure to move forces from MOOTW missions to warfighting missions and back again just as easily as they now move from defense to offense and back again in conventional war.
- *Versatile:* The revised organizational structures of Army forces will, with minimal adjustment and in minimum time, generate formations that can dominate at any point on the spectrum of operations.
- *Lethal:* The elements of lethal combat power remain fire, maneuver, leadership, and protection. When an Army force deploys, every element in the warfighting formation will be capable of generating combat power and contributing decisively to the fight. This will discourage and deter escalation and, if deterrence fails, allow the United States to prosecute a war with an intensity that ensures victory at the least cost to us and our allies.
- *Survivable:* As in the past, the Army will be prepared to enter any type of conflict and dominate the expanded battlespace, and it will do what is necessary to protect the force in such a manner that it will not only survive the conflict but dominate it.
- *Sustainable:* Sustainability is the capacity to keep up the fight over the course of the battle. The new types of operations envisioned will require new support structures and procedures, and the Army is committed to developing those structures as part of the total transition effort.

In terms of new developments, service in today's Army will be service on the leading edge of military technology and operations. The word "routine" is likely to disappear from the description of military service.

AN ERA OF POTENTIAL CONFLICTS

The end of the Cold War had three key strategic events: the collapse of international communism, the demise of the USSR, and an end to bipolar competition. These events, in turn, are affecting power and security relationships throughout the world. One result is the relative dispersal of power away from the states of the former Soviet Union toward other regional power centers. Another is the potential struggle within regions as the dominant states vie for position within the emerging power hierarchy. A third is that in many regions the "lid has come off" long-simmering ethnic, religious, territorial, and economic disputes.

In an appearance before Congress, George J. Tenet, director of the Central Intelligence Agency, declared the threat from terrorism real, immediate, and evolving. While state-sponsored terrorism appears to have declined over the past five years, transnational groups—such as the Al-Qaeda, with decentralized leadership that makes it harder to identify and disrupt—have emerged.

Osama bin Ladin and his Al-Qaeda terrorist network remain the most immediate and serious threat. Since 1998, Bin Ladin has declared all U.S. citizens legitimate targets of attack. As shown by the bombing of our embassies in

Semper Paratis, "Always Ready"

Africa in 1998, the Millennium plots in 1999, and the World Trade Center and Pentagon attacks in 2001, terrorists are capable of planning multiple attacks with little or no warning.

Afghanistan
The United States has dealt severe blows to Al-Qaeda and its leadership in Afghanistan. Despite the battles we have won in Afghanistan, we remain a nation at war, and the road ahead is fraught with challenges. The Afghan people, with international assistance, are working to overcome a traditionally weak central government, a devastated infrastructure, a grave humanitarian crisis, and ethnic divisions that deepened over the last 20 years of conflict. President Hamid Karzai will have to play a delicate balancing game domestically. Remaining Al-Qaeda fighters in the eastern provinces and ongoing power struggles among Pashtun leaders there underscore the volatility of tribal and personal relations that Karzai must navigate.

Although terrorism is our most important challenge today, President Bush has named Iraq, Iran and North Korea as states which are threats to the United States. There also remains uncertainty about the future of Russia and China—two major powers undergoing great change—plus other issues, such as the dynamics on the Korean peninsula, the prospects for lasting peace or continuing conflict in the Middle East, genocidal. ethnic, religious, and tribal conflict in Africa, the global impact of the proliferation of military technology, and an array of upcoming leadership changes.

Iraq

In spite of serious warnings from the United States and Great Britain, Iraqi leader Saddam Hussein refused to abandon his efforts to pursue weapons of mass destruction and missile development programs. He continued to finesse the United Nations and its weapons inspectors, and his government was linked to terrorist organizations. In early 2003, coalition forces primarily from the United States and Great Britain conducted a massive buildup of forces in Kuwait. In March 2003, these forces invaded Iraq and, in 30 days of often intense combat, removed Saddam Hussein and his diabolic leadership group from power and began the long-term task of reconstituting a peaceful, progressive government in that country.

As noted at the head of this chapter, the Army is trained and ready "to be persuasive in peace and invincible in war." Military operations conducted during this war provided evidence to soldiers that the Army's goals of having an army that is responsive, rapidly deployable, agile, versatile, lethal, survivable, and sustainable (as discussed earlier) may already be at hand. Public approval of the manner in which the Army and Marines conducted this campaign is among the highest in recent U.S. history.

The future role of the Army in Iraq will certainly be to assist in the transition to peace until other international arrangements can be put in place and become effective.

Iran

Iran's primary long-range goal is to establish itself as the pan-Islamic leader throughout the Middle East region and beyond. In pursuit of that goal it requires military forces that can deter or defeat Iraq, intimidate its Gulf Arab neighbors, and limit the regional influence of the West—particularly the United States. Iran is developing air, air defense, missile, mine warfare, and naval weapons capable of interdicting maritime access in the Gulf and through the Strait of Hormuz. These efforts reflect a clear intent to build an offensive capability well beyond Iran's defensive needs. However, Tehran's military buildup has been slowed recently by serious economic problems and a rapidly growing and youthful population, which do not bode well for a significant increase in military spending. As a result, Iran's military progress will be slow but steady, and many of its current conventional force shortcomings—particularly command and control, maintenance, training, and equipment—will linger. Over time, however, U.S. interests could be challenged by a hegemonic Iran seeking to dominate the region unless recent overtures bear fruit and U.S.-Iranian relations resume.

North Korea

North Korea retains the potential to inflict enormous destruction on South Korea, and a Korean war scenario remains America's primary near-term military concern in Asia. Given the early 2003 warlike tone of North Korea's government, war on the peninsula could erupt with little warning. Large civilian population and economic centers would be at risk from the outset of conflict. The key will be how North Korea's uncertain and unstable leadership handles the increasing internal pressures resulting from long-term economic and social deterioration. We must remain vigilant for both "implosion" and "explosion" possibilities and the impact this could have on U.S. forces in Northeast Asia.

China

The growth of Chinese power is the long-term key to security stability in Asia. China will continue to give priority to economic progress and modernization as it moves forward to a new era of regional influence. Should China become more assertive and aggressive in that role, the prospects for direct confrontation with other regional powers will increase accordingly. In a worst-case scenario, China would view the United States as a direct military threat.

On the other hand, in part to fund modernization, Beijing is cutting force structure, particularly within the Army, but it still retains forces that will be large and capable by regional and global standards.

Overall, China is one of the few powers with the potential to emerge as a large-scale regional threat to U.S. interests. Given Asia's growing global economic importance, its unsettled security picture, and the fact that four of the world's major powers—China, Russia, Japan, and the United States—all have interests and a presence there, the continued monitoring of Asia's security environment will remain a primary task for the U.S. defense community.

Russia

As China is the key to long-term stability in Asia, Russia is the key to stability in Eastern Europe. And like China, Russia also has the potential to emerge as a large-scale regional threat to U.S. interests within the next two decades. Accordingly, Russia's political and military future remains one of our key security concerns. For the near-term to mid-term outlook, we expect slow progress along the current reform path.

In the near future, real progress at Russian military reform will not occur until the economy improves sufficiently, domestic spending imperatives are satisfied, and the political and military leadership agree on the desired size, nature, and characteristics of the future force. It will take at least a decade before these circumstances occur.

Balkans

International peacekeeping forces in Bosnia and Kosovo continue to operate in a complex environment that poses significant challenges to the establishment of a stable and enduring peace. The Bosnian factions should continue to generally comply with the military aspects of the Dayton Accords and Stabilization Force (SFOR) directives. Ethnic Albanians in Kosovo continue to insist on independence. The threat to U.S. and allied forces in the Balkans from organized military forces remains low, but random violence could still occur unexpectedly.

South Asia
The tense rivalry between India and Pakistan over Kashmir is our most important security concern on the subcontinent. While neither side wants war, both see their security relationship in zero-sum terms. India's larger economy and more robust military is balanced by Pakistan's threat to retaliate with nuclear weapons if the two nations go to war. With frequent low-level clashes, the potential for miscalculation and rapid escalation is constant.

Latin America
The scourge of narco-trafficking, related money laundering, weapons and contraband smuggling, insurgency, and the recent disruption in the Venezuelan oil industry all combine to provide threatening conditions for some countries and governments of the region and for U.S. interests. The potential for more serious insurgency and more widespread terrorism and crime in several areas of Central and South America and the Caribbean continues to demand our vigilance.

In summary, although the United States will not likely see a global "peer competitor" within 20 years, the threats facing the United States in the next decade will be of an uncertain order of magnitude. The world remains a very dangerous and complex place, and there is every reason to expect U.S. military requirements to be at about the same level of the past several years, and that use of U.S. military forces will be required along the full spectrum of operations.

THE BEST TIME TO SERVE
As ironic as it may seem, morale in heavily engaged and deployed Army units is higher than in units doing peacetime training and garrison duties. This is probably because soldiers like doing constructive and visible Army missions. Although training is one of the Army's most important missions, actually performing the functions for which we are trained seems to be more rewarding.

The Army also seems to have stabilized in terms of its size and in the opportunities for professional advancement. Soldiers who work hard at their duties, perform to standard in training and conduct, and participate professionally in any operation are rewarded not only with decorations but also with promotion to higher ranks. The skills learned in the Army—both the technical skills and the skill of working on a team toward a cooperative goal—are treasures of a lifetime.

The Army also received a significant pay raise at the beginning of this millennium. Army salaries, when considering all the benefits and allowances and taking into account what they would cost if they had to be purchased out of a civilian salary, are now quite competitive. And pay increases with length of service and advancement in rank and responsibility.

Above all, Army duty is exciting, interesting, and personally rewarding. How many civilians get to be part of a world event? Very few. Soldiers do all the time. As U.S. interests in the world expand, the deployment of American forces to trouble spots around the world to deter enemies, protect international friends, and keep the peace between warring factions will continue to be missions worth training for and successfully executing.

The issues that soldiers are concerned about on a daily basis would fill thick volumes, with pay and entitlements; housing, including barracks and Army family housing; medical care for soldiers and their families; and a stable retirement system leading the list. Daily discussions about chow, guard duty, uniform costs, women in combat (or male attitudes toward them), homosexuals, the quality of training, leadership, supervision, field training exercises, the weather, separation hardships, marital discord, blisters and other ailments, orders, directives, and verbal instructions all point to the old adage that soldiers are happy when they have the opportunity to complain.

Some aspects of Army life are as follows:

• Soldiers of every race, gender, and creed are successful if treated equally and held to the same standards.

• Soldiers will get from combat training what they put into it.

• Most leaders and supervisors are competent; those who aren't fall by the wayside.

• Field training is critical to combat readiness.

• Separation from loved ones occurs in many occupational sectors of American society and must be understood and dealt with by the chain of command.

In recent years, members of the Army have had to deal with increasing deployments, assaults on their benefits, and, worse yet, fellow soldiers undermining the traditional key values by bad behavior. Nevertheless, in the Army family, plenty of good people do care and go about their business because it must be done. Selfless service calls for personal sacrifice and dedication to duty, regardless of the circumstances. No one gets rich on Army pay. If elements of the nation seem less than caring, well, that's just how it is, so don't sweat it.

Sergeant Major of the Army Jack Tilley had these final words of wisdom, "It is about believing in yourself, the Army, the mission, and in defending the Constitution of the United States." He also said, "September 11th [2001] changed our lives. You look at a flag now and know it stands for something more." It surely does.

4

Real-World Issues

Soldiers excel in their duty performance and have successful careers when they obey the requirements of law and Army policy and use a little common sense in other matters that can cause needless problems. Many of the issues confronting civilians also confront soldiers, but the Army has policies and rules to guide the conduct of soldiers. These rules apply to all ranks and address the following issues:

- Fraternization
- Equal opportunity
- Sexual harassment
- Extremism
- Homosexuality
- AIDS
- Marriage
- Divorce
- Spouse and family abuse
- Soldier pregnancy and single parenthood
- Indebtedness
- Alcohol and drug abuse

FRATERNIZATION
The Army has always had policies concerning senior-subordinate relationships. This is nothing new, and it is not just a problem relating to gender.

Army policy states that relationships between soldiers of different rank that involve or give the appearance of partiality, preferential treatment, or the improper use of rank or position for personal gain, and that are prejudicial to good order, discipline, and high unit morale, will be avoided.

Prohibited Relationships
Relationships between soldiers of different rank—regardless of military service—are prohibited if they:

- Compromise, or appear to compromise, supervisory integrity or the chain of command.

- Cause actual or perceived partiality or unfairness.
- Involve the improper use of rank or position for personal gain.
- Are exploitative or coercive in nature.
- Create an actual or predictable impact on discipline, authority, morale, or mission accomplishment.

Prohibited relationships between officers and enlisted people, trainers and trainees, and recruiters and recruits include:

- Any business relationships, except landlord-tenant relationships or one-time transactions.
- Borrowing or lending money, commercial solicitation, and any other type of ongoing financial or business relationship.
- Shared living accommodations other than those directed by operational requirements.
- Dating and other intimate or sexual relationships.
- Gambling.

The reason for this policy is clear. Officers have both punitive and reward power over the personnel in their units. Fraternization or inappropriate association by an enlisted soldier and his or her officers will surely be interpreted as an attempt to obtain favorable treatment. Since officers are legally bound not to fraternize with enlisted soldiers, it is best for enlisted soldiers not to seek these improper associations. Normal team-building associations such as community organizations, religious activities, family gatherings, unit-based social functions, and athletic teams or events are permitted and encouraged.

These prohibitions do not negate a leader's responsibility for the professional development of soldiers. Leaders cannot stop mentoring, coaching, and teaching soldiers because they fear being accused of fraternization or worse. They must continue to encourage individual study and professional development and to mentor the continued growth of their subordinates' military careers.

EQUAL OPPORTUNITY

Equal opportunity (EO) means exactly what the words indicate: Every soldier in the Army shall have an equal opportunity to serve his or her country and obtain the benefits of military service, including training, schooling, promotion, and assignments, without regard to race, religion, ethnic background, national origin, or gender.

Army policy is to base all personnel decisions on merit and excellence of duty performance. Equal opportunity does not mean creating quotas for promotions, assignments, or apportionment of duties based on a soldier's race or other defined category, for this, too, is against the law. Rather, the purpose of EO is for all soldiers to compete on an equal basis for schooling, promotions, and assignments. Soldiers who do their jobs best, who maintain the standards and values mentioned in the previous chapter, will win in these professional competitions regardless of their race or gender. In the Army, these rules are well understood and enforced. Equal opportunity for minorities in the military service has been a success story. It is seen as proof that the Army's EO policies are working, notwithstanding the existence of some individual acts of prejudice that unfortunately still occur.

Gender discrimination is defined as discrimination based solely on an individual's gender in a subgroup "female" or "male." Discrimination based on gender is often linked to a set of assumptions based on sex-role stereotypes concerning the abilities, competence, status, and roles of the particular subgroup, resulting in a disparate treatment of or impact on those groups. We've all seen it in one form or another—male soldiers serving as aides and drivers to male generals because of concerns about having women as their assistants, or an attractive female soldier in the operations shop rather than down in the motor pool working in her MOS.

To prevent the occurrence of discrimination, the Department of the Army has placed the responsibility for EO in the hands of unit commanders and has articulated the connection between EO and unit readiness by enforcing the policy through the traditional chain of command. AR 600-20, *Army Command Policy,* states:

> The chain of command, whether military or civilian, has the primary responsibility for developing and sustaining a healthy climate. This responsibility entails, but is not limited to, promoting positive programs that enhance unit cohesion, esprit, and morale; communicating matters with EO significance to unit personnel and higher headquarters; correcting discriminatory practices by conducting rapid, objective, and impartial inquiries to resolve complaints of discrimination; encouraging the surfacing of problems and preventing reprisal for those who complain; and taking appropriate action against those who violate Army policy.

Under current regulations, commanders have the legal authority to deal with cases of unlawful discrimination or sexual harassment (see the next section). AR 600-20, paragraph 4-4, "Soldier Conduct," provides that ensuring proper conduct of soldiers is a function of command. Commanders rely on all leaders in the Army to "take action against military personnel in any case where the soldier's conduct violates good order and discipline." Although this charge is not punitive, the commander's inherent authority to impose administrative sanctions and to prosecute specific offenses under the Uniform Code of Military Justice (UCMJ) provides commanders with sufficient authority to enforce Army policy against discrimination and harassment.

SEXUAL HARASSMENT

The Department of Defense defines sexual harassment as a form of sex discrimination that involves unwelcome sexual advances, requests for sexual favors, and other verbal or physical conduct of a sexual nature when:

- Submission to such conduct is made either explicitly or implicitly a term or condition of a person's job, pay, or career; or
- Submission to or rejection of such conduct by a person is used as a basis for career or employment decisions affecting that person; or
- Such conduct has the purpose or effect of unreasonably interfering with an individual's work performance or creates an intimidating, hostile, or offensive working environment.

This definition emphasizes workplace conduct. To be actionable as an "abusive work environment," harassment need not result in concrete psychological harm to the victim but need only be so severe or pervasive that a reasonable person would perceive, and the victim does perceive, the work environment as hostile or offensive. Any person in a supervisory or command position who uses or condones any form of sexual behavior to control, influence, or affect the career, pay, or job of a military member or civilian employee is engaging in sexual harassment. Similarly, any military member or civilian employee who makes deliberate or repeated unwelcome verbal comments, gestures, or physical contact of a sexual nature in the workplace is also engaging in sexual harassment and is subject to punishment under the provisions of the UCMJ.

Sexual harassment can include verbal abuse, profanity, off-color jokes, sexual comments, threats, barking, growling, oinking, or whistling at passers-by to indicate a perception of their physical appearance. It also includes nonverbal abuse such as leering, ogling (giving a person the "once over"), blowing kisses, licking lips, winking, leaving sexually suggestive notes, and displaying sexist cartoons and pictures. Unwanted physical contact such as touching, patting, hugging, pinching, grabbing, cornering, kissing, blocking a passageway, and back and neck rubs may also constitute sexual harassment.

EXTREMISM

In 1995, the Murrah Office Building in Oklahoma City was blown up by a former soldier as retaliation against the government's assault on the heavily armed compound of a religious cult the previous year. Later in the year, soldiers murdered two civilians in Fayetteville, North Carolina, because of their race. Although the Constitution guarantees freedom of speech and association, soldiers do not have the right to use these freedoms to infringe upon the rights of others.

Policy

Chapter 4–12 of AR 600-20, *Army Command Policy,* makes it clear that participation in extremist organizations or activities is inconsistent with the responsibilities of military service. It defines extremist organizations and activities as those "that advocate racial, gender, or ethnic hatred or intolerance; advocate, create, or engage in illegal discrimination based on race, color, sex, religion, or national origin; advocate the use of or use force or violence or unlawful means to deprive individuals of their rights under the United States Constitution or the laws of the United States, or any state, by unlawful means."

By regulation, soldiers are prohibited from the following actions in support of extremist organizations or activities:

1. Participating in a public demonstration or rally.
2. Attending a meeting or activity with knowledge that the meeting or activity involves an extremist cause when on duty, when in uniform, when in a foreign country (whether on or off duty or in uniform), when it constitutes a breach of law and order, when violence is likely to result, or when in violation of off-limits sanctions or a commander's order.
3. Fundraising.
4. Recruiting or training members (including encouraging others to join).
5. Creating, organizing, or taking a visible leadership role in such an organization or activity.
6. Distributing literature on or off a military installation the primary purpose and content of which concerns advocacy or support of extremist causes, organizations, or activities, and it appears that the literature presents a clear danger to the loyalty, discipline, or morale of military personnel or if the distribution would materially interfere with the accomplishment of a military mission.

Penalties for violations of these prohibitions include the full range of statutory and regulatory sanctions, both criminal (UCMJ) and administrative.

Command Authority

Commanders have the authority to prohibit military personnel from engaging or participating in any other activities that the commander determines will adversely affect good order and discipline or morale within the command. This includes, but is not limited to, the authority to order the removal of symbols, flags, posters, or other displays from barracks, to place areas or activities off-limits (see AR 190-24), or to order soldiers not to participate in those activities that are contrary to good order and discipline or morale of the unit or pose a threat to health, safety, and security of military personnel or a military installation.

HOMOSEXUALITY

In July 2000, the Department of Defense (DOD) distributed an official message on the subject of homosexual conduct policy. The new policy reiterated the prior one that the suitability of persons to serve in the Army is based on their *conduct* and their ability to meet required standards of duty performance and discipline.

Homosexuality remains incompatible with military service, notwithstanding the current policy of "Don't ask, don't tell." The revised policy adds the requirement "Don't harass." This means that soldiers must not harass others suspected of being homosexual. It is not up to the individual soldier to judge. If you have evidence that another soldier is engaging in homosexual conduct, bring the matter to the attention of your first sergeant and company commander.

Definitions
- *Bisexual:* A person who engages in, attempts to engage in, has a propensity to engage in, or intends to engage in homosexual and heterosexual acts.
- *Homosexual:* A person, regardless of sex, who engages in, attempts to engage in, has a propensity to engage in, or intends to engage in homosexual acts.
- *Sexual orientation:* An abstract sexual preference for persons of a particular sex, as distinct from a propensity or intent to engage in sexual acts.
- *Propensity:* Propensity to engage in homosexual acts means more than an abstract preference or desire to engage in homosexual acts; it indicates a likelihood that a person engages or will engage in homosexual acts.
- *Homosexual conduct:* A homosexual act, a statement by a soldier that demonstrates a propensity or intent to engage in homosexual acts, or a homosexual marriage or attempted marriage.

A "homosexual act" means any bodily contact, actively undertaken or passively permitted, between members of the same sex for the purpose of satisfying sexual desires, and any bodily contact (for example, hand holding, slow dancing, or kissing) that a reasonable person would understand to demonstrate a propensity or intent to engage in such an act.

A "statement by a person that he or she is a homosexual or bisexual or words to that effect" means language or behavior that a reasonable person would believe was intended to convey the statement that a person engages in, attempts to engage in, has a propensity to engage in, or intends to engage in homosexual acts. This may include statements such as "I am a homosexual," "I am gay," "I am a lesbian," "I have a homosexual orientation," and the like.

A "homosexual marriage or attempted marriage" means that a person has married or attempted to marry a person known to be of the same biological sex (as evidenced by the external anatomy of the person involved).

Separation Policy
Homosexual conduct is grounds for separation from the Army. Only a soldier's commander is authorized to initiate fact-finding inquiries involving homosexual conduct. A commander may initiate a fact-finding inquiry only when he or she has received credible information that there is a basis for discharge. Credible information exists when the information, considering its source and the sur-

rounding circumstances, supports a reasonable belief that a soldier engaged in homosexual conduct. It requires a determination based on articulable facts, not just a belief or suspicion. Credible information includes, for example, a reliable person's statement that he or she observed or heard a soldier engaging in homosexual acts or saying that he or she is a homosexual or bisexual or is married to a member of the same sex. Credible information also exists when a reliable person states that he or she heard, observed, or discovered a soldier making a spoken or written statement that a reasonable person would believe was intended to convey the fact that the soldier engages in, attempts to engage in, or has the propensity or intent to engage in homosexual acts.

A fact-finding inquiry may be conducted by the commander personally or by a person he or she appoints. It may consist of an examination of the information reported or a more extensive investigation, as necessary. The inquiry should gather all credible information that directly relates to the grounds for possible separation. Inquiries are limited to the actual circumstances directly relevant to the specific allegations. Commanders are responsible for ensuring that inquiries are conducted properly and that no abuse of authority occurs.

If a commander has credible evidence of possible criminal conduct, he or she follows the procedures in the *Manual for Courts-Martial,* ARs 27-10 and 195-2.

A basis for discharge exists if the soldier has engaged in a homosexual act, the soldier has said that he or she is homosexual or bisexual, the soldier has made some other statement that indicates a propensity or intent to engage in homosexual acts, or the soldier has married or attempted to marry a person of the same sex.

Commanders or appointed inquiry officers shall not ask, and soldiers shall not be required to reveal, whether a soldier is heterosexual, homosexual, or bisexual. However, upon receipt of credible information of homosexual conduct, commanders or appointed inquiry officials may ask soldiers if they engaged in such conduct. The soldier should first be advised of the DOD policy on homosexual conduct and his or her rights under the UCMJ.

The prohibition against homosexual conduct is a long-standing element of military law that continues to be necessary in the unique circumstances of military service. The armed forces must maintain personnel policies that exclude persons whose presence would create an unacceptable risk to the armed forces' high standards of morale, good order, discipline, and unit cohesion that are the essence of military capability. That exclusion must apply to persons who demonstrate a propensity or intent to engage in homosexual acts.

AIDS

The devastating effects of acquired immunodeficiency syndrome (AIDS) continue to be felt in the U.S. military community as well as throughout the nation and world.

Policy
Military readiness, medical, and personnel policies associated with HIV and
AIDS look to protect the Army's ability both to fulfill its constitutional role and
to confidentially identify, evaluate, and provide an appropriate level of care for
infected members.

Active soldiers are tested biennially for the AIDS virus, reserve component
soldiers every five years. Soldiers who are HIV-positive will not be deployed
outside the continental U.S. (Alaska, Hawaii, and Puerto Rico are considered
CONUS in this definition). The fact that HIV-positive soldiers are nondeploy-
able does not preclude their assignment to TOE or MTOE units, except for
Ranger and Special Forces units, which are totally closed. Soldiers who are
HIV-positive are eligible for all military professional development schools and
may also attend formal military training to qualify them for reclassification,
provided the schooling does not exceed 20 weeks.

Mandatory testing and HIV prevention awareness are being emphasized
Armywide. Soldiers and their families must learn to understand how to avoid
and prevent the spread of the disease. Immature soldiers should not make light
of the issue. Doing so downplays the important role of HIV and AIDS awareness and could result in avoidable infections, prolonged illness, and death.

For more information, request from the Association of the United States
Army a copy of its Institute of Land Warfare Paper No. 6, titled *AIDS and Its
Impact on Medical Readiness*. The author, Dr. (Col.) Edmund C. Tramont,
imparts information worth knowing. For example, Tramont says, "Acute diseases involving three organs of the body have most often affected military operations: the gastrointestinal tract, blood, and the genital tract [that is, diarrhea,
malaria, gonorrhea, etc.]. HIV, the cause of AIDS, infects two of these organ
systems. HIV is a fatal sexually transmitted disease that contaminates blood. As
such, its impact on medical readiness is broad and far-reaching."

MARRIAGE

Marriage of Junior Enlisted Soldiers
The old saying "If the Army wanted you to have a wife, it would have issued
you one" has gone by the boards. So has the quaint custom whereby a soldier
had to get his company commander's permission to get married. Although much
of this was done as a courtesy to inform the commander, it did give the company
commander—the "old man"—a chance to talk to the young soldier and to discuss the pros and cons of getting married at this particular stage of life.

Marriage is a commitment to fidelity, love, mutual support, and mutual
sacrifice. Junior-grade soldiers should make a serious self-assessment to determine whether they are ready to assume these responsibilities. There are several
areas to consider:

Money. Can you afford to be married? The wise soldier, like the wise civilian, makes a careful evaluation of whether his or her salary can support a marriage at this time.

Maturity. Sociologists tell us that the kinds of things you believe are important in a spouse when you are very young are likely to be different after about the age of 25. The wise soldier thinks twice about the real meaning of marriage and whether he or she is on solid emotional ground before making the commitment to being a husband or a wife. If you are a member of a church or religious faith, you should check with your chaplain, since many denominations now require multiweek prenuptial counseling before the clergyman will perform the marriage service. If your denomination requires this, take advantage of it, for it is in your and your fiancé's interest to do so.

Duty and Deployment. In recent years, America has experienced a large increase in the number of deployments to far-flung locations. In nearly all cases, deployments for married soldiers mean family separation. Although the Army has programs and family support groups for the spouses and families of deployed soldiers, all soldiers should consider the impact of their absence on their marital situation and the burdens this places on the spouse. For some, this will be no problem. For those who might have married too young or with too little income, it can spell unhappiness for both the soldier and the spouse.

Dual-Service Marriages. Some soldiers believe that if they marry a fellow soldier, they will not have to face the problems of separation during deployment or field exercises. This might be the situation at the moment of a marriage proposal, but it is not a guarantee that two soldiers will always share the same duty or even be in the same unit. The Army tries to assign married service couples to the same post or as close as possible within the same geographic location, depending on MOS vacancies, but you might not always end up in the same unit. Hundreds of dual-service couples have faced this situation without problems, but you should be aware of it before tying the knot. See chapter 12, "Assignments," for more details.

DIVORCE

Divorce is hard on everyone involved, and the military seems to have a larger number of divorces than the general American population. The Army has available a number of family counseling services. The Family Services Center (discussed later), the post or unit chaplain, or even your sergeants and officers can help if you want to save your marriage. If irreconcilable, then check with your local legal office to determine the legal requirements for divorce in your state.

SPOUSE AND FAMILY ABUSE

Do not ever, under any circumstances, abuse your spouse or children in any manner, physically or mentally. It is both a criminal and a moral offense. If you even suspect that you have tendencies to abuse family members less strong than you are, seek counseling immediately. The Army is a rough-and-tumble profession, and the Army requires tough soldiers. Keep the rough-and-tumble out of your family.

SOLDIER PREGNANCY AND SINGLE PARENTHOOD

For several years now, the Army has afforded pregnant soldiers options other than immediate discharge. Today, a pregnant soldier is faced with a number of choices based on Army policy, and she needs to understand these policies up front. These choices are spelled out in chapter 10, "Career Decisions."

Staying in the military as a mother of a newborn child does not afford the military mother special privileges. Although the Army is concerned for the welfare of the child, it does not adjust the assignment process to accommodate the new mother. Instead, the Army requires each soldier with dependents unable to care for themselves to file an approved family care plan. Because the soldier must be ready to deploy anywhere in the world on a moment's notice, the family care plan is necessary so that the Army knows that the child will be cared for in the event the mother is deployed overseas with her unit or assigned to an area where dependents are not authorized.

Married mothers usually face fewer problems, since the spouse will automatically have custody of the children and is assumed to be capable of caring for them if the mother is deployed or assigned to a no-dependents area. Unmarried military mothers have to make other guaranteed arrangements for children and document them in their family care plans, which are registered with the first sergeant.

INDEBTEDNESS

Nothing will make your first sergeant or company commander more upset than receiving letters from your creditors because you have bought more than your salary can pay for. This is not just a soldier problem, it's a DOD-wide problem affecting airmen, sailors, and marines as well, predominantly those in the junior enlisted grades.

Over 27 percent of first-term enlisted soldiers—and 36 percent of junior enlisted servicemembers who are single parents—are in serious debt, according to a March 3, 2000, news release of a study conducted by the DOD Office of Family Policy. The major culprits leading to indebtedness are:

- The "gotta-have-it-now" attitude.
- Undisciplined use of credit cards.
- Buying big-ticket items that are not really needed.
- Excessive entertainment.

The reason first sergeants and company commanders are upset with soldier indebtedness is because it takes so much of their time to deal with it. One military service, for instance, had the incredible record of 123,000 letters of indebtedness, 99,000 bad checks passed through the post exchange, and another 75,000 passed through the commissary—in one year! To reduce the size of this problem, the DOD has issued a compact disk training program called "Financial Tips" that is available at the education center.

A good source of information for soldier financial planning is Stackpole's *Armed Forces Guide to Personal Financial Planning*, 5th edition, which was written specifically to help servicemembers manage money and is chock full of sound advice. Likewise, Stackpole's *Servicemember's Legal Guide* is an excellent source of information on marriage, divorce, or the legal aspects of indebtedness.

ALCOHOL AND DRUG ABUSE
A drug is defined as "any substance which by its chemical nature alters structure or function in the living organism" (AR 600-85). This definition includes alcohol, glue, and aerosols, among many others. The harm and misery these substances have caused to soldiers are incalculable.

Soldiers who use drugs and those who sell drugs do not belong in the U.S. Army. A soldier who relies on alcohol to make it through the day or one who feels that he or she must turn to some drug to get by or get high should have the personal courage to quit or to seek help from the local Army Substance Abuse Program (ASAP).

Alcohol Abuse
AR 600-85 states that the use of alcohol is legal, provided the consumer is of legal age. Alcohol is socially acceptable, if used in moderation. Excessive use of alcohol is not condoned or accepted as part of any military event.

Drug Abuse
An NCO who is caught buying, selling, or using illegal drugs will be punished and separated from the Army. Junior enlisted personnel who abuse drugs may face the same consequences but more often receive nonjudicial punishment under Article 15 of the UCMJ, including loss of pay, reduction in grade, and the stigma of conviction attached to their official files.

Soldiers caught using drugs are referred to a mandatory ASAP for rehabilitation. However, the Army has a very strict "no-tolerance" attitude toward drug abuse, and ASAP treatment does not necessarily mean that the Army will not initiate separation action against the soldier. Don't do drugs.

PART II

The Soldier

5

Self Development

Everyone has room to improve. Every soldier in your pay grade is competing for that same promotion you desire. The farther you go up the ladder, the more you must compete for the next higher position. You must realize that you have control over how competitive you are. . . . Study one area, one task, once a week. It may take an hour or two away from your free time, but you will find the rewards will be worth it.

—CSM Walter J. Jackson in *Soldier's Study Guide*

The Army's system for promotion is discussed in detail in chapter 13. This chapter offers thoughts and proven methods for developing yourself in your current profession—soldier. Individual development is one of the keys to promotion, and the first step in that process is to set a goal for yourself.

SETTING PROFESSIONAL GOALS

Everyone wants to be promoted at some point in his or her career. No one can stay forever at the same rank. The Army's retention control points force you to move up or out. Look at where you want to be five years down the road and begin working to that end today. Waiting until you are a specialist or corporal to start working toward sergeant means that it will take you longer to acquire the necessary promotion points than soldiers who started when they were privates first class.

In all MOSs, some common elements are necessary for promotion. The three items common to all soldiers in the grades private to specialist are:

1. Develop MOS skills.
2. Qualify with your assigned weapon.
3. Maintain physical fitness.

With the new changes in the promotion system, much of your fate rests in your own hands. Work hard to identify yourself to the chain of command (and later the promotion board) as the best soldier.

Soldiers seeking promotion can directly influence their qualifications by making improvements in all three key elements. First, you should be perform-

48

ing duties in your primary MOS at the authorized or next higher grade. Take advantage of any opportunity to serve in a leadership position at the next higher grade. Second, attend any locally available military schools that you can at this stage in your career. The schools found at your installation can vary from air assault, combat life saver, NBC defense, or field sanitation. Finally, you should take advantage of every opportunity to attend military and civilian schools that improve your skills. Begin taking Army correspondence courses early in your career. Take college courses if you are in a position to do so. The additional military and civilian education you obtain on your own shows the chain of command that you are a self-starter seeking to improve yourself. Additionally, military and civilian schooling will improve your chances for promotion by converting educational credit into promotion points.

To keep things in perspective, however, remember that leaders look to your *duty performance* when recommending you for initial promotions. In an interview conducted in 1998, Sergeant Major of the Army Hall commented that he "would like every soldier to get a master's degree—a master's degree in soldiering."

Seek Advice

You should actively seek information and guidance from your chain of command, mentors, and career adviser. You must play an integral part in the decision and assignment process to help attain the goals you have set. Your career branch at the Total Army Personnel Command (PERSCOM) is also there to assist you in determining what is right for you, both professionally and personally. You should maintain communication with your branch to inquire about your next assignment or school. For information or assistance, contact DSN 221-4694 or check the PERSCOM home page at *www.perscom.army.mil*.

As mentioned in chapter 2, the Primary Leadership Development Course (PLDC) is the first level of the NCOES and is a requirement for promotion to the rank of sergeant. This course prepares specialists and corporals (E-4) for leadership and increased levels of responsibility. Promotions (chapter 13) are governed by AR 600-8-19, *Enlisted Promotions and Reductions.* Department of the Army (DA) controls the time in service (TIS) and time in grade (TIG) requirements for promotion. Commanders have the latitude to waive both TIS and TIG to promote outstanding soldiers ahead of their peers. DA controls the rate of promotion to sergeant (E-5) and staff sergeant (E-6), but the local battalion selects the soldiers for promotion at locally conducted promotion boards.

MOS KNOWLEDGE

The Army rewards selfless, dedicated, confident, competent service. If you are among the best in your MOS at your skill level, NCOs and officers will view your professional potential favorably. It will help promotion, school, and training selection boards identify and select you to be among the soldiers who will

Job training is continuous.

lead the Army in the 21st century. Ignoring your professional self-development can result in substandard job performance or, worse, mission failure at a critical time and place. Your knowledge in your occupational specialty, whatever it is, is important. Like all the MOSs in your unit, your technical expertise is essential to the accomplishment of your unit's mission. Be an expert in your MOS.

MILITARY EDUCATION
If you wait for the Army to send you to school to acquire military education promotion points, you have to go through PLDC (4 points per week) plus an additional 42 weeks of military school to reach the 200-point maximum in this promotion category (unless you opt for ranger and special forces training). The quickest way to achieve your 200-point goal is through the Army correspondence course program. Start earning points when you are a private or private first class, and have your military education maxed out when you are first eligible for promotion to sergeant. These same points carry over for promotion to staff sergeant.

Army Correspondence Course Program
A variety of exportable training courses specific to your CMF and MOS are available through the Army Correspondence Course Program. Courses and subcourses on specific topics developed by respective proponent schools are designed for your professional development. You may enroll in this program as

an individual student or via the group enrollment program. Students enrolling in individual study decide which courses to take and when to study the lessons and take the examination. Students register and enroll through the Army Institute for Professional Development (AIPD) Web site, *www.atsc.army.mil/accp/ aipd.htm.* Group enrollment allows a soldier to use these courses to supplement individual training. The program provides professionally designed training that a supervisor can readily administer, and it awards promotion points to those who successfully complete each subcourse. The group leader takes care of all administrative requirements.

A course consists of one or more subcourses designed to support a specific professional field, skill qualification development, or MOS-related tasks. Subcourses are issued in the sequence listed in each course. A subcourse is a basic unit of training covering one subject area, containing one or more lessons and a final examination.

The credit hour is the basic work unit for a correspondence course. The number of credit hours assigned to a subcourse is based on the estimated time required for an average student to read the material and complete all the exercises and the examination. *Five hours of subcourse work equates to one military education promotion point.*

AR 351-20, *Army Correspondence Course Program Catalog,* lists all courses and subcourses available to soldiers. One of the first courses you might consider taking is Primary Leadership Subjects—ACCP Course Number: 553BD21. Soldiers in the rank of private through specialist or corporal are eligible to take this course. The course covers subjects such as math skills, reading comprehension, study methods, management, and writing mechanics and composition. Soldiers in the grade of private first class, specialist, or corporal interested in progressing would also do well to take the Primary Leadership Development Preparatory Course. This course has two phases and consists of 22 subcourses.

Army Training Extension Courses

Army training extension courses (TECs) are oriented toward common skills and critical MOS tasks. Proponent schools develop TECs, and soldiers in the MOS validate them. This self-paced training medium is for individuals and groups. Generally, soldiers use TECs in groups as part of unit training or for individual study. The courses are usually distributed to unit learning centers, but you can requisition individual lessons. TECs are designed in various formats—printed, audiovisual, audio, and job performance aids. Printed lessons are, however, the most predominant form.

Other Sources for Individual Development

Two books written especially for soldier development and promotion are Walter J. Jackson's *Soldier Study Guide,* 4th edition (Mechanicsburg, PA: Stackpole

Books, 2000) and Audie G. Lewis's *Career Progression Guide for Soldiers* (Mechanicsburg, PA: Stackpole Books, 2003). Both books should be available in post exchange bookstores or military clothing sales stores or from the publisher.

IMPROVING BASIC LANGUAGE SKILLS

Reading and writing are critical skills for all soldiers. The Army depends on and must have in its ranks soldiers who read, comprehend, and communicate effectively in writing. Your ability to read, comprehend, and respond in writing to orders and directives from superiors is very important for all leaders. Your reading ability will be assessed when you attend the mandatory NCOES's PLDC, the first rung in the NCOES ladder. You must read at the tenth-grade level or face a likely consequence of nonenrollment.

If you have trouble reading and writing, get help at your local Army Education Center. An education counselor will assist you in identifying any literacy shortcomings. Once you know your reading and writing weaknesses, the counselor can help you enroll in courses designed to turn the weaknesses into strengths. It is better to discover and fix reading deficiencies and writing defects before some critical point in your career.

Much of Army writing is hard to understand and therefore wastes the time of the readers. When you write a military document, be sure to follow this important rule: Put the meaning of your communication in the first paragraph, in the first sentence, if possible. When you write clearly and simply, the material is easy to comprehend.

Common writing problems involve misuse of sentence structure, grammar, punctuation, mechanics, usage, tense, agreement, and "gobbledygook"—avoidable "padding" that hides meaning. Avoid gobbledygook; keep explanations of points you must make to a minimum. Use military jargon only if it is necessary. Avoid the overuse of acronyms. If you have to use acronyms, explain them before using them. One of the best sources to refine your writing skills is William A. McIntosh's *Guide to Effective Military Writing,* 3rd edition (Mechanicsburg, PA: Stackpole Books, 2003).

The best way to improve your writing skills and your reading ability is to read a variety of books, magazines, and newspapers. Reading stimulates the intellect and increases your understanding of people and events. Read more than one book on a subject; challenge yourself to comprehend complex ideas and issues. Stay tuned to topics that pertain to national events, such as human rights, free enterprise, democracy, liberty, and prosperity. Read stories in daily newspapers about business, politics, and environmental issues, about how these matters relate in the global marketplace, and how they affect other nations.

Stay informed. Read to understand America's role in the world, the Army's role in America, and your role in America's Army.

PERSONAL REFERENCE LIBRARY AND RECOMMENDED READING

What follows are the books, movies, and poetry that most affected my attitudes toward my service as an enlisted man and that I recommend to others. Most lend a historical perspective and deal with issues we are all faced with: duty, morale, ethics, training, and leadership, especially that of the small unit in extreme circumstances. Many look at leaders who are looking at themselves. Books that are on the Army reading list are marked with an asterisk (*).

Movies

Big Red One	*Kelly's Heroes*
Breaker Morant	*Saving Private Ryan*
Cross of Iron	*We Were Soldiers Once . . . and Young*
Gladiator	*Zulu*
Hamburger Hill	

Nonfiction

*Stephen Ambrose, *Band of Brothers*
John Baynes, *Morale*
*Tom Brokaw, *The Greatest Generation*
John Collins, *Common Sense Training*
*T. R. Fehrenbach, *This Kind of War*
Ernest F. Fisher, *Guardians of the Republic: A History of the Noncommissioned Officer Corps of the U.S. Army*
*Charles Heller and William Stoft, *America's First Battles: 1776–1965*
*David Hogan, *A Concise History of the U.S. Army: 225 Years of Service*
Elbert Hubbard, *A Message to Garcia*
*John Keegan, *The Face of Battle*
*Paul Kennedy, *Rise and Fall of the Great Powers*
Gerald Linderman, *The World Within War*
Dandridge (Mike) Malone, *Small Unit Leadership*
*Harold Moore and Joe Galloway, *We Were Soldiers Once . . . and Young*
Sam Watkins, *Co. Aytch*

Fiction

R. A. Heinlein, *Starship Troopers*
Jean Larteguy, *The Centurions*
*Anton Myrer, *Once an Eagle*
Guy Sager, *Forgotten Soldier*

Poetry

Rudyard Kipling, "The 'Eathen" and "If"
Robert W. Service, "The Quitter"

Other Works

Other recommended history and historical figure books include *The Civil War,* by renowned author Shelby Foote, and *Ernie's War, The Best of Ernie Pyle's World War II Dispatches,* edited by David Nichols.

Though they were not intended as literary works, the U.S. Constitution and the Bill of Rights are worth your time as well, as are other historic government documents. Read about civic matters to learn more about the U.S. government and the Army's role in it.

Stackpole Books, publisher of *Enlisted Soldier's Guide,* offers more than 100 other titles of interest to the military reader.

Soldiers, the official monthly magazine of the Army, is also a recommended source of feature information about unit activities and Army people. It is now published online at *www.dtic.mil/soldiers.* Although not an official publication of the army, *Army Times* weekly newspaper and *Army* magazine, the monthly journal of the Association of the U.S. Army, are important publications containing professional information.

Official Doctrine and Guidance

You should also read material about specific subjects that become increasingly important to professional soldiers. Study the following: Field Manual 6-22 [FM 22-100], *Military Leadership;* FM 3-22.9 [FM 23-9], *M16A1 Rifle Marksmanship;* FM 3-22.20, [FM 21-20], *Physical Fitness Training;* FM 7-10 [FM 25-101], *Battle Focused Training;* AR 27-10, *Military Justice;* STP 21-1, *Soldier's Manual of Common Tasks Skill Level 1*; and STP 21-24SMCT 1, *Soldier's Manual of Common Tasks Skill Level 2.* All these publications should be available in your company or at your local MOS library and are available online at the Training and Doctrine Digital Library at *www.atsc.army.mil.*

EXPLORING THE INFORMATION SUPERHIGHWAY: THE ARMY ON-LINE AND THE WORLD WIDE WEB

The Army has entered the information superhighway, with dozens of sites currently on-line and more established daily. Computer literacy is becoming important for soldiers of all ranks, because it enables them to receive and transmit text and supporting communications across vast electronic networks. No longer do you have to thumb through old copies of the *Army Times* or look for the latest PERSCOM message to find information vital to your career. Just go to the PERSCOM home page and view the most up-to-date information concerning your MOS. Entire books are on-line at the Center of Military History's home page. Need to prepare a class on the most current techniques to breach a minefield? Try the Center for Army Lessons Learned. It's all there—you just have to look.

The Internet
The Internet is the worldwide free-enterprise network of computers that links distant sites. It is a combination of tens of thousands of computer servers linked to computer users via telephone lines or direct circuits, all connected through the world's telephone companies. Each server is a separate "site" with a unique numeric name. Another name for part of the Internet is the World Wide Web, shortened to www or the Web.

Web Pages
A Web page is the graphical presentation of a document on the Web. Usually each page contains one type or grouping of information with "links" to other subpages or to other Web pages at different sites. Web pages can be as simple as text pages or can be as complex as pages with pictures, animated images, video clips, and attached sound files.

U.S. Army On-line
Listed below are some of the more popular Web sites that deal with military issues. No longer do you have to wait in the dark for the word to be passed down on Army issues. You can now go to the source.

Adjutant General Directorate
www-perscom.army.mil/tagd/index
APFT Score Converter Download Page
members.aol.com/DavidWCobb/APFT16
Armor Magazine
www.entelechy-inc.com/docs/knoxdoc/armormag/index
Army Alumni Association Database
www.army.mil/vetinfo/vetloc
Army and Air Force Exchange Service
www.aafes.com
Army Career and Alumni Program (ACAP)
www.acap.army.mil
Army Continuing Education System
www-perscom.army.mi/tagd/aces/aces.htm
Army Correspondence Course Program
www.atsc.army.mil/accp/aipd.htm
Army Emergency Relief
www.aerhq.org
Army Enterprise Strategy
www.hqda.army.mil/enterprise/
Army home page
www.army.mil

Army Housing Division
147.103.22.141
Army Institute for Professional Development (AIPD)
206.135.244.97/accp/aipd
Army Knowledge Online Access Page
www.us.army.mil
Army Publishing Agency (USAP.A)
www-usappc.hoffman.army.mil
Army Reserve Personnel Center
www.army.mil/usar/arpercen/arpercen
Army Retirement Services
www.odcsper.army.mil/prod/retire/retire
Army Sergeants Major Academy
bliss-usasma.army.mil
Army Training Digital Library
www.atsc-army.org/atdls.html
Army Training Information Management Program (ATIMP)
www.atimp.army.mil
Army Training Requirements and Resources System
www.asmr.com/atrrs/index
Army Training Support Center
www.atsc-army.org/atschomel-ssi
Army Training XXI
www.dcst.monroe.army.mil/atxxi/atxxi-hp
Army Vision 2010
www.army.mil/2010
Association of the United States Army
www.ausa.org
Battle Command Training Program
leav-www.army.mil/bctp
Brigade/Battle Staff NCO home page
leav-ftp.army.mil/bcbst/NCBOS.HTM
CALL (Center for Army Lessons Learned) Newsletters
call.army.mil/cal/homepages/newsltr.html
Career Branch Newsletters
www-perscom army.mil/enlist/cb-let.htm
Center for Army Leadership
www-cgsc.army.mil/cal/index.htm
Center for Army Leadership home page
www-cgsc.anny.mil/cgsc/cal/cal
Center for Army Lessons Learned (CALL)
call.army.mil/call

Center of Military History (CMH)
www.army.mil/cmh-pg/default
Combat Developments Directorate for Combat Service Support (CSS)
cascom-www.army.mil/multi
Command and General Staff College
www-cgsc.army.mil
Common Task Training
atscweb.atsc-army.org/dev/itsd/ctt.htm
Corps and Division Doctrine
www-cgsc.army.mil/cgsc/cdd/cdd
Defense News
www.defensenews.com
DefenseLINK
www.dtic.mil/defenselink
Department of Veterans Affairs
www.va.gov
Electronic Access to Military History
www.kuhttp.cc.ukans.edu/history/milhst
Enlisted Leader Development Network
www-cgsc.army.mil/cal/eldn/eldnfr.htm
Enlisted MOS Structure Charts
www-perscom.army.mil/gendocs/enlcmf.html
Enlisted Promotions, PERSCOM
www-perscom.army.mil/select/enlisted.htm
FAMILY Demographics Database
www.usarmycfsc.com
FAMILY System, Soldier and Family Demographics
www.asmr.com/pam/family1
GulfLINK
www.dtic.dla.mil:80/gulflinkl>
Headquarters, Department of the Army
www.hqda.army.mil
Joint Language Training Center
jltc.army.mil
Leader XXI
www-cgsc.army.mil/cgsc/call/do/homepagl
Louisiana Maneuvers (LAM)
140.139.18.189/lamhome1
Medals and Ribbons
www.dtic.mil/soldiers
Military Acronyms
www.ha.osd.mil/main/acronym.html

Military Family Institute
www.marywood.edu
Military Internet Resources
kuhttp.ccukans.edu/history/ehawk/arm_index
Military Network
www.military-network.com
Military Review Magazine
www-cgsc.army.mil/milrev/index
National Guard Association
www.ngaus.org
NCOES Information Paper
www-perscom army.mil/enlist/guide/ncoes.htm
Noncommissioned Officers Web site
www.geocities.com/Pentagonl4227
Office of the Chief, Army Reserve (OCAR)
www.army.mil/usar/ocar
Pentagon Library
www.hqda.army.millpenlibweb/homepage
Per Diem
www.dtic.mil/perdiem
PS Magazine—Preventive Maintenance Monthly
www.logsa.army.mil/psmag/pshomel
Soldier Support Network
www-ssn.ria.army.mil
Soldiers Magazine On-line
www.dtic.mil/soldiers
Total Army Personnel Command
www-perscom.army.mil
TRADOC Retention Management Division
www-tradoc army.mil/dcsbos/reup
Trainer On-line
www.atsc-army.org/trainonll
Training Quarterly
call.army.mil/call/homepages/trngqtr.htm
TRICARE Support Office home page
www.ochampus.mil
TRICARE Support Office OCHAMPUS
www-qa-sun.ochampus.mil.index2
U.S. Army National Guard
www.dtic.mil/defenselink/guardlink
U.S. Army Reserve
www.army.mil/usar

U.S. Personal Management Retirement Programs
www.opm.gov/retire
USAJOBS (OPM)
www.usajobs.opm.gov
Warfighter XXI
call.army.mil: 1100/~bctd/wfxxi/wfxxi-hp
World War II—"50 Years Ago"
www.webcom.com/~jbd/ww2

PROFESSIONAL ASSOCIATIONS

Association of the U.S. Army

The Association of the U.S. Army (AUSA) is a private, nonprofit organization established in 1950. It supports active and reserve component members, Army civilians, retirees, and Army families. Its goals are as follows:

- People support for those in the Army.
- Industry support of the Army.
- Public education about the Army.
- Professionalism within the Army.

AUSA's legislative affairs office stays on top of issues that affect soldiers during and after service. The association pushes for pay equity, adequate military housing, cost-of-living allowances, and standard subsistence allowances for all personnel, as well as full reimbursement of expenses for official travel and changes of station, quality medical and dental care, and an upgraded retirement system.

Regular membership costs are stepped according to grade: $20 per year for grades E-1 through E-4, $25 for E-5 through E-7, and $30 for E-8 and E-9. Among its membership benefits are opportunities to participate in chapter activities and discount product and service programs. AUSA also offers MasterCare, a TRICARE supplement; accidental death and dismemberment coverage; a group term life insurance program; a discount eyewear program; discount car rental and lodging programs; and its own Visa card.

For more information, check the AUSA website at *www.ausa.org* or call (800) 336-4570. You can also write to Association of the United States Army, 2425 Wilson Blvd., Arlington, VA 22201, or e-mail them at *ausa.info@ausa.org*.

Noncommissioned Officers Association

The Noncommissioned Officers Association (NCOA) is a federally chartered, nonprofit, fraternal association founded in 1960. The NCOA seeks to promote health, prosperity, and scholarship among its members and their families through legislative and benevolent programs to improve benefits for soldiers, veterans, and their families and survivors. Through its office near the Pentagon,

NCOA actively lobbies Congress, the White House, the Department of Veterans Affairs, the military services, and other federal agencies to fulfill its goals. It monitors state and local administrative and legislative activities affecting NCOA members, conducts a nationwide outreach program for hospitalized veterans, and operates fellowship and intern programs for undergraduate college students.

Annual membership for NCOs costs $30. The association offers many member benefits, including a certified merchants program and a buying network. Members also receive *NCOA Journal* and may qualify for the NCOA Visa card. Also offered are a health insurance supplement, a motor club that provides roadside assistance and towing, property and casualty insurance, and free accidental death and dismemberment insurance.

For more information, write to Noncommissioned Officers Association, ATTN: Membership Processing, P.O. Box 105636, Atlanta, GA 30348-5636; call (800) 662-2620; or check the website at *www.ncoausa.org*

National Guard Enlisted Association
The National Guard Enlisted Association (EANGUS) exists to promote the status, welfare, and professionalism of the enlisted members of the National Guard of the United States and promote adequate national security.

EANGUS has a home page on the Internet at *www.eangus.org*. Users can access the congressional database system, Senate, House, EANGUS's *New Patriot* magazine and newsletter, *Congressional Quarterly, Legislative Updates,* and more. E-mail capability puts you in touch with the various departments at the national office that can answer your questions regarding membership, events, and legislative issues.

Membership in EANGUS has its benefits, including discount vision care, travel benefits, rental cars, long-distance telephone programs, college counseling, comprehensive résumé services, credit cards, auto insurance, and other insurance programs.

For more information, call toll-free (800) 234-EANG, or write to Enlisted Association of the National Guard of the United States, 1219 Prince St., Alexandria, VA 22314; E-mail address: *natloffc@eangus.org*.

6

Marksmanship

Every soldier must be a proficient marksman with his or her assigned weapon. Proper shooting is a physical skill that, like riding a bicycle, can be learned. When practiced often for short periods, it becomes a skill that will be retained. Marksmanship is learned on the zero range and the qualification range; in combat, it is the individual soldier's ultimate defense. Marksmanship fundamentals include assuming a steady position, aiming, breathing in a controlled manner, and squeezing the trigger. Knowing these fundamentals develops fixed and correct firing habits for instinctive application.

The mechanics for zeroing the M16A1 and M16A2 are in STP 21-1 SMCT, *Soldiers Manual of Common Tasks,* and are not presented here. Only the prone supported position is described below. The basic techniques described, however, apply to all positions.

FUNDAMENTALS

Position
To assume the prone position, face the target, spread your feet a comfortable distance apart, and drop to your knees. Using the butt of the rifle as a pivot, roll onto your nonfiring side. Place the rifle butt in the pocket formed by the firing shoulder, grasp the pistol grip in your firing hand, and lower the firing elbow to the ground. Adjust your left and right elbows until your shoulders and feet are about level to provide the steadiest possible position. Your elbows provide additional support, and your feet, shoulder-width apart, add stability. Rest the handguard in the "V" formed by the thumb and forefinger and across the heel of your nonfiring hand with the hand on the sandbag, ensuring that all the weapon's weight is on the sandbag and not on your elbows. Place the butt of the stock firmly into the pocket formed by the firing shoulder. Wrap your hand around the hand grip. The three lower fingers come around the pistol grip and meet the thumb to form the grip. The grip should be like a good, firm handshake. If you put on a "death grip," the muscle tension will cause you to shake.

Your body must lie in a relaxed, flat position. Point your toes out so your feet lie sideways, flat against the ground. Start with your feet and think about the position of all body parts, working up to your fingers. If you are using muscles to hold your position, you will shake. Keep your forearm vertical under the rifle, straight up and down. When you angle your arms, you are using muscles to hold them still. Gravity will do this for you if you keep your forearm vertical.

Place your cheek firmly against the stock of the rifle, putting your eye close to and directly behind the rear peep sight. You can tell that you have a good position when there is absolutely no movement of the weapon when you sight on the target, exhale, hold your breath, and squeeze the trigger. This way, your head rides with the rifle as it recoils, and it will not kick you. It just pushes your shoulder, and you ride with it.

Aim

You begin the aiming process by aligning the rifle with the target when assuming a firing position. Point the rifle naturally at the desired point of aim. If you use muscles to adjust the weapon onto the point of aim, you will find that they automatically relax as the rifle fires, and the rifle will move toward its natural point of aim, which is the point at which the rifle naturally rests in relation to the aiming point. Because this movement begins just before the weapon discharges, the rifle is moving as the bullet leaves the muzzle. This causes inaccurate shots with no apparent cause (recoil disguises the movement). Since the rifle becomes an extension of your body, it is necessary to adjust your position until the rifle points naturally at the preferred aiming point on the target.

Once you are in position and aimed toward your target, the method for checking for natural point of aim is to close your eyes, take a couple of breaths, and relax as much as possible. Upon opening your eyes, your sights should be positioned at the aiming point (target). You can change the deviation of the natural point of aim by shifting your body left or right. Elevation can be changed by leaving your elbows in place and sliding your body forward or rearward. This raises or lowers the muzzle of the weapon, respectively. By adjusting the weapon and body as a single unit, rechecking, and readjusting as needed, you can achieve a true natural point of aim.

Once your natural point of aim is established, aim your weapon at the exact point on the target.

Four aspects contribute to aiming: your shooting eye, the rear sight, the front sight, and the target. The distance between the sights does not change. The distance from your eye to the rear sight can change when you have different stock welds. The relationship between your eye and the rear sight is important. Once you find the right position for your eye, note the relationship between your nose and the stock or action of the rifle. Each time you aim, put your nose in the same place. This will help you keep your sight picture consistent. This is called a stock weld. When zeroing, it is critical to use the same aim point, regardless of the strike of the shot group, so that you do not chase the shot groups trying to hit center using holdoff.

Aiming involves four elements: sight picture, sight alignment, aiming point, and focus.

Sight Picture

In aiming, you are concerned with correctly pointing your rifle so the bullet will hit the target when you fire. To do this, you must have the rear sight, the front sight post, and the target or aiming point in their proper relationship. This is known as sight picture. A correct sight picture is obtained when the sights are aligned and the aiming point (target) is in the correct relationship to the front sight post. The sight picture includes two basic elements: sight alignment and placement of the aiming point.

Sight Alignment

Alignment is critical. Any movement you make during firing that changes the relationship of the front and rear sights by one-tenth of an inch will cause a miss on a 300-meter target by 5 feet. When you look through the rear aperture, your mind must form an imaginary pair of crosshairs, one vertical and one horizontal. Align these crosshairs with the front sight post. Bring the top of the front sight post up even with the horizontal line and centered, ensuring that there is an equal amount of the front sight post on each side of the vertical line.

Although a small misalignment can cause problems, don't "get wrapped around the axle" with the thousandths of an inch—just do it correctly. Remember, it must be done the same way each and every time.

CORRECT SIGHT PICTURE	CORRECT SIGHT ALIGNMENT	CORRECT PLACEMENT OF AIMING POINT

Aiming Point

When zeroing, the aiming point is the center mass of the black 250-meter scaled silhouette of the 25-meter target. If the aiming point is correctly positioned, an imaginary vertical line drawn through the center of the front sight post will appear to split the aiming point.

1. Position the front sight just to the right or left of the target, just far enough so the whole target next to the front sight post can be seen.

2. Raise or lower the front sight post so the top of the sight is halfway between the top and bottom of the target.
3. Smoothly move the front sight straight over to the target, without raising or lowering the post, and stop when the post is centered on the target.

If the sight picture gets too blurry, relax, blink your eyes, take a breath, and start over at step 1.

Focus

Remember that the human eye cannot focus on two objects at the same time. A correct sight picture has the rear sight and target blurry and the front sight in focus. The line of sight goes from the eye through the rear sight aperture (the mind forms the imaginary crosshairs). The front sight post is then brought into the line of sight and correctly aligned with the imaginary crosshairs. This is critical to good shooting and scores. Whether shooting at 25, 100, or 600 meters, you must always focus on the *front* sight post.

Dominant Eye

Some shooters have problems aligning the target with the sights because of their eyesight. To determine which eye is dominant, extend one arm to the front and point the index finger skyward to select an aiming point. With both eyes open, align the index finger with the aiming point; then close one eye at a time while looking at the aiming point. With one eye, the finger will appear to move off the aiming point; with the other eye, the finger will stay on the aiming point. The dominant eye is the eye that does not move the finger from the aiming point. Some individuals may have difficulty aiming because of interference from the dominant eye, if this is not the eye used in the aiming process. Such individuals must close the dominant eye while shooting.

Breathe

If you don't breathe during weapon firing, you will shake. There is a correct way to breathe when shooting. Try this exercise: Take a breath. Let it out. While exhaling, notice that there is a point at which you don't feel it necessary to continue exhaling or to start breathing in again. Now try it again. This time, when you get to that point, stop breathing for a second or two. It's easy!

This is the place in your breathing cycle where you want to take your shot. Since you can hold it for only a second or two at most, you must time the rise and fall of the rifle, the sight alignment and picture, and the trigger squeeze to coincide with that point. Notice that when you inhale, the muzzle of the rifle drops. It rises again when you exhale. When your chest expands, your shoulder rises; your forearm that supports the rifle does not move, so the muzzle drops. You must time this rise and fall so that the target is sighted at that point.

SEQUENCE FOR BREATHING AND FIRING

1. Breathe. Inhale and exhale to the natural respiratory pause. Check for consistent head placement and stock weld. Ensure that eye relief is correct. At the same time, begin aligning the front blade with the target at the desired point of aim.

2. Relax. As you exhale, relax as many muscles as possible while maintaining control of the weapon and position.

3. Aim. If you have a good, natural point of aim, the rifle points at the desired target during the respiratory pause. If the aim is off, make a slight adjustment to acquire the desired point of aim. Avoid "muscling" the weapon toward the aiming point.

4. Squeeze. As long as the sight picture is satisfactory, squeeze the trigger. The pressure applied to the trigger must be straight to the rear without disturbing the lay of the rifle or the desired point of aim.

Squeeze

Squeeze is nothing more than squeezing the trigger straight to the rear without disturbing the sight picture. You begin the trigger squeeze and continue until the rifle fires, while maintaining sight alignment. The part of the finger that should touch the trigger is the pad of flesh directly opposite the quick of the fingernail—not the fingertip, and no further back than the first joint.

When you pull the trigger, you must apply steadily increasing pressure until the gun fires. The shot should come as a surprise every time. If you anticipate and flinch, you will never be able to shoot well. The normal reflex action of the body is such that you will miss if the trigger is not squeezed. Your concentration should be so centered on sight alignment, focus, and trigger control that you can ignore the recoil and just let it happen.

Follow-through

You will have less tendency to jerk, flinch, and buck if you follow through after your shot. Follow-through is the act of continuing to apply all the marksmanship fundamentals as the weapon fires as well as immediately after it fires. Follow-through involves:

- Keeping the head in firm contact with the stock (stock weld).
- Keeping the finger on the trigger all the way to the rear.
- Continuing to look through the rear aperture or scope tube.
- Keeping muscles relaxed.
- Avoiding reaction to recoil and noise.
- Releasing the trigger only after the recoil has stopped.

Hearing Protection

The biggest mistake you can make is not wearing hearing protection. Not only can you damage your hearing, but the noise will be loud, and you will begin to associate the noise with the recoil. In your mind, the noise and the recoil will be one and the same.

Acting as a Coach

If you are acting as a coach, watch for the following:

- Ensure that the firer assumes a good steady position.
- Make sure that the firer applies correct pressure during trigger squeeze.
- Determine whether the firer flinches, jerks, or bucks by watching the firer's head, shoulder, trigger finger, and nonfiring hand and arm.
- Make sure that the firer breathes correctly by watching his or her back occasionally.
- Make sure that the firer releases pressure on the trigger and lowers his or her rifle when the trigger is not squeezed within 3 to 5 seconds.
- Check shoulder placement of the rifle butt and pressure in the shoulder pocket. It should be snug; the top of the butt should be level with the top of the shooter's shoulder and not falling off the side of the shoulder.
- Check that the back of the nonfiring hand is fully supported by the sandbag.

References

FC 23-11, *Unit Marksmanship Trainer's Guide*
FC 23-29, *Weaponeer Training Device*
FM 23-9 M16A1, *Rifle and Rifle Marksmanship*
SH 23-9-3, *BRM Trainers Guide*
STP 21-1 SMCT
TM 9-1005-249-10 (M16A1)
TM 9-1005-319-10 (M16A2)

7

Physical Fitness and Weight Control

The real value of being physically fit is as clear today as it was on distant battlefields long—and not so long—ago. In Vietnam, for example, soldiers from the 101st Airborne Division assaulted an enemy-infested hill 11 times, captured it, and destroyed an entrenched enemy. The victory showed the willpower and guts of physically fit warriors who would not quit.

Mental toughness goes hand in hand with physical fitness. Soldiers who fought and won more recent battles can attest to the value of physical strength and mental endurance. Soldiers today—active and reserve—must be fit to fight.

Infantrymen, medics, cooks, mechanics, tankers, engineers, artillerymen, and air defenders all serve on the same team. Each soldier in America's Army is expected to get and stay prepared, because a need to deploy is likely to arise.

According to Army policy, soldiers must train to accomplish their wartime Mission Essential Task List (METL). A unit METL includes all its critical wartime tasks. So, soldiers should have in their physical training programs events that fully prepare them to accomplish METL, or wartime, tasks.

In an artillery unit, one physically demanding METL task might be to load a 202-pound, 8-inch explosive projectile into a howitzer. In an armored unit, a METL task could be to remove, repair, and replace a track pad on a disabled M-1 tank. An airborne infantry METL might read: "On order, parachute at night with full combat load from a C-141 jet aircraft, then move on foot to find, close with, and kill the enemy." By now, you should fully grasp the importance of physical fitness to the accomplishment of a unit's METL.

THE FIVE COMPONENTS OF FITNESS

The five components of fitness give soldiers the ability to handle military emergencies.

1. Cardiorespiratory endurance enables the body to deliver nutrients and remove waste at the cellular level.
2. Muscular strength is applying the greatest amount of force possible in a single movement.

3. Muscular endurance is the ability to perform repeated movements with moderate resistance for given periods of time.
4. Flexibility is the ability to move joints of the body through their entire range of motion.
5. Body composition deals with the proportion of lean body mass (muscle, bone, and essential organ tissue) to body fat.

THE SEVEN PRINCIPLES OF EXERCISE

PROVRBS (pronounced "proverbs")—progression, regularity, overload, variety, recovery, balance, and specificity—are the principles behind a proper physical training program. These principles lead to a positive training effect and physical excellence each time you exercise. Violate any principle, and your program will be less rewarding.

Progression

The intensity of each successive exercise period must gradually be increased so that physical strength improves gradually (progress). A safe improvement rate is about a 10 percent increase in cardiorespiratory and muscular ability every 10 days. That is, you should strive to reduce your elapsed time on a run by about 10 percent every 10 days to two weeks until you achieve the desired goal. You should try to increase the number of endurance-related exercises such as push-ups and sit-ups by about 10 percent during the same period, and you should push and pull toward the same level of improvement in muscular strength during the period.

Regularity

Exercise must be performed at regular intervals, at least three to five times a week. Soldiers must also rest, sleep, and eat properly on a regular basis.

Overload

Overloading means going for the "max" during each exercise session and doing so safely to achieve a positive training effect. Overloading means working your heart at a relatively high percentage of its maximum capacity, based on your current physical condition, sex, and age. This is called the training heart rate. Your unit master fitness trainer (MFT) can help you determine your rate so that you train at the proper intensity when running or doing other aerobic exercises. Overloading also means working to muscle failure when doing muscular strength or endurance routines. With push-ups and sit-ups, this means using several timed sets (such as a 60-second set, followed by a 20-second rest, followed by a 45-second set, followed by a 20-second rest, followed by a 30-second set, and doing as many repetitions per set as possible). Over time, as you become more fit, your training heart rate intensity is increased and the timed sets are lengthened.

Unit physical training can be done anywhere.

Variety
Variety means breaking up the weekly training routine with various exercises to reduce boredom and increase motivation. A program can include different kinds of runs, such as ability group runs, circuit training, slow distance runs, fast continuous runs, relays, and so forth. Strength and endurance workouts can be outdoors or at the gym and include free weights, Nautilus machines, Kaiser or pneumatic machines, universals, mat routines, partner-resisted exercises, timed sets, sandbag circuits, and so forth. Of course, units should train collectively, so periodic cohesion runs and formation routines should be included.

Recovery
Recovery provides a 24- to 48-hour rest between exercising the same muscles. Hard days of training should be alternated with easier days, or the muscles exercised each day should be alternated. Improper recovery leads to muscle fatigue, which can cause injury. During rest periods, muscle damage is repaired and waste is metabolized.

Balance
Balance entails balancing the principles of exercise so that they lead to the five components of fitness. It means that as you progress through your exercise program, you should balance upper-body and lower-body routines, back muscle and abdomen routines, and rest and recovery periods. For example, balance endurance runs with sprints so that you can run fast and far for as long as possible.

Specificity

The last principle, specificity, involves what the balance principle seems to tell you to avoid: working on a specific ability. Specificity, however, deals with specific muscles and muscle groups or with a specific kind of run to address areas that need improvement.

Suppose you were an infantry scout who had real trouble climbing over tall obstacles. You would need to focus on your lack of upper-body climbing strength without violating the other principles of exercise. By adding a rope-climbing routine to your overall exercise program, you would comply with the principles of exercise and overcome a specific METL-related deficiency.

Most soldiers are required to participate in an organized physical training program. The program will undoubtedly emphasize the "big three" of the Army's Physical Fitness Test (APFT)—push-ups, sit-ups, and running—but it should also offer a variety of calisthenics and individual fitness training.

DESIGNING AN INDIVIDUAL FITNESS PROGRAM[1]

Many soldiers do not know how or what to do to increase their physical fitness beyond the present level. This is not because they are uncaring, but because many were never taught how. Many organizations and schools still conduct physical training (PT) en masse, which normally consists of push-ups, sit-ups, and a run. Additionally, many remedial PT programs are not geared to deficiencies, concentrating instead on running rather than the soldier's weakness.

The following individual PT program was developed for soldiers with little time to devote to PT. It is a modification of a successful PT program found in a light infantry battalion and is based on the principles found in FM 21-20. This program may help you increase your physical readiness without a major cost in time.

The program was validated using 40 students in an ROTC program. Students exercised three times per week for 20 to 25 minutes, not including the run. The following results were achieved: after one month, the average Physical Fitness Test score for students increased by 15 to 20 points, from an average of 192 to 212; at the end of three months, students went from an average of 212 points to 243; the next three months saw average scores climb to 267, with the low score 242 and the high 300. Since this is an individual program, it is designed to fit every soldier's physical ability. The program takes a soldier gradually to a higher level of physical fitness.

Individual Fitness Program Analysis

Take a look at your last APFT. From your scores, you can determine where your starting point for your individual fitness program should be. If you haven't

---

[1]Published by the author in *NCO Journal* (summer 1993) and republished in *NCO Journal* (summer 1997).

taken an APFT in the last three to four months, you may want to assess your physical abilities before beginning the program.

To conduct a self-assessment, do as many correct push-ups and sit-ups as you can in a one-minute period, and then run as hard as you can for a timed half mile. Multiply your push-up and sit-up scores by 1.25 to find an entry point into the charts. Multiply your half-mile time by four.

The Program
The following, if done correctly, will bring you to muscle failure. This exercise regime is designed to be done every other day, as your muscles need 24 to 48 hours to recover from hard usage.

To get your starting numbers of exercises, look at the charts below. The numbers along the top of the charts are the numbers of push-ups or sit-ups that you performed. Follow the number down the column to give you the number of repetitions of each exercise you should begin with in your individual program.

PUSH-UP IMPROVEMENT
APFT NUMBER PUSH-UPS

#	10	15	20	25	30	35	40	45	50	55	60	65	70	75	80	85
Push-ups	4	6	8	10	12	14	16	18	20	22	24	26	28	30	32	34
Diamonds	2	3	4	5	6	7	8	9	10	11	12	13	14	15	16	17
Wide-arm	2	3	4	5	6	7	8	9	10	11	12	13	14	15	16	17
Turn and bounce	5	6	7	8	9	10	12	14	16	18	20	22	24	26	28	30

SIT-UP IMPROVEMENT
APFT NUMBER SIT-UPS

#	10	15	20	25	30	35	40	45	50	55	60	65	70	75	80	85
Sit-ups	4	6	8	10	12	14	16	18	20	22	24	26	28	30	32	34
Crunches	4	5	6	7	8	8	9	9	10	10	11	12	13	14	15	16
Flutter kick	5	6	7	8	9	10	12	14	16	18	20	22	24	26	28	30
Leg spreader	5	6	7	8	9	10	12	14	16	18	20	22	24	26	28	30

Running

Using the following running chart will help you both increase your aerobic and anaerobic stamina and better your 2-mile-run time. Enter the table using your 2-mile-run time, or multiply your half-mile assessment by four. For example, if your run time is 26:15, enter the chart at +26. This program is designed to be run every other day, although there is no harm in running more than three times per week.

RUNNING IMPROVEMENT

Minutes	+12	+13	+14	+15	+16	+17	+18	+19	+20	+21	+22	+23	+24	+25	+26
1/8 mile	—	—	—	—	—	:48	:51	:55	:59	1:03	1:07	1:10	1:14	1:18	1:22
1/4 mile	1:07	1:15	1:23	1:30	1:37	1:45	1:52	2:00	2.08	2.15	2.23	2.30	2.37	2:45	3.00
1/2 mile	2:45	3:00	3:15	3:30	3:45	4:00	4:15	4:30	4:45	5:00	5:15	5:30	5:45	6:00	6:15
Fast run	—	—	—	—	—	1/2 mi	1/2 mi	1/2 mi	1/2 mi	1/2 mi	1/2 mi	1/2 mi	1/2 mi	1/2 mi	1/2 mi
	—	—	—	—	—	4:00	4:15	4:30	4:45	5:00	5:15	5:30	5:45	6:00	6:15
	—	—	1 mi	1 mi	1 mi	1 mi	1 mi	1 mi	1 mi	1 mi	1 mi	1 mi	1 mi	1 mi	1 mi
	—	—	6:30	7:00	7:30	8:00	8:30	9:00	9:30	10:00	10:30	11:00	11:30	12:00	12:30
	2 mi	2 mi	2 mi	2 mi	2 mi	2 mi	2 mi	2 mi	2 mi	2 mi	2 mi	2 mi	2 mi		
	11:30	12:30	13:30	14:30	15:30	16:30	17:30	18:30	19:30	20:30	21:30	22:30	23:30		
	2+ mi	2+ mi													
	14:30	15:30													
Long run															

Sprint Day

This program will increase your anaerobic ability and decrease your run time. Enter the sprint portion of the chart at your run time row. Do four sprints each of two distances, alternating your sprints between the distances. Begin with the lesser distance for your speed. Attempt to beat the time listed. Rest one minute before you run the longer sprint. Rest two minutes between the longer and shorter sprints. If you feel that you are not being properly stressed, and as you develop your wind, decrease the amount of rest time between sprints. For those with run times of +17 to +26, when the 220 sprint goal is met, move up to the quarter-mile (440) and half-mile (880) runs.

Fast Run Day

Begin with the lesser distance for your speed. When you beat the time for that distance, move to a longer distance within the same column. When you surpass the time for the distance at the bottom of the column, move to the left one column, maintaining the same distance. When you move one column to the left on the fast run, move your sprint goals to the same column.

Long and Slow Run

Run at least 30 minutes for a good cardiovascular workout. Run for time during this session, not necessarily for distance.

Sequence of Exercises: Push-up and Sit-up Improvement

1. Regular push-ups x 3 sets with 1 minute rest between sets. Form is important; if you can't do the push-ups properly, go to your knees and continue until you have finished the sets. After 3 workouts, add 2 push-ups to each set. (*Example:* Start with 6 push-ups on Wednesday, and go to 8 push-ups the next Wednesday.)

2a. Regular sit-ups x 3 sets with 1 minute rest between sets. If you can't do all the sit-ups properly, lower the angle of your legs until they are almost parallel to the ground. After 3 workouts, add 2 sit-ups to each set. (*Example:* Start with 8 sit-ups on Wednesday, and the next Wednesday, go to 10 sit-ups.)

2b. Alternative to sit-ups: Add 1 set of all 10 crunches every third workout. (*Example:* Start with 6 crunches on Wednesday, and the next Wednesday, go to 7 crunches). See the next section on proper crunch position.

3. Diamond push-ups: Put your hands together under your chest in a diamond shape. Perform the push-ups. Go to your knees if necessary. Add 1 diamond after every 3 workouts.

4. Wide-arm push-ups: Place your hands as far apart as possible. Perform the push-ups. Go to your knees if necessary. Add 1 wide-arm after every 3 workouts.

5. Add 1 set of all 10 crunches every third workout. (*Example:* Start with 6 crunches on Wednesday, and the next Wednesday, go to 7 crunches.) See illustration on crunch positions. *Note:* If you do exercise 2b instead of sit-ups, do 1 less repetition of the crunch.

6. Turn and bounce: Start with your arms parallel to the ground, palms facing up. The exercise is an 8-count movement at a slow cadence. Pivot slowly at the waist to the right for 4 counts and then to the left for 4 counts. Add 2 turns and bounces after every 3 workouts.

7. Flutter kicks: Put your hands under your buttocks. Lift your feet 6 to 8 inches off the ground to start. Begin by lifting your legs in sequence 6 to 18 inches. Keep legs slightly bent to reduce the strain on your back. One repetition equals 4 counts. Add 2 flutter kicks after every 3 workouts.

8. Leg spreaders: Put your hands under your buttocks. Lift your feet 6 to 8 inches off the ground to start. Begin by spreading your legs 18 to 30 inches, then back together. Keep legs slightly bent to reduce the strain on your back. One repetition equals 4 counts. Add 2 leg spreaders after every 3 workouts.

Crunches

Start with your arms crossed across your chest, hands grasping your shoulders. Use the stomach muscles to crunch up, not the neck and shoulder. Try not to stop between sets.

ARMY PHYSICAL FITNESS TEST

Soldiers taking the APFT are encouraged to make a maximum effort and to pass and excel. The test is administered at least every six months for active duty, and yearly for reserve component soldiers. Described in detail in chapter 14 of FM 21-20, the APFT includes timed push-ups, sit-ups, and a 2-mile run (or alternative aerobic event in certain circumstances).

Push-up Event

The push-up measures the endurance of the chest, shoulder, and triceps muscles. The first event is a two-minute push-up test. The push-ups must be properly completed to be counted as valid repetitions. The starting position is as follows:
- Hands are placed a comfortable distance apart.
- The body must remain in a generally straight line.
- Arms are straight and fully extended.
- Feet may be up to 12 inches apart.

To execute a repetition, bend your elbows, evenly lowering your body until your upper arms are parallel with the ground. Then straighten your arms until they are fully extended. Throughout the repetition, your body should remain generally straight, and your hands and feet must not break contact with the ground. Only your hands and feet may touch the ground during this exercise. If you fail to maintain proper form for the entire repetition, it will not be counted.

Sit-up Event

The second event is a two-minute sit-up test that measures the endurance of the abdominal and hip-flexor muscles. To assume the starting position for this exercise, do the following:
- Lie flat on your back.
- Bend your knees so that your feet are flat on the ground and a 90-degree angle is formed by the upper and lower portions of your legs.
- Place your feet together or up to 12 inches apart.
- Clasp your hands behind your head with your fingers interlocked.

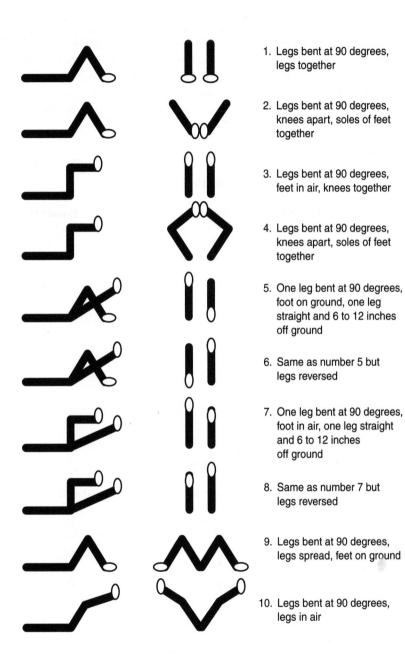

1. Legs bent at 90 degrees, legs together

2. Legs bent at 90 degrees, knees apart, soles of feet together

3. Legs bent at 90 degrees, feet in air, knees together

4. Legs bent at 90 degrees, knees apart, soles of feet together

5. One leg bent at 90 degrees, foot on ground, one leg straight and 6 to 12 inches off ground

6. Same as number 5 but legs reversed

7. One leg bent at 90 degrees, foot in air, one leg straight and 6 to 12 inches off ground

8. Same as number 7 but legs reversed

9. Legs bent at 90 degrees, legs spread, feet on ground

10. Legs bent at 90 degrees, legs in air

Crunches Exercise Positions

To execute a correct repetition, raise your body to the vertical position with the base of your neck above the base of the spine. Lower your body so your back touches the ground. The repetition will not be counted if you fail to reach the vertical position, arch your back, raise your buttocks off the ground, fail to keep your fingers interlocked and behind your head, or allow your knees to exceed a 90-degree angle. Another soldier will assist you during this exercise by holding your feet firmly on the ground.

PUSH-UPS

Age Group	Male Min.	Male Max.	Female Min.	Female Max.
17–21	42	71	19	42
22–26	40	75	17	46
27–31	39	77	17	50
32–36	36	75	15	45
37–41	34	73	13	40
42–46	30	66	12	37
47–51	25	59	10	34
52–56	20	56	9	31
57–61	18	53	8	28
62+	16	50	7	25

SIT-UPS

Age Group	Male/Female Min.	Male/Female Max.
17–21	53	78
22–26	50	80
27–31	45	82
32–36	42	76
37–41	38	76
42–46	32	72
47–51	30	66
52–56	28	66
57–61	27	64
62+	26	63

Two-mile Run
The two-mile run or alternative aerobic event measures cardiorespiratory and leg muscle endurance. Instructions for each APFT event in FM 21-20 must be read verbatim before each event is administered. The current APFT standards are shown on the following charts.

TWO-MILE RUN

Age Group	Male Min.	Male Max.	Female Min.	Female Max.
17–21	15:54	13:00	18:54	15:36
22–26	16:36	13:00	19:36	15:36
27–31	17:00	13:18	20:30	15:48
32–36	17:42	13:18	21:42	15:54
37–41	18:18	13:36	22:42	17:00
42–46	18:42	14:06	23:42	17:24
47–51	19:30	14:24	24:00	17:36
52–56	19:48	14:42	24:24	19:00
57–61	19:54	15:18	24:48	19:42
62+	20:00	15:42	25:00	20:00

ARMY FITNESS REGULATIONS
Army Physical Fitness Badge
The Army Physical Fitness Badge is awarded to soldiers attaining a score of 90 points in each event, for a total of 270 points. Under the current standards, soldiers must score 270 points annually to continue to wear the badge. Doing well on the APFT also assists soldiers in obtaining promotion points up to the rank of staff sergeant, ranging from 50 points to 10 points. Fit soldiers also receive verbal commendations and other accolades, are retained in service and selected for advanced military schooling, and can be promoted if they meet other selection criteria, including presenting a sharp military appearance.

Medical Profiles
Soldiers on permanent profile may be unable to take some or all of the APFT events for medical or other authorized or unavoidable reasons. In order to get credit for the APFT, however, the two-mile run or an alternative aerobic event must be taken and passed. Alternative aerobic events include the 800-yard swim, 6.2-mile bicycle ride (in one gear), and 2.5-mile walk. Like the run, the alternative events must be completed unassisted in a prescribed amount of time

relative to age and gender. Unlike the run, the other events are not scored; test takers either pass or fail the event. Soldiers who fail any or all of the events must retake the entire test. In case of test failure, commanders may allow soldiers to retake the test as soon as they are ready. Soldiers without a medical profile will be retested no later than three months following the initial APFT failure.

Failure to Pass

In compliance with Army retention policy, soldiers who have six months or more time in service who fail two consecutive record APFTs must be processed for separation for unsatisfactory performance under chapter 13 of AR 635-200, *Enlisted Personnel*. Receipt of a "chapter 13" for fitness failure indicates that the soldier is unqualified for service because he or she will not develop sufficiently to participate in further training or become a satisfactory soldier. It also means that failures would be likely to recur, and the soldier is unlikely to be able to perform duties effectively in the future, as well as lacking the potential for advancement or leadership. Entry-level soldiers (those with less than six months time in service) who repeatedly fail diagnostic and record APFTs may be separated under chapter 11 of the *Enlisted Personnel* regulation. A "chapter 11" covers inability, lack of reasonable effort, or failure to adapt to the military environment.

WEIGHT CONTROL

AR 600-9, *The Army Weight Control Program,* states that each soldier (commissioned, warrant, or enlisted) is responsible for meeting service weight-control standards. To help soldiers meet their responsibility, height and weight screening tables are published in the weight-control regulation. The regulation's proponent agency, the Office of the Deputy Chief of Staff for Personnel (ODC-SPER), recommends that soldiers strive to remain at least 5 percent below their individual screening table weight maximum. Soldiers should individually attain and maintain an acceptable weight and body composition through self-motivation or involvement in an official weight-control program. For some, the weight-control guidance is easy to follow. For others, weight can be a real problem.

Dealing with Body Fat

If a soldier consistently exceeds the personal weight goal, he or she should seek the assistance of master fitness trainers for advice in proper exercise and fitness and healthcare personnel for a proper dietary program. Soldiers exceeding the screening table weight or identified by the commander or supervisor for a special evaluation will have their body fat measured using the tape-test method. When men are tape-tested, they have the abdomen and neck measured; women have the hips, forearm, neck, and wrist measured. All measurements are taken three times and must be within one-quarter of an inch to be considered valid.

Weight-Control Program

To help soldiers fight fat, the Army provides educational and other motivational programs to encourage personnel to attain and maintain proper weight and body fat standards. Programs include nutrition education sessions conducted by qualified healthcare personnel, as well as exercise programs. Commanders will enforce body fat standards and monitor, measure, and, if necessary, place individuals into the Army Weight Control Program and continue to monitor them, in compliance with AR 600-9. Soldiers entered into the program are not allowed to reenlist or extend their enlistment, are considered nonpromotable, and are not assigned to command positions (e.g., squad leader, platoon sergeant, first sergeant, or command sergeant major).

Further, overweight soldiers are denied attendance at professional military or civilian schooling. AR 351-1, *Individual Military Education and Training,* states that personnel who do not meet body fat standards are not authorized to attend professional military schooling. All soldiers scheduled for attendance at schooling will be screened prior to departing the home station or losing command. Their height and weight will be recorded on their temporary duty orders, DD Form 1610, or on their permanent-change-of-station (PCS) packet. Soldiers exceeding established screening weights will not be allowed to depart their commands until the commander has determined that they meet the standards.

School commandants will take the following action upon determining that a student has arrived exceeding established body fat composition standards. Soldiers arriving at any Department of the Army (DA) board select school or those who PCS to a professional military school who do not meet body fat standards will be processed for disenrollment and removed from the DA board select list. Personnel arriving at professional military schools (other than DA board select or PCS schools) who do not meet body fat composition standards will be denied enrollment and reassigned in accordance with AR 600-9.

Actions to initiate mandatory bars to reenlistment, or initiation of separation proceedings for soldiers who are eliminated for cause from NCOES courses, will be in accordance with AR 601-280, *Army Reenlistment Program,* and AR 635-200, *Enlisted Personnel.* Additionally, soldiers who by the definition in AR 600-9 are considered weight-control failures will be processed for separation from the Army.

Soldiers who are entered into the weight-control program and then successfully meet their body fat reduction goal will be removed from the program and monitored for a year. Failure to meet the standards at any time during the monitoring period will result in initiation of separation action.

Soldiers who consider themselves too fat—or who come close to qualifying for the Army Weight Control Program—should look at modifying their lifestyles and eating habits for life. Soldiers interested in an improved diet may seek guidance in appendix C of AR 600-9, "Nutrition Guide to the Weight Control

WEIGHT FOR HEIGHT TABLE
(SCREENING TABLE WEIGHT)

Height (in inches)	Male Age				Female Age			
	17–20	21–27	28–39	40+	17–20	21–27	28–39	40+
58	—	—	—	—	109	112	115	119
59	—	—	—	—	113	116	119	123
60	132	136	139	141	116	120	123	127
61	136	140	144	146	120	124	127	131
62	141	144	148	150	125	129	132	137
63	145	149	153	155	129	133	137	141
64	150	154	158	160	133	137	141	145
65	155	159	163	165	137	141	145	149
66	160	163	168	170	141	146	150	154
67	165	169	174	176	145	149	154	159
68	170	174	179	181	150	154	159	164
69	175	179	184	186	154	158	163	168
70	180	185	189	192	159	163	168	173
71	185	189	194	197	163	167	172	177
72	190	195	200	203	167	172	177	183
73	195	200	205	208	172	177	182	188
74	201	206	211	214	178	183	189	194
75	206	212	217	220	183	188	194	200
76	212	217	223	226	189	194	200	206
77	218	223	229	232	193	199	205	211
78	223	229	235	238	198	205	210	216
79	229	235	241	244	203	209	215	222
80	234	240	247	250	208	214	220	227

Note: For screening purposes, body fat composition is to be determined in accordance with appendix B, AR 600-9.

ALLOWABLE BODY FAT

Age Group:	17–20	Age Group:	21–27
Male (% body fat):	20	Male (% body fat):	22
Female (% body fat):	30	Female (% body fat):	32

Age Group:	28–39	Age Group:	40 & older
Male (% body fat):	24	Male (% body fat):	26
Female (% body fat):	34	Female (% body fat):	36

Program." According to the guide, proper nutrition and regular exercise are necessary to help you lose weight and improve your state of fitness. It says, "Invest in yourself." Here are some examples of how this can be done:

• Make a decision to lose weight and shape up.
• Get motivated.
• Develop a strategy (diet, exercise routine, lifestyle changes).
• Carry out this strategy and enjoy the payoff—a healthy appearance, an improved self-image, a sense of accomplishment, and a feeling of pride.

Studies show that the average American man eats 2,360 to 2,640 calories per day. The average woman eats between 1,640 and 1,800. Reducing calories taken in leaves fewer calories for the body to burn to lose weight. Army Master Fitness Training Course material states that a healthy man can safely take in as few as 1,500 calories per day, and a healthy woman can consume as few as 1,200.

Vegetables, fruits, and complex carbohydrates, such as whole-grain breads, are "secret weapons" for anyone trying to maintain a healthy diet. They are filling and satisfying because they are high in fiber and generally lower in calories.

8

Continuing Civilian Education

Enlisting in today's Army usually comes with a monetary bonus for civilian education. That education can start while you are on active duty if your duty assignment and location permit. In addition, civilian education counts for a maximum of 100 promotion points. Each college credit hour gained through an accredited source is worth $1^{1}/_{2}$ promotion points, and an associate's degree (normally 60 credit hours) garners you an additional 10 points, for a total of 100 points.

ARMY CONTINUING EDUCATION SYSTEM

The Army Continuing Education System (ACES) through its many programs promotes lifelong learning opportunities and sharpens the competitive edge of Army, 2010 and beyond. ACES is committed to excellence in service, innovation, and deployability. Today's soldier can take advantage of numerous educational programs. The comprehensive Web site for Army education is at *www.armyeducation.army.mil.*

Your *Army Continuing Education System Record,* DA Form 669, can serve a very important purpose during your military career—or it can collect dust. Maintained at your local Army Education Center, it contains information used by education counselors to document your pursuit of higher education. Semester after semester throughout your career, you should (whenever the mission allows) contribute course completion slips to your record. Consider that you would be making regular deposits to an intellectual savings account that would grow with enormous interest—the kind that Army promotion boards and civilian employers will have for you as your educational value increases.

You should invest in yourself. The Army does, and benefits in the process. The Army Continuing Education System mission is, in part, to improve the combat readiness of the Army by planning, researching, and implementing educational programs and services to support the professional and personal development of quality soldiers and their adult family members, according to AR 621-5. In support of the mission, ACES supports five goals, three of which apply to soldiers, as follows:

- Develop confident, competent leaders.
- Support the enlistment, retention, and transition of soldiers.
- Provide personal development opportunities for soldiers.

The ACES meets its mission goals by providing quality educational programs and services throughout the Army. Education and training mutually support and enhance the combat readiness of the Army and are essential elements in the NCO Development Program. ACES programs and services are designed to expand soldiers' skills, knowledge, and behavior. Programs and services discussed later in this chapter contribute to the three pillars of leader development: institutional training, operational assignments and self-development.

Individual development, supported by ACES, is a planned, progressive, sequential program that leaders use to enhance and sustain the leadership plan discussed earlier.

Under the guidelines of AR 621-5, soldiers should meet the following educational objectives:

- Master academic skills needed to perform duties of their primary MOS and meet prerequisites for the NCO Education System.
- In cases of exception to the enlistment rule regarding having a high school diploma, earn a high school diploma or equivalent before completing a first enlistment.
- Earn a college degree, license, or professional certificate in an MOS related discipline, as recommended in DA Pamphlet 600-25, *The NCO Professional Development Guide.*

ARMY EDUCATION CENTER COUNSELORS

Counselors help soldiers establish realistic educational goals and provide counseling through the attainment of the goals. They also help soldiers get the maximum benefit from limited tuition assistance and other resources. Soldiers who are new to an installation are required by AR 621-5 to receive education counseling within the first 30 days of their arrival and then receive follow-up counseling as needed.

Soldiers should not need a regulatory push to receive educational counseling; however, they should take advantage of the valuable advice and assistance that counselors provide. Counselors help with school selection, application procedures, prerequisite assessments, and financial aid.

When they cannot help locate financial aid for formal courses of instruction, counselors can recommend free alternative methods of obtaining educational credit. (See DANTES, CLEP, and GRE, under "Independent Study and Examination Programs for College Credit.")

HIGH SCHOOL COMPLETION PROGRAM

The High School Completion Program (HSCP) is an off-duty program that provides soldiers and adult family members the opportunity to earn a high school diploma or equivalency certificate. It is open to all non-high school graduates. Tuition assistance (TA) is authorized for soldiers up to 100 percent of the tuition costs of courses. ACES will pay TA only to accredited institutions and will not pay fees covering such items as books, matriculation, graduation, and parking.

COLLEGE DEGREE PROGRAMS

Thousands of degree programs are available to soldiers—too many to list here. But you may use dedicated resources to find out more information about obtaining an associate's, bachelor's, or master's degree in arts or science.

If you want to take college courses but are concerned about your ability to comprehend course material, use DA Pamphlet 351-20, *Army Correspondence Course Program Catalog*. It is filled with offerings that will teach you the basics of many subjects. For example, suppose you want to earn an electrical engineering degree. You could contact your local education center to request the basic electricity course listed in the pamphlet. The course is open to "any student who meets the basic qualifications for correspondence study." After successfully completing 17 sequential electricity subcourses, you should be fully prepared to enroll in a college course that deals with the subject of electricity. Apply this method to other subjects, and you will see the value of "boning up" through correspondence studies.

SERVICEMEMBERS OPPORTUNITY COLLEGES ARMY DEGREE PROGRAM

Under the Servicemembers Opportunity Colleges (SOC), there are degree and certification programs in which a soldier can be awarded a degree or certificate for an academic or technical course of study. The programs were developed to provide common curricula in disciplines related to Army MOSs.

The SOC is a network of schools across the country and overseas that have recognized and responded to soldiers' expectations for postsecondary education. The schools must have liberal entrance requirements, allow soldiers to complete courses through nontraditional modes, provide academic advisement, offer maximum credit for experiences obtained in service, have residence requirements that are adaptable to the special needs of soldiers, have a transfer policy that recognizes traditional and nontraditional learning obtained at other schools, promote the SOC, and provide educational support to servicemembers. Under the Servicemembers Opportunity College Army Degree Program (SOCAD), the college must limit the residence requirement and offer a flexible curriculum.

The SOCAD student agreement gives the soldier a one-time evaluation of everything the soldier has done that can be credited toward the college degree and lists what the soldier must take to graduate. The SOCAD colleges require a soldier to take no more than 25 percent of his or her coursework with that college to receive their degree—not necessarily on campus, but from their offerings and elsewhere. Once a soldier completes residency, future courses taken at other colleges will be accepted and applied toward the soldier's original degree plan.

eArmyU

Another new initiative toward assisting soldiers in achieving their educational goals is *eArmyU*. This program is entirely online, offering soldiers a stream-lined "portal" approach to a variety of postsecondary degrees and technical cer-tificates. All courses allow soldiers to study on their own schedule. Highly motivated soldiers can complete degree and certification requirements regard-less of work schedules, family responsibilities, and deployments.

eArmyU Benefits

eArmyU provides soldiers 100 percent tuition assistance (TA) up to $4,500 annually for books; fees for online courses; a technology package (laptop com-puter, printer, email account and Internet access); maintenance and warranty of equipment; and 24/7 help desk assistance. After completing the required 12 semester hours in two years, the technology package becomes the soldier's property. Added to the existing education programs and services available, this online program helps to ensure all soldiers have the opportunity to fulfill their personal and professional educational goals while simultaneously building the technology, critical thinking, and decision-making skills required to fully trans-form the Army.

Soldier Eligibility

To be eligible for participation in this program, soldiers must be regular active duty or active guard reserve enlisted soldiers with at least three years remaining on their enlistment. Soldiers may extend or reenlist to meet this requirement. More information on *eArmyU* can be found at *www.eArmyU.com.*

COLLEGE CREDIT FOR MILITARY EXPERIENCE

Army Education Center counselors can help you complete DD Form 295, *Application for the Evaluation of Learning Experiences during Military Ser-vice.* The completed form is used to inform institutions, agencies, and employ-ers about in-service educational achievements. Schools use the form to determine how many and what kinds of college credits to award soldiers based on military education, training, and experience. Your pursuit of a degree should include completing and forwarding DD Form 295 to the college or university of your choice.

The American Council on Education (ACE) evaluates Army service school courses and recommends the number of semester hours of credit that civilian schools may award based on a soldier's military training and experience. Exam-ples include vocational, lower-level baccalaureate and associate's degree, upper-level baccalaureate, and graduate-level credits. These recommendations are published in the *Guide to the Evaluation of Educational Experiences in the Armed Services (ACE Guide)*.

INDEPENDENT STUDY AND EXAMINATION PROGRAMS FOR COLLEGE CREDIT

If you are working on an undergraduate (associate's or bachelor's) degree, you should know about independent ways to earn credit. Credit can be earned through the following programs: Defense Activity for Nontraditional Education Support (DANTES), including the College Level Examination Program (CLEP) and Defense Subject Standardized Tests (DSST); American College Testing Proficiency Examination Program (ACTPEP); Graduate Record Examination (GRE); and Annenberg Project and Center for Public Broadcasting (AP/CPB).

The DANTES, CLEP, DSST, ACTPEP, GRE, and AP/CPB offerings all require independent study. Many subject packets include texts, workbooks, and audio- or videotapes that are used in conjunction with the paper materials. Most of the for-credit tests offered by these programs and agencies are each worth three or four semester hours of credit. The GRE, which includes a general exam and subject exams, is worth much more credit. The GRE sociology examination, for example, is worth 30 semester hours of undergraduate credit—15 lower division (100 and 200 level), and 15 upper division (300 and 400 level).

DANTES independent study and examination program services are available to all eligible active-duty soldiers. One important aspect of the DANTES is the CLEP, which also enables students to earn credit by examination. The examinations measure knowledge of the basic concepts and applications involved in courses that have the same or similar titles. They are divided into two types: general examinations and subject examinations.

The general examination measures college-level achievement in five basic areas of the liberal arts: English composition, social sciences and history, natural sciences, humanities, and mathematics. Test material covers the first year of college, often referred to as the general or liberal education requirement. Subject examinations measure achievement in specific college courses and are worth course credit. Examples of test titles include Introduction to Business Management, General Psychology, Western Civilization, and American Literature.

Each civilian educational institution has its own criteria for using CLEP test scores to determine credit. You should have official transcripts forwarded to the registrar of the college or university at which you desire to receive credit (some institutions require that a minimum number of semester hours of classwork be completed before CLEP credit will be accepted). Another subject test that, like CLEP, substitutes for college classroom work is the DANTES Subject Standardized Tests.

GI BILL

Valuable educational benefits offered under the GI Bill are available today for would-be college graduates and for those soldiers who wish to pursue certain kinds of training. Originally named the Servicemen's Readjustment Act of 1944, the GI Bill was signed into law by President Franklin D. Roosevelt on June 22, 1944. The bill, now called the Montgomery GI Bill after its latest champion, Congressman G. V. Montgomery, takes the form of the Montgomery Active Duty GI Bill and the Montgomery Selected Reserve GI Bill. The post-Vietnam Veterans Educational Assistance Program (VEAP) is also covered by the Montgomery GI Bill. A wide range of benefits valued at hundreds of dollars per month for up to 36 months is available. You are urged to take full advantage of the benefits to which you are entitled.

Montgomery Active Duty GI Bill

The Montgomery Active Duty GI Bill (chapter 30, U.S. Code) provides up to 36 months of benefits. Soldiers covered by Category I of this program are those who first entered active duty after June 30, 1985, and who contributed a nonrefundable $100 a month for the first 12 months of service. Active-duty members may begin using their benefits after completing two years of service. Members of the National Guard who are in the Active Guard and Reserve Program also are covered by this contributory program, but they must have entered service after November 29, 1989, and must not have previously served on active duty.

Montgomery Selected Reserve GI Bill

The Montgomery Selected Reserve GI Bill (chapter 106, U.S. Code) is available to members of the Army Reserve and the Army National Guard. It applies to members who entered selected reserve status after June 30, 1985. To receive up to 36 months of entitlements under this program, members must have made a six-year commitment that began after September 30, 1990. Members also must have completed Initial Active Duty for Training, be high school graduates or have equivalent certificates, and serve in an active reserve or National Guard unit and remain in good standing. With few exceptions, benefits under this program expire 10 years from the date of eligibility for the program or on the day the member leaves the Selected Reserve.

Monetary Value of the GI Bill

As indicated above, the monetary value of the benefit program you qualify for will depend on various factors, including the date you entered the military, your status in the military, how long you have been or were in service, and the character of a previous discharge or separation. Also, if you are in a contributory program, the amount of money the government will contribute depends on how much you contribute, up to a maximum matching contributory amount.

In-service benefits are worth less, monetarily, than post-service benefits and normally cover only tuition and fees. But here is a kicker: Under current federal law, if you receive a college or university assistantship, fellowship, or grant that pays or offsets part or all of your tuition and fees or research expenses, you may still be entitled to receipt of education benefits—meaning that monthly entitlements received from the DVA are yours to keep.

Various rules and certain service- or usage-oriented restrictions cover the programs and situations described above. Visit your Army Education Center or local DVA office, obtain counseling, and get the most recently published copies of the following:

- Pamphlet 27-82-2, *A Summary of DVA Benefits.*
- Pamphlet 22-90-2, *Summary of Educational Benefits.*
- Pamphlet 22-90-1, *Avoiding VA Education Overpayments.*

When you decide to apply for benefits, first make sure that the education or training program you choose is approved by the DVA. Then complete and submit DVA Form 22-1990 at least two months before the beginning of the program. If you choose to use some of your benefits while in service, your commander and local education assistance officer must sign the form. Depending on your personal situation, you also may need to provide a copy of your marriage license, divorce decrees from any previous marriages, and children's birth certificates. The level of your educational benefits may be increased according to the number of legal dependents you have.

Except for the Selected Reserve program, educational benefits expire 10 years from the date of your last discharge or release from active duty. The DVA can extend the 10-year period by the amount of time you were prevented from training during the period because of a certified disability or detention by a foreign government power. Certain other exceptions apply as well and are covered in DVA Pamphlet 22-90-2.

You may use GI Bill benefits for the following purposes:

- To seek an associate's, bachelor's, master's, professional, or doctoral degree at a college or university.
- To participate in a cooperative training program.
- To participate in an accredited independent study program leading to a college degree.
- To take courses leading to a certificate or diploma from a business, technical, or vocational school.
- To work and train in an apprenticeship or job-training program offered by a company or union.
- To take a correspondence course.
- To participate in a program abroad that leads to a college degree.
- To take remedial, deficiency, and refresher courses, under certain circumstances.
- To receive tutorial assistance for a deficiency (such as in math), if you attend school at least half-time.

- To participate in the DVA work-study program, provided you attend school or train three-quarters or full-time.

Soldiers with private pilot's licenses are entitled to benefits leading to more advanced flying certification. This program has been extended indefinitely.

You may be entitled to benefits under more than one program, or you may be eligible for vocational rehabilitation if you have a service-connected disability. In either case, you are strongly encouraged to discuss your educational plans with a local DVA counselor. If local counselors are unavailable, contact DVA regional offices. DVA toll-free telephone service is available in all 50 states, Puerto Rico, and the U.S. Virgin Islands. Call (800) 827-1000.

OTHER FINANCIAL AID

The U.S. Department of Education (DOE), in *The Student Guide,* informs you and your family members about federal student aid programs and how to apply for them. The department advises you to contact the financial aid administrator at the school that you, your spouse, or your children are interested in and ask about the total cost of education. Ask the state higher education agencies about state aid. Check the local library for state and private financial aid information. Check with companies, foundations, religious organizations, fraternities or sororities, and civic organizations such as the American Legion. Also ask about aid through professional associations.

The Student Guide is free and may be available at the local Army Education Office.

A FINAL THOUGHT ON EDUCATION

Buy bonds. Series EE savings bonds may be entirely tax free when used for education. If you have children and are worried about the rising cost of education, purchasing bonds on a regular basis is a smart way to invest in their future and protect your financial security. For example, assuming an annual interest rate of 6 percent, putting just $50 a month into bonds for a 1-year-old child who will begin college at age 18 will yield $17,356. Investing $100 a month will yield $34,712. If you are a soldier with a 12-year-old who will begin college in 6 years, putting $50 a month into bonds will provide $4,227; $100 a month will yield $8,454—minimum.

If you are a young soldier, you may purchase bonds for yourself, hold them five years or so, then use them to augment other financial aid you will apply toward a bachelor's or master's degree.

Beginning with Series EE bonds purchased in 1990, the interest earned can be excluded from federal income tax if you pay tuition and fees at colleges, universities, and qualified technical schools during the same year the bonds are cashed. The exclusion applies not only to your own educational expenses but also to those of your spouse and any other dependents, according to the Savings Bonds Public Affairs Office in Washington, D.C. Some restrictions apply. Contact your unit savings bond coordinator for more information.

9

Leadership Competencies

It is perfectly reasonable and possible for a soldier to aspire and be promoted to the rank of corporal or sergeant during his or her first term of enlistment. Such a promotion, however, requires that the soldier possess certain leadership competencies—that is, be competent to lead.

The Army defines leadership as "the process of influencing people by providing purpose, direction, and motivation while operating to accomplish the mission and improve the organization." Leadership, despite the great strides in technology, remains the same—influencing and motivating people to get a job done. The new FM 6-22 (FM 22-100), *Army Leadership,* consolidates five current manuals and one Department of the Army pamphlet on various aspects and levels of leadership. The new manual discusses character-based leadership, clarifies values, establishes attributes as part of character, and most importantly focuses on improving people and organizations for the long term. Rather than provide a one-size-fits-all leadership model, Army leadership doctrine now outlines three levels of leadership—*direct, organizational,* and *strategic;* and it identifies four skill domains that apply at all levels: *interpersonal, conceptual, technical,* and *tactical.* The discussion on actions outlines for each level what leaders do—what turns character into leadership.

Although the concept "be, know, do" remains the centerpiece of the 1999 edition of *Army Leadership* by providing a specific framework with 23 dimensions that describes a leader of character and competence, leadership doctrine now flows from the axiom: *Leaders of character and competence act to achieve excellence by providing purpose, direction, and motivation.* Above all, the new doctrine anchors leaders of character and competence in moral bedrock—Army Values.

Character describes who a person is inside, and at the core of Army leaders are Army Values. Those values—*loyalty, duty, respect, selfless service, honor, integrity*, and *personal courage* (LDRSHIP)—capture the professional military ethos and describe the nature of our soldiers. Our common values help us understand the purpose of our missions and devise appropriate methods to accomplish them. Values are the foundation of all that we are and do.

Added to Army values is practice of leadership that involves exercising will, initiative, self-discipline, intelligent judgment, and cultural awareness. These mental attributes, combined with the physical attributes (military and professional bearing, physical and health fitness, and emotional self-control; balance and stability components), when put into practice, form a leader's behavior.

The new definition of leadership focuses on *behavior,* something that can be seen and evaluated. *Influencing, operating* and *improving* are basic leadership actions. Leaders demonstrate influence through communicating, decision making, and motivating. A leader's influence obviously applies in the day-to-day business of operating—accomplishing missions. As part of operating, a leader is responsible for detailed, suitable planning; careful, proficient executing; and continual assessing and adjusting. Assessing change is essential to improving an organization. This new doctrinal emphasis means that a leader's influence today involves preparing for tomorrow. The traditional measure of leadership is whether an organization performed its tasks, fulfilled its obligations, and accomplished its missions—all short-term goals.

The Army has identified three areas of leadership competency. The first area deals with the *behavior* of the leader: the traits the leader must have. The second area is *knowledge:* what the leader must know. The third area is *skills:* how a leader must do the job of leading. Together these areas are known as skills, knowledge, and behavior (SKB), or "be, know, do."

Within the area of skills and knowledge, there are nine further competencies: communication, supervision, teaching and counseling, soldier team building, technical and tactical proficiency, decision making, planning, use of available systems, and professional ethics.

The necessary behavior, skills, and knowledge of leaders in the grades of corporal and sergeant are shown in the following lists. Use them as the basis for your preparation for promotion, as well as when acting in a leadership position.

BEHAVIOR (BE)
To be a leader in today's army means that you must be a soldier who behaves like a leader—one who:
- Enforces standards.
- Sets the example.
- Accomplishes the mission.
- Takes care of soldiers.
- Is dedicated and selfless.
- Accepts responsibilities for self and subordinates.
- Obeys lawful orders.
- Is honest and courageous.
- Maintains physical and mental toughness.
- Shows competence and self-confidence.

- Acts fairly and equitably with subordinates.
- Is loyal to the nation and the Constitution.
- Is loyal to superiors and subordinates.
- Shows initiative and motivation.

KNOWLEDGE (KNOW)

Leaders must *know* or learn the principles and/or policies in each leadership competency.

Communication

- Listening and watching principles (FM 6-22 [FM 22-100]).
- Speaking principles (TSP NCOES and USASMA RB 350-25).
- Reading grade level - 10 (TABE and AR 25-30).
- Writing grade level - 10 (TABE and AR 25-30).

Supervision

- Duties, responsibilities, and authority of NCOs (FM 7-27.7 [TC 22-6]).
- Wear and appearance, drill and ceremony (AR 670-1 and FM 3-21.5 [FM 22-5]).
- Unit standing operating procedure.
- Army Training System and responsibilities of trainers (FM 7-0 [FM 25-100] and FM 7-10 [FM 25-101]).
- Operator's manuals for equipment (TM-10 series).
- Unit supply procedures (AR 735 series).
- Army safety program (AR 385 series).
- EO/sexual harassment policy (AR 600-20).

Teaching and Counseling

- Common tasks skill levels (STP 21-1).
- Common leader combat skills.
- Army training system and responsibilities of trainers (FM 7-0 [FM 25-100] and FM 7-10 [FM 25-101]).
- Performance counseling of individuals (FM 6-22 [FM 22-100]).
- After-action review techniques (FM 7-10 [FM 25-101] and TC 25-20).
- Individual Training Evaluation Program (AR 350-37).

Soldier Team Development

- Concept of team building (FM 6-22 [FM 22-100]).
- Principles of leadership (FM 6-22 [FM 22-100]).
- Factors of leadership (FM 6-22 [FM 22-100]).
- Human stress factors (FM 6-22 [FM 22-100]).
- Customs and traditions of unit.

- Army enlisted promotion system (AR 600-20 and AR 600-8-19).
- Noncommissioned Officer Education System (AR 351-1).
- Disciplinary actions (UCMJ).
- Physical fitness training (FM 3-22-20 [FM 21-20]).

Technical and Tactical Proficiency
- Marksmanship training (FM 3-22.9 [FM 23-9]).
- Operation, characteristics, and employment of weapons and equipment.
- Appropriate MOS skill level tasks and standards (*Soldier's Manual* & AR 611-201).
- Appropriate common tasks skill level (STP 21-1 and STP 21-24).
- Land navigation/map reading (FM 3-22.26 [FM 21-26]).
- Movement techniques (FM 3-21.75 [21-75], FM 3-21.8 [7-8], FM 3-21.10 [7-10], 3-21.20 [7-20]).
- Operation of MILES in tactical training (TC 25-6.)
- Equipment operator's manuals (TM-10 series).
- Unit collective tasks (ARTEP/AMTP).
- Common leader combat skills.

Decision Making
- Problem-solving process (FM 6-22 [FM 22-100]).
- Ethical decision-making process (FM 6-22 [FM 22-100]).
- Military decision-making process (FM 101-5).

Planning
- Planning principles (FM 7-0 [FM 25-100]).
- Training schedules and event plans (FM 7-10 [FM 25-101]).
- Higher headquarters training objectives.
- Backward planning process (FM 6-22 [FM 22-100]).

Use of Available Systems
- Computers, automated systems, information management, and analytical techniques affecting battalions and higher-level commands.

Professional Ethics
- Soldierly qualities (FM 1 [FM 100-1]).
- Professional Army ethics (FM 1 [FM 100-1]).

SKILLS (DO)
In each of the nine competencies, a leader in the grade of corporal or sergeant must be able to *do* the tasks listed.

Communication
- Receive and interpret information from superiors and subordinates.
- Issue clear and concise oral and written orders.
- Write performance counseling statements.
- Provide input on personnel matters affecting subordinates.
- Participate in after-action reviews.

Supervision
- Enforce Army standards of appearance and conduct.
- Control and account for individuals and units.
- Supervise collective training.
- Supervise and/or lead and evaluate individual training.
- Lead team in performance of collective tasks.
- Supervise maintenance of equipment, living areas, and workplaces.
- Enforce the Army Safety Program.
- Enforce the Army equal opportunity and sexual harassment policies.

Teaching and Counseling
- Teach and coach CTT (Sgt.).
- Teach and coach MOS skill level 1 tasks.
- Teach common leader combat skills.
- Teach performance-oriented training.
- Coach subordinates in proper execution of tasks.
- Evaluate tasks to standards.
- Provide feedback through performance counseling and after action reviews (AARs).

Soldier Team Development
- Develop cohesion at appropriate level.
- Foster loyalty and commitment.
- Build spirit and confidence.
- Instill discipline.
- Take care of subordinates.
- Lead physical fitness training.
- Develop and mentor subordinate NCOs.

Technical and Tactical Proficiency
- Qualify with weapon; train and supervise or direct marksmanship training.
- Be proficient with mission-essential weapons and equipment.
- Perform MOS skill levels 1 and 2 tasks to standard (Sgt.).
- Perform MOS skill level 1 tasks to standard (Cpl.).
- Navigate and lead appropriate echelon movement.
- Employ MILES equipment.
- Perform PMCS on individual and platoon/section/squad weapons and equipment.
- Train and lead collective tasks for element.

Decision Making
- Interpret information and make decisions affecting subordinates.
- Use problem-solving process.
- Use ethical decision-making process.
- Exercise initiative in tactical situations.

Planning
- Plan METL-based individual and collective training.
- Use backward planning process.

Use of Available Systems
- Use and control automated systems and information management at different echelons.

Professional Ethics
- Lead by example.
- Practice professional Army ethics.
- Demonstrate high moral standards.

Soldiers learn leadership every day. Simply by watching other leaders and performing their duties, they will learn leadership. Those who deliberately apply the process—study examples of leadership, reflect on their own experiences, apply lessons learned, and seek comments—become better leaders now and for the future.

Leadership skills are one of the lifelong benefits of military service. The skills are worth learning well. They are indispensable while on active duty and invaluable when you return to civilian life.

Additional information on leadership is found in FM 6-22 [FM 22-100] *Army Leadership*.

10

Career Decisions

Just as one day you enlisted, someday you will face separation. So what you do in the meantime is vital to your future (and, if you are married, your family's future). Have you remained qualified to reenlist? What are your "re-up" options? Do you want to reenlist? What if you choose not to re-up? Whatever you do, begin considering your options at least a year out—even though you may change your mind at the last minute.

If you separate, you will most certainly need to go to work unless a lottery jackpot or some other bonanza drops in your lap. If you choose not to re-up but have a remaining service obligation, you still have military career decisions to make about joining the Army Reserve or the Army National Guard. If you choose to remain in service to the nation full-time, do *you* have what it takes to become a professional NCO or warrant or commissioned officer?

If you enlisted when you were 18 or 19 years old, and you continue your Army career, you will be only 38 or 39 when you become eligible for retirement. Would you like to draw an Army retirement check before age 40, knowing that that check will arrive monthly for the rest of your life?

Soldiers must be in the grade of promotable sergeant or higher to be eligible to serve 20 years. Soldiers not promoted beyond the grade of sergeant may serve only 15 years. And promotable corporals and specialists—those who do not get promoted before their separation dates—may serve no more than 13 years. Also remember that at the 15-year mark you will have another decision to make regarding your retirement options: whether to opt for a 50 percent retirement at 20 years, or get a $30,000 lump-sum, taxable payment, plus the 40 percent option at the 20-year mark.

THE REENLISTMENT DECISION

If you decide that the Army is right for you, you should consider all options when reenlisting. Begin early. Visit your unit retention office. Discuss your decision with your fellow soldiers. Seek counseling from your immediate supervisor and others in your chain of command. Talk to your family. Consider at least the following:

Soldiers Reenlisting at the World Trade Center

- Why you are reenlisting.
- How reenlisting can enhance your career.
- Whether you will receive a Regular or Selective Reenlistment Bonus.
- MOS training and schooling, or MOS reclassification options.
- Travel and assignment options.
- Your promotion potential.
- The needs of the Army and the nation.

Reenlistment Bonuses

The Army offers reenlistment bonuses as a means of encouraging soldiers in certain critical MOSs to reenlist or extend their current enlistments. Critical MOSs are determined by the needs of the Army. The Army updates the list of critical MOSs regularly and publishes it through the DA Circular 611 series. Your unit's retention NCO should be able to provide you with the list.

The Selective Reenlistment Bonus (SRB) Program is available to all soldiers, regardless of rank, who hold a primary MOS designated as critical. Soldiers reenlisting through the SRB Program are eligible for reenlistment bonuses up to $20,000 if they reenlist or extend for a minimum of three years. They may receive a maximum of three such SRBs during their military careers, and only one in each established time zone. The zones, based on time of active military service, are zone A, extending from 21 months to 6 years; zone B, from 6 to 10 years; and zone C, from 10 to 14 years of active military service.

The actual amount of the SRB is determined by a formula based on the soldier's monthly basic pay. The bonus cannot exceed six times the monthly pay, multiplied by the number of years of additional obligated service, nor can the bonus exceed $20,000. The SRB is based on the current needs of the Army and on current reenlistment trends in specific MOSs. The more critical the Army's need, the higher the SRB. Consequently, sometimes no MOS qualifies for the maximum rate.

The following examples illustrate how the program operates: A soldier receiving basic pay of $800 a month reenlists under the SRB Program for four years; the bonus amount for his MOS is the maximum, six times the monthly basic pay. The SRB bonus would be ($800 × 6) × 4 = $19,200. If, however, the soldier was receiving a basic pay of $1,000 a month, the SRB would not be ($1,000 × 6) × 4 = $24,000; instead, this soldier would receive the maximum allowable bonus—$20,000. Since qualifying MOSs and their SRB rates fluctuate based on the needs of the Army, interested soldiers should contact their retention office to obtain current information. The SRB is paid in addition to any other pay and allowance to which the soldier is already entitled.

Training and Duty Station Options

If you decide to remain on active duty, you have a number of options. Upon reenlistment, you can elect additional training, a particular duty station elsewhere, or current duty station stabilization.

Options for the first-termer include airborne training, U.S. Army Intelligence and Security Command electronic warfare training, U.S. Army Information Systems Command training, language training, and other MOSs that have openings for new soldiers who qualify. Other options include volunteering for Special Forces, a combat arms unit of choice, and the U.S. Army 3rd Infantry (Old Guard).

Soldiers willing to reenlist or extend their enlistment can also apply for a number of interesting career development programs: explosive ordnance disposal, presidential support activities (working at the White House), technical escort (for chemical, ammunition, and EOD specialists), Army bands, instructors at service schools, drill sergeants, and recruiters. Selection of a new duty station may also be an option for your reenlistment. You may be eligible for the overseas area option, the CONUS-to-CONUS station option, or, if overseas, the CONUS station of choice option.

Information and requirements for each career program are contained in AR 614-200; reenlistment NCOs and career counselors can also be of assistance to the soldier who wishes to explore some of the more unusual career options in the Army.

OTHER MILITARY OPPORTUNITIES

Your career choices at the end of your first term are not limited to reenlisting in the Army or returning to civilian life. You may elect to serve in the Army

Reserve or Army National Guard while pursuing a civilian career. Or you may decide to seek a commission or a warrant through Officer Candidate School, Warrant Officer Entry Courses, the U.S. Military Academy, or an ROTC program. All Army installations have reenlistment NCOs and in-service recruiters who can provide more detailed information about these options.

Army Reserve

The Army Reserve is a federal military force composed of the Ready Reserve and the Standby Reserve. The Ready Reserve is made up of combat support and combat service support units available for quick mobilization in times of national emergency or war. The Standby Reserve is a pool of soldiers who have a remaining military obligation and are eligible for recall to active duty.

Through the Ready Reserve, the former soldier can supplement his or her civilian income while taking full advantage of the leadership training he or she received while on active duty. Reservists receive four days' pay for each weekend of reserve training, which is usually held monthly. An additional requirement is a two-week annual training session. Salary ranges depend on time in service and pay grade.

Each soldier leaving active duty who enlists in the Ready Reserve within 60 days of discharge from the Army retains his or her active rank, pay grade, and time-in-grade status. Privileges include $200,000 Servicemen's Group Life Insurance (SGLI), space-available dental care, and commissary and post exchange privileges.

Army National Guard

The Army National Guard is a federal-state military force. Its primary mission is to maintain combat divisions and support units available for active duty in time of national emergency or war. Under its state mission, the Guard protects life and property and preserves state internal security.

Pay and benefits are essentially the same for the Guard as for the Army Reserve. One unique feature of the Guard is its Officer Candidate School (OCS) program. This one-year program provides training on weekends through the state OCS. Guard members can also attend the active Army OCS and earn a commission in 14 weeks.

Officer Candidate School

Enlisted personnel who elect to remain on active duty may be eligible to apply for OCS training. Applicants must meet the following criteria:

- Be between $19^1/_2$ and 29 years of age upon enrollment.
- Not be assigned to a Cohesion, Operational Readiness, and Training (COHORT) unit.
- Have completed at least two years (60 semester hours) of college.
- Achieve a minimum score of 90 on the Officer Selection Battery (OSB).

During their assignment at OCS, candidates are paid at the E-5 level unless they held higher rank prior to their assignment.

The 14-week program is rigorous and requires a high level of physical fitness, mental fortitude, and dedication to succeed. Upon completion of the course, graduates who choose to accept a commission are commissioned as second lieutenants.

Warrant Officer Entry Course

Warrant officers are highly specialized experts and trainers who operate, maintain, administer, and manage the Army's equipment, support activities, and technical and tactical systems for their entire careers. The career progression of warrant officers is designed to encourage them to seek in-depth knowledge of particular systems and activities and maintain proficiency in their particular skills.

The Warrant Officer Entry Course, located at Fort Rucker, Alabama, trains selected enlisted personnel in the fundamentals of leadership, ethics, personnel management, and tactics. Following completion of the rigorous six-week course, warrant officers go on to additional specialized training in their particular MOSs.

To qualify for entry to the Warrant Officer Entry Course, a soldier must fit the following criteria:

- Be a sergeant or higher rank.
- Have earned a high school diploma or GED equivalency.
- Have served three years' active enlisted service prior to appointment.

Warrant officers may serve in a variety of MOSs, but there is an emphasis on maintenance and aviation specialties. For additional information, consult DA Pamphlet 350-1 or contact your unit reenlistment officer.

U.S. Military Academy

Soldiers who wish to attend the U.S. Military Academy at West Point may seek direct nomination under the provisions of AR 351-12 if they meet the entrance requirements without further study. For additional information on direct nomination, write to the Admissions Office, U.S. Military Academy, West Point, NY 10966.

An alternative for solders who need additional academic preparation to compete for an appointment is provided through the U.S. Military Academy Preparatory School (USMAPS). Located at Fort Monmouth, New Jersey, USMAPS provides academic, military, and physical training. The 10-month school, divided into two semesters, emphasizes English and mathematics in the academic arena. The sole function of USMAPS is to mold its students into qualified West Point cadets. Its success rate is impressive—approximately 95 percent of its graduates gain admission to West Point. To qualify for admission, a soldier must meet the following criteria:

- Be a U.S. citizen.
- Be at least 17 but not yet 21 years old on 1 July of the year entering the school.
- Be unmarried and without dependents.
- Be physically qualified (pregnancy is a disqualifying factor).
- Be a high school graduate (or the equivalent).
- Have high moral character.

To apply, soldiers must submit a complete application package no later than 15 March of the year in which they hope to enter the school. The packet consists of the following:

- A letter of application.
- A legible copy of the most recent Medical Examination (SF 88) and Report of Medical History (SF 93), neither more than one year old.
- A complete high school transcript, or a copy of the GED certificate with test scores.
- College transcripts for any college credit received.
- General technical (GT) score from the Army classification battery of tests administered before induction into the Army.
- ETS date. (The soldier must have enough time in service remaining to complete the school; if not, he or she must extend or reenlist before arriving at the school.)
- Most recent APFT score, not more than one year old.
- Results of the SAT.
- A recent photograph.
- An evaluation by the immediate commanding officer.
- A handwritten, one-page essay on the questions "Why I Wish to Attend USMAPS" and "What Are My Goals in Life?"

Further information can be obtained by writing Admissions, USMAPS, Fort Monmouth, NJ 07703-5509, or phoning (201) 532-1807 (civilian) or 992-1807 (DSN).

ROTC

One other option for the soldier is to separate from the service under a special ROTC scholarship program. In this program, the soldier may earn a degree, be commissioned a second lieutenant, and return to active duty. The Army provides for 200 soldiers annually to be discharged from the service early to attend college full-time under the Army ROTC program. The ROTC program offers two- and three-year scholarships for active-duty enlisted personnel. Through the "Green to Gold" program, these soldiers become civilians specifically to enter the ROTC program, complete a baccalaureate program, and then be commissioned as officers in the Regular Army or the Army Reserve. Once discharged, the soldier forfeits the pay and benefits of active duty, but he or she may still use any veterans educational benefits earned while on active duty. In addition, a monthly stipend of $100 is provided, as well as full payment of college tuition and fees and a standard allowance for books and supplies.

The ROTC cadet is not a soldier in civilian clothes. The former soldier leads the life of a normal college student with few additional responsibilities. Cadets must complete prescribed military science courses, a minimum of one semester of foreign language, ROTC Advanced Camp (a paid six-week training program between the junior and senior years), and any other training identified by the Secretary of the Army as a requirement for commissioning.

Returning to active duty as a Regular Army second lieutenant is not a guarantee. Based on the needs of the Army, some cadets are commissioned as second lieutenants in the U.S. Army Reserve instead. Cadets select the branch of service in which they would prefer to serve, but branch selection is also not guaranteed; again, the needs of the Army must take precedence. Active-duty service can sometimes be delayed up to two years at the request of the individual in order to complete postgraduate studies; educational delays are also based on the needs of the Army at the time of commissioning.

To qualify for consideration for one of the 200 scholarships, a soldier must have completed at least one year but not more than two years of college. One hundred twenty-five soldiers are selected for three-year scholarships, and 75 others are selected for two-year scholarships. Scholarships cover the *time remaining to finish the degree.* To be eligible, the soldier must meet the following criteria:

- Be a U.S. citizen.
- Be on active duty at least until 1 June of the year in which he or she will begin full-time college study in September.
- Be less than 25 years of age on 30 June of the year in which he or she will receive a commission. (This requirement can be adjusted up to four years based on time spent on active duty. For instance, a soldier with two years' active-duty service would have to be younger than 27 on 30 June year of commissioning.)
- Be medically qualified. (Medical qualifications for ROTC are more stringent than those for general active-duty service.)
- Demonstrate strong leadership potential.
- Have a GT Aptitude Area score of at least 115.
- Have a cumulative grade point average of 2.0 on a 4.0 scale for all college work completed thus far.
- Have passed the APFT within the past year with a minimum score of 180 and a minimum of 60 points in each event.
- Be accepted as an academic junior for the two-year scholarship, or as an academic sophomore for the three-year scholarship, by an institution offering Army ROTC.

If a servicemember has a bar to reenlistment, plans on studying for the ministry, has completed one undergraduate degree and is working on a second, or is in the weight-control program, he or she is ineligible for the scholarship program.

Soldiers may apply to the program between 15 December (of the preceding year) and 31 March of the year in which they wish to enroll in school. Applications, available as early as 15 October, should be submitted early in this period so that any missing information or documents can be supplied before the 1 April deadline. Incomplete packets will not be considered. The application packet can be requested from U.S. Army ROTC Cadet Command, ATTN: ATCC-C. Fort Monroe, VA 23651-5000.

Soldiers accepted into the program will be assigned an early discharge date prior to the beginning of the school program. At their discharge, they will enlist for eight years in the U.S. Army Reserve. School time counts toward the reserve obligation. Upon graduation from college, all scholarship recipients apply for an Army commission. Those receiving a reserve commission may finish their obligation in a local reserve unit or apply for active duty. Those receiving a Regular Army commission return to active duty. If they later terminate their Army career *before* the original eight-year obligation has expired, they must finish the remaining obligation with the reserve.

Some limitations are placed on what a scholarship recipient may study. Fields of study are grouped into six categories: engineering, physical science, business, social sciences, nursing, and other (such as humanities, medical fields, and pre-law). The Army needs highly trained, technical officers, so the preponderance of scholarships go to enlisted soldiers planning on entering technical fields.

For the soldier interested in a possible career as an Army officer, or for the soldier who simply wants to make the road toward the baccalaureate degree shorter by attending college full-time, the ROTC Scholarship Program offers a viable alternative.

THE SEPARATION DECISION
Whether you decide on an Army career or separation after your first enlistment, sooner or later you must quit the service. In this section, we consider the various types of discharges, the operation of the U.S. Army Transfer facilities, and veterans' rights.

Separations
How and why a soldier is separated from the Army depends on many factors, according to AR 635-200, *Enlisted Personnel*. Separation policies in AR 635-200 promote readiness of the Army by providing an orderly means to accomplish the following:

- Ensure that the Army is served by individuals capable of meeting required standards of duty performance and discipline.
- Maintain standards of performance and conduct through characterization of service in a system that emphasizes the importance of honorable service.
- Achieve authorized force levels and grade distribution.
- Provide for the orderly administrative separation of soldiers in a variety of circumstances.

AR 635-200 provides the authority for separation of soldiers upon expiration of term of service (ETS); the authority and general provisions governing the separation of soldiers before ETS to meet the needs of the Army and its soldiers; the procedures to implement laws and policies governing voluntary retirement of soldiers for length of service; and the criteria governing uncharacterized separations and the issuance of honorable, general, and under other than honorable conditions discharges.

The following are the authorized types of separation under the provisions of AR 635-200:

Chapter 4—Separation for Expiration of Service Obligation. A soldier will be separated upon expiration of enlistment or fulfillment of service obligation.

Chapter 5—Separation for Convenience of the Government. A chapter 5 separation covers the following: involuntary separation due to parenthood; lack of jurisdiction as ordered by a U.S. court or judge thereof; aliens not lawfully admitted to the United States; personnel who did not meet procurement medical fitness standards; failure to qualify medically for flight training; personality disorders; concealment of arrest record; and failure to meet Army body composition and weight-control standards.

Chapter 6—Separation Because of Dependency or Hardship. Soldiers of the active Army and the reserve components serving on active duty or active duty for training may be discharged or released because of genuine dependency or hardship. Dependency exists when death or disability of a member of a soldier's (or spouse's) immediate family causes the family or one of its members to rely on the soldier for principal care or support. Hardship exists when in circumstances not involving death or disability of a member of the soldier's (or spouse's) immediate family, separation from the service will materially affect the care or support of the family by alleviating undue and genuine hardship.

Chapter 7—Defective Enlistments, Reenlistments, and Extensions. This chapter provides the authority, criteria, and procedures for the separation of soldiers because of minority, erroneous enlistment or extension of enlistment, defective enlistment agreement, and fraudulent entry.

Chapter 8—Separation of Enlisted Women for Pregnancy. Chapter 8 provides authority for voluntary separation of enlisted women because of pregnancy. A pregnant soldier is faced with a number of choices, the most basic of which is whether to separate from the Army. This decision can be very difficult because of its far-reaching ramifications. Once the soldier has decided to be retained on active duty, she will be expected to complete her full enlistment before she is again give the choice of continuing in the military or returning to civilian life.

Being the mother of a newborn child does not afford the soldier special privileges, but normally she will not receive PCS orders for an overseas assignment during the pregnancy. Such orders can often be deferred or deleted (for up to one year) if they should be issued. After the child is born and the mother is released from normal postnatal care, however, the military mother is given no unique consideration for assignments. She is expected to fulfill the needs of the Army just like any other soldier. This means that she could receive orders for worldwide assignments, including to dependent-restricted overseas areas.

The Army is concerned for the welfare of the child, but it does not adjust the assignment process to accommodate the new mother. Instead, the Army requires each soldier with dependents who are unable to care for themselves to file an approved Family Care Plan. Failure to complete an adequate plan will result in a bar to reenlistment. The plan specifies what actions the soldier has taken to ensure care for her dependents in the event she is assigned to an area where dependents are not authorized. In addition, she is expected to make provisions for the care of her dependents while she is away or on military duty (both on a daily basis and in the event of a necessary temporary duty).

One other consequence of the pregnant soldier's decision to continue in the military is the possibility of involuntary separation. If the soldier cannot handle her normal duties during the pregnancy or once she is a new mother, she may be separated from the service involuntarily. Such decisions are made on the grounds of unsatisfactory performance of duty or misconduct, whichever is appropriate. Involuntary separation is covered by AR 635-200, paragraphs 5-8 and 13-2, in addition to chapter 14. If a soldier in an entry-level status becomes pregnant, she will be evaluated by a medical officer to determine whether she can fully participate in the training required for the MOS. If it is determined that she cannot participate in the training, she will be involuntarily discharged. Otherwise, the soldier will be retained unless she specifically requests discharge under AR 635-200, chapter 8.

The soldier will be provided medical care during and after the pregnancy. Again, she has a choice. She may remain at her present duty assignment and receive care through a military facility within 30 miles of that location; if such care is not available, she will be treated through a civilian doctor and civilian facilities. Or she may choose to take ordinary leave, advance leave, and excess leave so that she may return to her home or other appropriate and desired location for her maternity care and the birth of her child. Once labor begins, her leave status changes to convalescent leave for the period of labor, hospitalization, and postpartum care. Convalescent leave for postpartum care is limited to the amount of time the doctor specifies as essential for the medical needs of the mother. Generally, postpartum convalescent leave does not exceed 42 days. Leave status and the pregnant soldier are covered in AR 630-5, chapter 9, section II.

If the soldier decides to return home to deliver the baby, it is her responsibility to first ensure that military facilities near her home have obstetrical care available. Many military facilities do not provide such care. The soldier cannot choose to return home for maternity care and have the government pay for that care at a civilian facility. This is prohibited in AR 40-3, except for bona fide medical emergencies that justify the use of a civilian facility. Using civilian facilities away from the duty location means that the soldier, not the government, is normally responsible for the medical bills. The health benefits adviser at the nearest military medical facility is the best source for further information on this matter.

If the pregnant soldier chooses to separate from the Army, she receives an honorable discharge and any benefits applicable to soldiers with the amount of time in service she has at the time of separation. Separation due to pregnancy is authorized under chapter 8 of AR 600-200.

Unit commanders must counsel women who are eligible for pregnancy separation. Army chaplains and the American Red Cross also offer counseling, and the JAG office can instruct the soldier in legal matters regarding the birth and care of her child. The soldier will have at least a week to consider her options but must indicate her choice of either separating or remaining on active duty in writing.

Whether the soldier is allowed to reconsider her choice depends on the choice she initially made. If she originally chose to stay on active duty but then decides to separate, the Army must separate her. If she originally elected to separate and then decides she wants to remain in the Army, the case will be reviewed, and a decision whether to retain her will be made based on the best interests of the Army.

An abnormal pregnancy places a difficult burden on the woman involved. The Army allows a woman the option of seeking a discharge in the event of a miscarriage, abortion, or premature delivery if she had been pregnant for at least 16 weeks at the time the pregnancy terminates.

Medical treatment for obstetrical and postpartum care is provided at government expense through a military medical facility. The separating soldier may not use Tricare or civilian medical facilities at government expense. In fact, the pregnant soldier is required to sign a statement before she decides to separate from the military, clearly stating that she understands that under no circumstance can Tricare, any military department, or the DVA reimburse her civilian maternity care expenses; the statement further clarifies that she understands that any costs for civilian care will be her personal financial responsibility. Therefore, careful planning must be made to ensure that she settles in an area where military medical facilities provide maternity care. The separating pregnant soldier will be authorized postpartum care for up to six weeks after the birth of the child.

Chapter 9—Alcohol or Other Drug Abuse Rehabilitation Failure. A soldier who is enrolled in the Alcohol and Drug Abuse Prevention and Control Program (ADAPCP) for substance abuse may be separated because of inability or refusal to participate in, cooperate in, or successfully complete such a program.

Chapter 10—Discharge for the Good of the Service. A soldier who has committed an offense or offenses punishable by a bad conduct discharge or dishonorable discharge under the provisions of the UCMJ and the *Manual for Courts-Martial* may submit a request for discharge for the good of the service. The request does not prevent or suspend disciplinary proceedings. (See AR 635-200, pages 43–45 for details.)

Chapter 11—Entry-Level Status Performance and Conduct. This chapter provides guidance for the separation of personnel because of unsatisfactory performance or conduct (or both) while in entry-level status. It covers inability, lack of reasonable effort, or failure to adapt to the military environment.

Chapter 12—Retirement for Length of Service. A soldier who has completed 20 years' active federal service and who has completed all required service obligations is eligible to retire. Upon retirement, the soldier is transferred to the U.S. Army Reserve Control Group (Retired) and remains in that status until active service time plus control group time equals 30 years, and then is placed on the retired list. A Regular Army soldier who has completed at least 30 years of active federal service will, upon request, be placed on the retired list.

Chapter 13—Separation for Unsatisfactory Performance. A soldier may be separated per this chapter when unqualified for further military service because of unsatisfactory performance, under the following circumstances: (1) the soldier will not develop sufficiently; (2) the seriousness of the circumstance is such that retention would have an adverse impact on military discipline, good order, and morale; (3) it is likely that the soldier will be a disruptive influence; (4) it is likely that the circumstances will continue to recur; (5) the ability of the soldier to perform duties, including potential for advancement or leadership, is unlikely; (6) the soldier meets retention medical standards.

Chapter 14—Separation for Misconduct. This chapter establishes procedures for separating personnel for misconduct because of minor disciplinary infractions, a pattern of misconduct, commission of a serious offense, conviction by civil authorities, desertion, and absence without leave. A discharge under other than honorable conditions is normally appropriate for a soldier discharged under this chapter.

Chapter 15—Separation for Homosexuality. This chapter, which has undergone microscopic review during the last several years, remains in effect with changes based on recent policy guidance. Homosexual conduct is grounds for separation from the Army. (See the section on homosexuality in chapter 4 for more information.)

Types of Discharge
Honorable Discharge
An honorable discharge is given when an individual is separated from the military service with honor. An honorable discharge cannot be denied to a person solely on the basis of convictions by courts-martial or actions under Article 15 of the UCMJ. Denial must be based on patterns of misbehavior and not isolated instances. An honorable discharge may be awarded when disqualifying entries in an individual's service record are outweighed by subsequent honorable and faithful service over a greater period of time during the current period of service. Unless otherwise ineligible, a member may receive an honorable discharge if he or she has, during the current enlistment or extensions thereof, received a personal decoration or is separated by reason of disability incurred in the line of duty.

General Discharge
A general discharge is issued to an individual whose character of service has been satisfactory but not sufficiently meritorious to warrant an honorable discharge. Such persons would have, for example, frequent punishments under Article 15 of the UCMJ or be classified as general troublemakers.

Other than Honorable Discharge
Discharges that fall within this category are given for reasons of misconduct, homosexuality, security, or the good of the service and are covered by AR 635-200. No person shall receive a discharge under other than honorable conditions unless afforded the right to present his or her case before an administrative discharge board with the advice of legal counsel.

Uncharacterized Separations
There are two types of uncharacterized separations: those given when a soldier is in entry-level status, and those given because of void enlistments or inductions.

Bad Conduct or Dishonorable Discharge
A soldier will be given a bad conduct discharge pursuant only to an approved sentence of a general or special court-martial. A soldier will be given a dishonorable discharge pursuant only to an approved sentence of a general court-martial. The appellate reviews must be completed, and the affirmed sentence duly executed. Dishonorable and bad conduct discharges result in expulsion from the Army.

TRANSITION ACTIVITIES
U.S. Army transfer facilities provide an informal, quiet atmosphere centrally located at a post where personnel being separated may be processed within

acceptable time limits. AR 635-10 prescribes that overseas returnees, except retirees, be separated on the first workday after their arrival at the separation transfer point, when possible. Personnel being released from active duty who are discharged before ETS or the period for which ordered to active duty are separated by the third workday after approved separation. All others are separated on their scheduled separation dates, except for those individuals who elect to be separated on the last workday before a weekend or a holiday.

Medical Examination

There is no statutory requirement for soldiers to undergo a medical exam incidental to separation. It is Army policy, however, to accomplish a medical examination if a soldier is active Army and retiring after 20 or more years of active duty. An examination is also required if a soldier is being discharged or released and requests a medical examination, if review of the soldier's health record by a physician or physician's assistant warrants an exam, or if an examination is required by AR 40-501.

Each soldier undergoing separation processing will have his or her medical records screened by a physician, regardless of whether a separation physical has been requested. *A separation physical may be one of the most important medical examinations of your life.* Separation physicals end in a personal interview with a doctor. That interview is the proper time to bring up every single medical fact incident to military service. This interview substantiates service connection should a soldier, after discharge, request disability compensation from the DVA based on military service. Above all, each soldier being separated from the service should make a copy of his or her medical and dental records and keep them after discharge.

Army Career and Alumni Program

The Army Career and Alumni Program (ACAP) is a transition and job assistance initiative located at military sites worldwide. Each ACAP site includes a transition assistance office (TAO) and a job assistance center (JAC), which are available for active and reserve component soldiers, Army civilians, and military and civilian family members.

Transition Assistance. The TAO is the first step in the transition process. It synchronizes current pre-severance transition services on an individual basis to help personnel leaving the Army. The office staff provide eligible clients with transition advice and serve as a focal point for problems.

Job Assistance. The JAC provides clients with job search training, individual assistance and counseling, and a referral service. It conducts individual, small-, and large-group workshops to help soldiers prepare for interviews, evaluate job offers, track job leads, and develop their resumes.

Ideally, the TAO and JAC like to see you 180 days before your separation or retirement date. If that is not possible, you are eligible to be seen at the ACAP office until you are discharged from the Army.

Army Employment Network
The Army Employment Network (AEN) is an ACAP database that contains information about companies that are committed to considering Army personnel for employment. The AEN provides the company name, location of all branches of the company, total number of personnel hired annually, types of positions for which a company hires, points of contact, and, in some cases, a listing of currently available positions. The network is linked to regional and federal Office of Personnel Management computers that list federal jobs, and is also tied to the DVA.

For more information about the ACAP, call toll-free in the continental United States (800) 445-2049. If you are stationed overseas, call DSN 221-0993. If you are an NCO, you should visit your local ACAP office and learn more about the program, then relate the information to every soldier you supervise.

Enlisted Voluntary Release Program
If you or someone you know is in an MOS affected by the Enlisted Voluntary Release Program, take an educated look at what is being offered. Consider the entire benefits package, not just the money associated with the Special Separation Bonus (SSB) or Voluntary Separation Incentive (VSI). Many soldiers opt for the SSB "Cadillac bonus" without taking into consideration the investment or tax advantage of the VSI. If a soldier is set financially and does not have to concern himself or herself with meeting future financial needs, the SSB might be the correct option. If, however, a soldier is like the majority of people who must make ends meet on a monthly basis, the VSI is probably the more sensible exit bonus. The VSI pays less immediately but is worth far more over time.

Terminal Leave
Deciding whether to take terminal leave may not be an easy decision; it depends on how much leave a soldier has accrued at the time of separation, how much leave he or she may have previously cashed in for pay, and what plans the servicemember has for job-hunting activities, travel, or vacation.

Personnel taking terminal leave will be allowed to finish processing at the local transfer activity before departure on leave. On the day of separation, a telephone call from the soldier, verifying his or her status and whereabouts, is all that is needed to finish the outprocessing procedure.

Discharge Certificates
Your DD Form 214, *Certificate of Release or Discharge from Active Duty,* is the most important document you will receive during your outprocessing and is one of the most important documents you will ever receive during your military career. At the time of your separation, you will receive copies 1 (original) and 4 (carbon) of DD Form 214. Be sure to make copies of these forms and protect the originals. *Do not let the originals out of your possession.*

Travel and Transportation Allowances

Separated soldiers are authorized travel allowances from their last duty station to their point of entry. Shipment and storage of household goods incident to separation are authorized on a one-time basis, and are subject to weight limitations and other controls. Specific information relative to shipment and storage of household goods is contained in DA Pam 55-2, *Personal Property Shipping Information.* See chapter 14 for weight limitations.

Wearing the Uniform

Wearing of the uniform by separated soldiers is a privilege granted in recognition of faithful service to the country. Former members of the Army who served honorably during a declared or undeclared war and whose most recent service was terminated under honorable conditions may wear the Army uniform in the highest grade held during such war service. The uniform may be worn only for the following ceremonies and when traveling to and from such ceremonies:

- Military funerals, memorial services, weddings, inaugurals, and other occasions of ceremony.
- Parades on national or state holidays, or other parades or ceremonies of a patriotic nature in which any active or reserve U.S. military unit is taking part.

Wearing of the Army uniform at any other time or for any other purpose is prohibited.

VETERANS' RIGHTS AND BENEFITS

The benefits discussed in this section are available to all veterans regardless of status. All Veterans Administration (VA) benefits (with the exception of insurance and certain medical benefits) payable to veterans or their dependents require that the particular period of service on which the entitlement is based be terminated under certain conditions. Honorable and general discharges qualify the veteran as eligible for benefits; however, dishonorable discharges and bad conduct discharges issued by general courts-martial are a bar to VA benefits. Other bad conduct discharges and discharges characterized as other than honorable may or may not qualify. Qualification depends on a special determination made by the VA and is based on the facts of each case.

In order to prove your eligibility for VA benefits, you must have the following:

- A complete copy of your medical records.
- DD Form 214, *Discharge Certificate.*

Conversion of SGLI to VGLI

A servicemember has 120 days after separation to apply for Veterans Group Life Insurance (VGLI), with no medical examination requirements. Beyond the

120 days, a soldier has one year to apply, with exam requirements. During the 120 days after separation, the SGLI coverage continues without premiums. Five years after separation, the VGLI expires and is not renewable. However, before it expires, it can be converted to an individual commercial policy at standard rates without physical examination or other proof of good health. A conversion notice and a list of participating insurance companies will be sent to you. Hundreds of companies participate in the conversion program.

Employment
Priority referral for job openings and training opportunities is given to eligible veterans, with preferential treatment for disabled veterans. In cooperation with VA regional offices and Veterans Outreach Centers, the job service assists veterans who are seeking employment by providing information about such opportunities as job marts, on-the-job training, and apprenticeship training.

Veterans seeking employment with the federal government may receive special opportunities, such as the following:

- A five-point preference is given to those who served during any war, in any campaign, in an expedition for which a campaign medal has been authorized, or for 180 consecutive days between January 31, 1955, and October 15, 1976.
- A 10-point preference is given to those who were awarded the Purple Heart, have a current service-connected disability, or are receiving compensation, disability retirement benefits, or pension from the VA.
- A veteran with a 30 percent or more disability may receive appointment without a competitive examination, with a right to be converted to a career appointment and with retention rights during reductions in force.

Educational Benefits
See your ACES counselor for details on the GI Bill (also covered in chapter 8), VEAP, and other educational benefits programs.

GI Loans
The purpose of VA GI loans is multifacted. They can be used to buy a home or a residential unit in certain condominium projects; to build, repair, alter, or improve a home; to refinance an existing home loan; to buy a manufactured home (with or without a lot); to buy a lot for a manufactured home that is already owned; to improve a home through installation of a solar heating and/or cooling system or other weatherization improvements; to purchase and simultaneously improve a home with energy-conserving measures; to refinance an existing VA loan to reduce the interest rate; to refinance a manufactured home loan in order to acquire a lot; or to simultaneously purchase and improve a home. Eligibility requirements vary, based on period of service with the exception that all eligible veterans must have been discharged under conditions other than dishonorable.

The loan terms are subject to negotiation between the veteran and the lender. The repayment period or maturity of GI home loans may be as long as 30 years. Newly discharged veterans are mailed certificates of eligibility shortly after discharge. Other veterans may secure their certificates by sending VA Form 26-1880, *Request for Determination of Eligibility and Available Loan Guaranty Entitlement,* along with the required supporting documents, to the VA regional office nearest them. Active-duty personnel may also take advantage of these loans.

Unemployment Compensation

The purpose of unemployment compensation for veterans is to provide income for a limited time to help meet basic needs while employment is sought. The amount and duration of payments vary because they are governed by state laws, although benefits are paid from federal funds. Veterans should apply immediately after discharge at the nearest state employment service, not at the VA. A copy of DD Form 214 is needed to establish the type of separation from the service.

One-Time Dental Treatment

In addition to dental conditions that qualify for treatment because of service connection, veterans are entitled to a one-time dental treatment without review of service records to establish service connection. This treatment must be applied for within 90 days of separation. Do not fail to take advantage of this important benefit. Contact the local VA office for a copy of VA Form 10-10, *Application for Medical Benefits.*

Disability Compensation

If you believe that you have a condition that may entitle you to VA compensation, file your claim at the time of separation. If the VA, upon reviewing your medical records, finds that you do have grounds for seeking compensation, an appointment for a physical exam will be made for you at the VA hospital closest to your home. Your claim will be processed based on the examination results.

Medical Benefits

The DVA offers a wide spectrum of medical benefits to qualified veterans: aids and services for the blind, alcohol treatment, domiciliary care, drug treatment, hospitalization care for dependents or survivors, nursing home care, outpatient dental treatment, outpatient medical treatment, and prosthetic appliances.

Eligibility criteria for hospitalization gives top priority to veterans needing hospitalization because of injuries or diseases incurred or aggravated in line of duty in active service. Veterans who are receiving compensation or who would be eligible to receive compensation (except for retirement pay) and need treatment for an ailment connected with their service are admitted as beds are available. Under certain circumstances, veterans who were not discharged or retired for disability or who are not receiving compensation and who apply for treatment of a nonservice-connected disability may be admitted to a VA hospital. Any veteran with a service-connected disability may receive VA outpatient medical treatment.

Vocational Rehabilitation
Generally, a veteran is eligible for vocational rehabilitation for 12 years following discharge or release from active service. A four-year extension is possible under certain circumstances, and further extensions may be granted for veterans who are seriously disabled, as determined by the DVA. Eligible disabled veterans may receive training up to a total of four years or the equivalent in part-time or a combination of part-time and full-time training. Eligibility for this training is determined by the VA.

Correspondence and Records
Keep a file of every paper the VA sends you. Your dealings with the VA will require patience and persistence; the required degree of each will depend to a large extent on how busy your local VA office is. Invariably, VA personnel are courteous, and they try to be helpful, but processing your claim may take months.

Burial
Burial is available to any deceased veteran of wartime or peacetime service (other than training) at all national cemeteries having available grave space, except Arlington Cemetery. The veteran must have been discharged under conditions other than dishonorable.

Eligible veterans' dependents may receive a headstone or grave marker without charge, shipped to a designated consignee. The cost of placing the marker in a private ceremony must be borne by the applicant. The VA may partially reimburse (up to the average actual cost of a government headstone or marker) costs incurred by an applicant acquiring a nongovernment headstone or marker for placement in a cemetery other than a national cemetery.

RETIREMENT OPTIONS
Under the defense authorization bill for fiscal year 2000, servicemembers now have a choice between retirement plans. Now, at the 15-year mark, soldiers can opt for either the current "Redux" retirement of 40 percent at 20 years' service plus a $30,000 lump-sum, taxable payment paid immediately, or select the pre-"Redux" 50 percent retirement system. Both options have merits, and neither is universally better than the other.

References

AR 612-10, *Reassignment Processing and Army Sponsorship (and Orientation) Program*

AR 614-30, *Overseas Service*

AR 635-10, *Processing Personnel for Separation*

AR 635-200, *Enlisted Personnel*

DA Pam 600-5, *Handbook on Retirement Services*

DA Pam 600-8, *Management and Administrative Procedures*

VA FS 1S-1, *Federal Benefits for Veterans and Dependents*

PART III

Quick Reference

11

Army Traditions

Traditions are tied directly to Army history, dating to 14 June 1775, when the Army began to take shape in Pennsylvania, Maryland, and Virginia. In 1776, the Continental Congress established the Board of War and Ordnance, which later became the War Department, now called the Department of the Army. Soldiers are the defenders of the Constitution, and Army traditions, customs, and courtesies are based on this role.

The men and women serving in today's Army are members of a proud profession long in history and rich in heritage and tradition. Soldiers perpetuate Army traditions by being model citizens, by respecting one another, and by showing symbols of national unity such as the U.S. flag.

MILITARY COURTESY

Military courtesy is the respect shown to superiors by subordinates and the mutual respect demonstrated between senior and subordinate personnel. It is basic to military discipline and founded on respect for and loyalty to authority. Military courtesy has an effect on every aspect of military life.

The Salute

The most common military courtesy is the salute. Although many forms of salutes are authorized, depending on the arms you may be carrying and the situation involved, the most common salute is the hand salute. A sharp, crisp salute shows pride in recognizing the comrade in arms; conversely, a sloppy or halfhearted salute shows a lack of pride and is a poor reflection on the soldiers rendering it.

The hand salute is required whenever you recognize an officer. Exceptions are made when the situation so requires—in public transportation (such as buses and planes) or in public places (such as theaters), or when the salute would be impractical (at work, when driving a vehicle, or when actively engaged in athletics). Even though saluting an officer is not required by military regulation when both soldier and officer are in civilian clothes, the soldier who renders this courtesy is following long-standing military tradition.

Army Salute

When the overseas cap, cold weather cap, or beret is worn, the hand salute is to the forehead—except when wearing glasses, when the tip of the fingers should touch the corner of the frame. When the utility cap, camouflage cap, or helmet is worn, the salute is to the visor.

Every soldier should learn the following guidelines:
- If running, slow to a walk before saluting.
- Always hold your salute until it is returned by the officer.
- Never salute while holding an object in your right hand.
- Render the greeting of the day in a firm, crisp voice. A confident "Good morning, sir (or ma'am)" demonstrates pride in yourself.
- In formation, salute only on the command "Present arms." Keep in mind that if you are in charge of a fatigue detail or formation, you are responsible for rendering the courtesies for the group.

The salute itself should be made in one movement, raising the right arm so that the upper arm is horizontal and bending the elbow so that the tip of the forefinger touches the forehead slightly to the right of the right eyebrow. The fingers and thumb should be extended, with the fingers "joined," or touching one another. Neither the palm nor the back of the hand should be visible from a front view.

If you wear eyeglasses, the fingertip of your right hand should touch the point on the glasses where the front frame joins the temple or earpiece. When you are wearing a utility cap, a service cap, or a helmet, your fingertip should touch the visor of the headgear.

On some occasions, you should salute the officer twice. Specifically, if you salute an officer and the officer stays in your general vicinity but does not converse directly with you, all military courtesies have been fulfilled. When the officer spends a few moments talking with you, however, you should salute a second time at the end of the conversation. This custom can be considered a preliminary greeting followed by a farewell.

When a vehicle passes carrying an officer that you recognize, you should render a salute. Likewise, if an official vehicle passes displaying vehicle plates or flags that depict the rank of the passenger, you should salute.

The salute is also used to show respect to the American flag, when the flag passes or during the retreat ceremony.

The best advice on saluting is to render the salute whenever any doubt exists as to whether the salute is actually required. Rendering the salute is a matter of pride.

Correct Use of Titles

Each member of the armed forces has a military rank: private to general in the Army and Marine Corps, airman to general in the Air Force, and seaman to admiral in the Navy. The accompanying chart shows the ranks used in the U.S. Armed Forces.

Rank becomes a soldier's military title by force of regulation and custom. In official documents, a member's rank or title always accompanies his or her name, and it is also used in conversation. By custom, military titles are used between civilians and the military, just as the custom has been established to use

ENLISTED INSIGNIA OF GRADE

AIR FORCE	ARMY	MARINES	NAVY
Chief Master Sergeant of the Air Force (CMSAF)	Sergeant Major of the Army (SMA)	Sergeant Major of the Marine Corps (SgtMajMC)	Master Chief Petty Officer of the Navy (MCPON)
Chief Master Sergeant (CMSgt) — Command Chief Master Sergeant	Command Sergeant Major (CSM) — Sergeant Major (SGM)	Sergeant Major (SgtMaj) — Master Gunnery Sergeant (MGySgt)	Fleet/Command Master Chief Petty Officer — Master Chief Petty Officer (MCPO)
Senior Master Sergeant (SMSgt) — First Sergeant (E-8)	First Sergeant (1SG) — Master Sergeant (MSG)	First Sergeant (1stSgt) — Master Sergeant (MSgt)	Senior Chief Petty Officer (SCPO)
Master Sergeant (MSgt) — First Sergeant (E-7)	Platoon Sergeant (PSG) or Sergeant First Class (SFC)	Gunnery Sergeant (GySgt)	Chief Petty Officer (CPO)
Technical Sergeant (TSgt)	Staff Sergeant (SSG)	Staff Sergeant (SSgt)	Petty Officer First Class (PO1)
Staff Sergeant (SSgt)	Sergeant (SGT)	Sergeant (Sgt)	Petty Officer Second Class (PO2)
Senior Airman (SrA)	Corporal (CPL) — Specialist (SPC)	Corporal (Cpl)	Petty Officer Third Class (PO3)
Airman First Class (A1C)	Private First Class (PFC)	Lance Corporal (LCpl)	Seaman (Seaman)
Airman (Amn)	Private E-2 (PV2)	Private First Class (PFC)	Seaman Apprentice (SA)
Airman Basic (AB) (no insignia)	Private E-1 (PV1) (no insignia)	Private (Pvt) (no insignia)	Seaman Recruit (SR)

OFFICER INSIGNIA OF GRADE

AIR FORCE	ARMY	MARINES	NAVY
General of the Air Force	General of the Army	(None)	Fleet Admiral
General	General	General	Admiral
Lieutenant General	Lieutenant General	Lieutenant General	Vice Admiral
Major General	Major General	Major General	Rear Admiral (Upper Half)
Brigadier General	Brigadier General	Brigadier General	Rear Admiral (Lower Half)
Colonel	Colonel	Colonel	Captain
Lieutenant Colonel	Lieutenant Colonel	Lieutenant Colonel	Commander
Major	Major	Major	Lieutenant Commander

OFFICER INSIGNIA OF GRADE

AIR FORCE	ARMY	MARINES	NAVY
Captain	Captain	Captain	Lieutenant
First Lieutenant	First Lieutenant	First Lieutenant	Lieutenant Junior Grade
Second Lieutenant	Second Lieutenant	Second Lieutenant	Ensign

	SILVER AND BLACK	SCARLET AND SILVER	
	W-5 ... W-4 ... W-3	W-5 ... W-4 ... W-3	W-4 ... W-3
	Chief Warrant Officer / Chief Warrant Officer / Chief Warrant Officer	Chief Warrant Officer / Chief Warrant Officer / Chief Warrant Officer	Chief Warrant Officer / Chief Warrant Officer
(None)	SILVER AND BLACK	SCARLET AND GOLD	
	W-2 ... W-1	W-2 ... W-1	W-2 ... W-1
	Chief Warrant Officer / Warrant Officer	Chief Warrant Officer / Warrant Officer	Chief Warrant Officer / Warrant Officer

COAST GUARD

Coast Guard officers use the same rank insignia as Navy officers. Coast Guard enlisted rating badges are the same as the Navy's for grades E-1 through E-9, but they have silver specialty marks, eagles and stars, and gold chevrons. The badge of the Master Chief Petty Officer of the Coast Guard has a gold chevron and specialty mark, a silver eagle, and gold stars. For all ranks, the gold Coast Guard shield on the uniform sleeve replaces the Navy star.

the title "doctor," "professor," or "governor." A person who has earned a military title carries it permanently and, if desired, into retirement.

When addressing another soldier, preface the soldier's last name with his or her rank. "Sergeant Jones," "Sergeant Major Smith," "Private Henderson," "Major Brown" are appropriate means of addressing soldiers conversationally.

When referring to persons not present, always use ranks and names. Use of last names only is disrespectful; use of pay grades (e.g., "I was talking to an O-4," or "It was an E-7") is unmilitary and degrading. All soldiers have earned their ranks, from the newest private first class to the most senior general; use them accordingly.

Titles of Commissioned Officers
Lieutenants are addressed officially as "Lieutenant." This applies to both first lieutenants and second lieutenants. The same applies to colonels and lieutenant colonels, both of which are addressed officially as "Colonel." Likewise, all generals are addressed as "General," regardless of whether they are brigadier, major, or lieutenant generals.

When not using the rank title, "Sir" is used for all officers. "Ma'am" is used to address women officers when "Sir" would be used with male officers. All chaplains are officially addressed as "Chaplain," regardless of their military rank or professional title.

Titles of Warrant Officers
The warrant officer (all five grades) officially ranks below second lieutenant and above cadet. He or she is extended the same privileges and respect as a commissioned officer and differs only in that there are certain regulated restrictions on command functions. The warrant officer is the Army's top-grade specialist and is addressed as "Mister" or "Miss," as appropriate. Under informal conditions, a chief warrant officer may be addressed as "Chief."

Titles of Cadets
Cadets of the U.S. Military Academy and the ROTC often serve summer internships with regular units where they experience military life during their training. In written communications and in conversations when they are not present, cadets are addressed as "Cadet." In direct conversation, they are addressed as "Mister" or "Miss."

Titles of Noncommissioned Officers
Sergeants major are addressed as "Sergeant Major." A first sergeant is addressed as "First Sergeant." Other sergeants, regardless of rank, are addressed as "Sergeant." Corporals and specialists are addressed with those titles. Privates first class are addressed with the abbreviation of their rank: PFC. Privates E-1 and E-2 are called "Private." The full titles of all enlisted members are used in official communications.

The Place of Honor

The place of honor is on the right. When a junior walks, rides, or sits with a senior, the junior takes position abreast and to the left of the senior. The junior should walk in step with the senior, step back and allow the senior to be the first to enter a door, and render similar acts of courtesy to the senior. The same applies when riding in a van or sedan. The junior enters the right door first and sits on the left seat; the senior enters second and sits to the right of the junior.

Courtesies to Officers

A number of customs and courtesies for showing respect to officers have evolved over the years. For instance, an officer entering a room is shown courtesy. The first soldier to recognize the officer calls the other personnel in the room to attention, but the soldier does not salute. A salute is rendered indoors only when the soldier is reporting. Soldiers should remain at attention until the officer gives an "at ease" command. Do not call the room to attention if the entering officer is junior in grade to an officer already in the room. Coming to attention in the work environment is required at the start of the day when the commander or senior person first enters the building. It is not required thereafter. If at all practical, however, when an officer not commonly working directly with a soldier is in the work environment and addresses the soldier directly, the soldier should stand.

Outside of the work environment, standing at attention is always expected of the soldier when he or she is talking with an officer. Frequently the officer will instruct the soldier to stand at ease. When the conversation is completed, the soldier should return to attention, salute, and voice an appropriate acknowledgment of the conversation, such as, "Yes, ma'am," or "Good afternoon, sir."

One final recommendation on rendering courtesies to officers: You should regard "requests," "desires," or "wishes" expressed by a commanding officer as orders. Frequently, the wording is softened as a courtesy to the subordinate, but the intent is the same as an order.

Appointments with Commanding Officers

Soldiers are authorized under the Army's "open-door policy" to speak with each commander in their chain of command. It is usually under the most serious conditions that this is done, when a soldier believes that he or she has been wronged or has some important information that the commander may need to know.

Soldiers are usually able to get help with difficulties from offices on post or from their NCO support channel, which is the squad or section leader, the platoon sergeant, or the first sergeant. However, it is essential to discipline that each soldier knows that he or she has the right to appeal directly to the commander for redress of wrongs.

When a soldier believes that a matter requires a commander's attention, he or she should make an appointment to see the commander. The first sergeant can make appointments to see the company commander and can coordinate appointments with the battalion commander by going through the battalion command sergeant major. Just inquire, "May I see the commanding officer?" Often it is appropriate to state the reason, unless the matter is extremely private. Once an appointment is made with the commander, be sure to arrive promptly for the meeting, and render all military courtesies.

TABOOS

Do Not Defame the Uniform. When you wear your uniform, you are acting in a capacity of a member of the government of your country. Do not defame yourself, your uniform, your unit, or your country by behaving badly while wearing the uniform or by wearing the uniform in any manner other than as prescribed. Be especially strict with yourself when in foreign countries.

Never Slink Under Cover to Avoid Retreat. Now and then, thoughtless people are observed ducking inside a building or under cover just to avoid a retreat ceremony and the moment of respect it includes. Never slink away from an opportunity to pay respect to our flag and our national anthem. The flag and anthem are the symbols of what soldiers and, indeed, the whole Army exist to protect.

Proffer No Excuses. Never make excuses or explain a shortcoming unless an explanation is demanded. The army demands results. Soldiers of all grades make mistakes, and when that happens, admit the mistake, correct the error if possible, and find out how to do it right the next time. Admitting and bearing the consequences of a mistake will earn you the respect of colleagues and superiors alike.

Never Lie to a Superior. The fourth "rule" of the 1759 Standing Orders for Rogers Rangers says: "Tell the truth about what you see and what you do. There is an army depending on us for correct information. You can lie all you please when you tell other folks about the rangers. But don't ever lie to a ranger or officer." This applies to noncommissioned, warrant, and commissioned officers.

Avoid "Going Over a Superior's Head." It is both a customary and a legal right for soldiers to discuss grievances with their chain of command. Except for the most exceptional cases, it is bad form for a soldier to take a problem or grievance to the battalion commander without first having sought relief with the platoon leader and platoon sergeant or the first sergeant and company commander.

Do Not Associate Inappropriately. It is a long-standing Army tradition that enlisted soldiers do not associate socially with officers. Enlisted soldiers do not gamble, borrow or lend money, or drink intoxicants with officers. Dating is strictly forbidden. See chapter 4 for more details on this matter.

Never Lean on a Superior's Desk. When called before a senior commissioned or noncommissioned officer, avoid leaning or lolling against the senior's desk. Stand erect until offered a seat.

Never Keep Anyone Waiting. Report at once when notified to do so. Never keep anyone waiting unnecessarily. This is certainly an old Army tradition. The failure of a soldier to appear at his or her place of duty is a punishable offense.

Do Not Carry an Umbrella While in Uniform. There is a long-standing taboo against soldiers in uniform carrying umbrellas. Women soldiers, however, may carry and use umbrellas when in uniform and not in formation. The logic of this taboo for men has never been explained. Accept it on faith.

COURTESY TO THE FLAG

Four common sizes exist for the national flag. The garrison flag, flown on special occasions and holidays, measures 20 by 38 feet. The post flag, flown for general use, is 10 by 19 feet. The storm flag, used in inclement weather, is 5 by 9.5 feet. The last size is that of the grave-decorating flag, which measures 7 by 11 inches.

In addition to the national flag, we can speak of the national color, the national standard, and the national ensign. The national color, carried by dismounted units, is a 3-by-4-foot flag trimmed on three sides by a golden yellow fringe measuring 2.5 inches in width. The national standard is identical to the national color, except that it is carried by a mechanized, motorized, or mounted unit. The national ensign is a naval term designating a flag of any size used to indicate the nationality of ship personnel. The term *flag* does not technically refer to colors, standards, or ensigns. Other terms associated with flags are also a part of military tradition. The *hoist* is the width, the *fly* is the length, and the *truck* is the ball at the top of the flagstaff.

Honor the Flag; Honor Yourself

Honoring the nation's flag is an integral part of military customs and courtesies. The hand salute is rendered to show respect when the flag passes in front of a soldier in uniform. You should initiate the salute when the flag is approaching and is within six paces, and then you should hold the salute until the flag has passed six paces. If you are walking past a stationary flag, the same six-pace rule applies. In addition, you should turn your head in the direction of the flag. Soldiers marching in formation render salute only on command. If you are indoors when the flag passes, do not render the hand salute.

A soldier in civilian clothes still honors the flag with a salute, but it is modified to a "civilian salute," with the right hand placed over the heart. If headgear is worn with civilian clothing by a male soldier, the headgear is removed with the right hand and held over the heart; a female soldier in civilian clothing wearing headgear does not remove the headgear but still places her right hand over her heart.

The national flag should never be dipped low as a means of salute or greeting. The only exception is made for military vessels under specific international courtesies. Organizational flags, including the U.S. Army flag, are dipped lower than the national flag during the playing of the national anthem, "To the Color," or a foreign national anthem.

Out of respect for the flag, you should never use it as part of a costume, on a float, or on a vehicle, unless it is displayed on a staff. No lettering of any kind should ever be added to the flag. When a flag is damaged, soiled, or weathered, it should be burned or disposed of in a dignified manner. No portion of the flag should ever be allowed to touch the ground; if it does, the flag is considered soiled. The proper way of folding the flag should be followed exactly (see illustration).

Another means of showing respect to the flag is the Pledge of Allegiance, first adopted by Congress in 1942. The tradition surrounding the pledge specifies that it should be said while standing at attention, with the right hand over the heart. The Pledge of Allegiance is normally not recited in military formations or in military ceremonies.

Raising and Lowering the Flag

Military customs and traditions govern the raising and lowering of the flag, as well. Reveille is the daily military ceremony honoring the flag at the beginning of the day. Retreat is the counterpart when the flag is lowered at the end of the day. Reveille is a bugle call, often recorded and played over a public-address system on military installations today. The flag is hoisted quickly to the top of the flagpole, beginning on the first note of reveille. Retreat ceremonies, full of traditions, are discussed in the following section.

The flag is sometimes flown at half-staff as a salute to the honored dead. Memorial Day, the last Monday in May, is one occasion when the flag is flown at half-staff from reveille to 1200 hours. A 21-gun salute is then fired before the flag is raised to the top of the staff until retreat. Whenever the flag is to be flown at half-staff, it should first be hoisted to the top of the staff and then lowered to the midpoint. Likewise, before lowering the flag, it should be hoisted the full height of the staff and then lowered and properly folded.

Full details on flag courtesies can be found in AR 840-10.

CUSTOMS

The customs of the service make up the unwritten "common law" of the Army. These customs are rich in tradition, and every soldier should know and observe them.

Retreat Ceremony

The purpose of the retreat ceremony is to honor the national flag at the end of the day. Often the evening gun is fired at the time of retreat so that soldiers throughout the installation will be aware of the ceremony even if they are outside the range of the bugle. The evening gun is also used to mark the end of the work day.

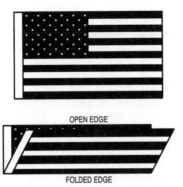

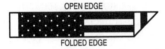

FOLD THE LOWER STRIPED SECTION OF THE FLAG OVER THE BLUE FIELD.

FOLD THE FOLDED EDGE OVER TO MEET THE OPEN EDGE.

START A TRIANGULAR FOLD BY BRINGING THE STRIPED CORNER
OF THE FOLDED EDGE TO THE OPEN EDGE.

FOLD THE OUTER POINT INWARD PARALLEL WITH THE
OPEN EDGE TO FORM A SECOND TRIANGLE.

CONTINUE FOLDING UNTIL THE ENTIRE LENGTH OF THE FLAG IS FOLDED
INTO A TRIANGLE WITH ONLY THE BLUE FIELD AND MARGIN SHOWING.

TUCK THE REMAINING MARGIN INTO THE POCKET FORMED BY THE
FOLDS AT THE BLUE FIELD EDGE OF THE FLAG.

THE PROPERLY FOLDED FLAG SHOULD RESEMBLE A COCKED HAT.

Folding the American Flag

Retreat is not necessarily observed at the same time at each installation. The post commander sets the time of the sounding of both reveille and retreat.

During the retreat ceremony, the evening gun is fired at the last note of retreat. At that time a band, a bugler, or recorded music plays the national anthem or sounds "To the Color." Soldiers begin lowering the flag on the first note of the national anthem or "To the Color" at a rate that ensures that the lowering is completed with the last note of music. Then, following strict customs, the flag is folded and stored until reveille the next morning.

Special respect is rendered to the flag and to the national anthem during retreat by soldiers all across the installation, not merely by those participating directly in the ceremony. Under no circumstances should a soldier run into a building to avoid rendering this courtesy to the flag.

During the playing of the national anthem, soldiers in uniform should stand at attention, facing the flag if visible, or the music if the flag is not visible. A salute should be rendered on the first note and held until the final note. The same courtesy applies to "To the Color." When indoors, the salute is omitted. Soldiers in civilian clothing render the "civilian salute" in the same manner as to the flag. Women never remove headgear.

All vehicular traffic should stop during the retreat ceremony. For cars and motorcycles, the driver and passengers should get out of the vehicle and show proper respect. For other vehicles, such as buses or armored vehicles, the ranking soldier should get out and render the appropriate salute. All other passengers should sit quietly at attention inside the vehicle. Commanding officers of tanks or armored cars can salute from the vehicle.

The same respect should be rendered to the national anthems of friendly nations when they are played during official occasions.

Bugle Calls

In addition to reveille and retreat, several other bugle calls play important roles in military tradition. In general, bugle calls can be divided into four categories: alarm, formation, service (which includes reveille and retreat), and warning.

First call is the first bugle of the day. Considered a warning call, it alerts you that reveille is about to take place and that you will be late if you're not ready within the next few minutes.

The last bugle call of the day is *taps,* a service call dating back to Civil War days. Taps is traditionally used at military funerals as well, giving the final bugle call for the fallen soldier.

"To the Color" is the alternative music used during the retreat ceremony. It signals that the flag is being lowered. You should render the salute during "To the Color," as you would during the national anthem. Both are meant to honor the flag.

Tattoo is usually played near 2100 hours and has traditionally been the call for lights-out in 15 minutes.

Unit Customs

Individual units foster pride and esprit de corps by observing a variety of customs that set them apart from the rest of the Army. Since it is a matter of personal honor for a soldier to know in which battles his or her unit took part, soldiers joining a new unit should learn its history. A quick check with the post library is often the best way to start.

Units perpetuate their history through their organizational properties, mottoes, and insignia. A unit's organizational properties include flags and standards (including battle honors and campaign streamers) and other physical representations of its heritage. Many units claim regimental silver with a unique history as part of their organizational property. For example, the 23rd Infantry's silver bowl was made from the metal of 5,610 combat infantryman's badges earned by the 23rd's infantrymen during the first 18 months of combat in Korea. Perhaps the most famous regimental silver property is the 31st Infantry's "Shanghai Bowl," which was presented to the regiment by the citizens of Shanghai after the Boxer Rebellion.

Unit mottoes provide another link with the past. The 19th Infantry's motto, "The Rock of Chickamauga," recalls the regiment's service at the Battle of Chickamauga. The 7th Cavalry's motto and song, "Garry Owen," was brought to the regiment in the 1860s by Irish immigrants. The 22nd Infantry's motto "Deeds, Not Words" speaks for itself.

Many units have acquired Infantry's nicknames as a result of past service. The 31st Infantry is known as the "Polar Bears" as a result of duty in northern Russia after the end of World War I. The 28th Infantry's "Lions of Cantigny" recalls the regiment's service at the first American offensive battle in World War I.

Unit insignia also embody unit traditions. For example, shoulder-sleeve insignia, first authorized during World War I, were originally conceived to foster esprit de corps and heighten the individual soldier's identification with his unit. The 81st Infantry Division was the first division to develop a sleeve insignia, that of a black wildcat on a circular path. The idea was so well received by the headquarters of the American Expeditionary Force that General Pershing directed the other divisions to develop their own distinctive cloth patches.

The Army Song

Another tradition that literally brings soldiers to their feet is the Army song. When you hear it being sung or being played, the appropriate action is to stand at attention. The melody is that of the "Caisson Song," composed in the early 1900s by then Lt. Edmund L. Gruber, who later was promoted to brigadier general. But the words for "The Army Goes Rolling Along" were selected much later. The eight-year process began in 1948 with a nationwide contest to create an official Army song. Within four years, the Army had also enlisted the aid of several music composers, publishers, and recording studios. Their joint efforts produced the new lyrics, set to the music of the old "Caisson Song." "The Army Goes Rolling Along" became the official Army song when it was dedicated on Veterans Day, 11 November 1956, at Army installations throughout the world.

The Army Goes Rolling Along

Verse: March along, sing our song
                   with the army of the free.
                   Count the brave, count the true
                   Who have fought to victory.
                   We're the Army and proud of our name!
                   We're the Army and proudly proclaim:

1st Chorus: First to fight for the right
                   And to build the nation's might,
                   and THE ARMY GOES ROLLING ALONG.
                   Proud of all we have done,
                   Fighting till the battle's won,
                   and THE ARMY GOES ROLLING ALONG.

Refrain: Then it's hi! hi! hey!
                   The Army's on its way,
                   Count off the cadence loud and strong:
                   For where'er we go, you will always know
                   That THE ARMY GOES ROLLING ALONG.

2nd Chorus: Valley Forge, Custer's ranks,
                   San Juan Hill and Patton's tanks,
                   And the Army went rolling along.
                   Minutemen from the start,
                   Always fighting from the heart,
                   And the Army keeps rolling along.

Refrain: Then it's hi! hi! hey!
                   The Army's on its way,
                   Count off the cadence loud and strong:
                   For where'er we go, you will always know
                   That THE ARMY GOES ROLLING ALONG.

3rd Chorus: Men in rags, men who froze,
                Still that Army met its foes,
                And the Army went rolling along.
                Faith in God, then we're right
                And we'll fight with all our might
                As the Army keeps rolling along.

Refrain: Then it's hi! hi! hey!
                The Army's on its way,
                Count off the cadence loud and strong:
                (two! three!)
                For where'er we go, you will always know
                That THE ARMY GOES ROLLING ALONG.
                (Keep it rolling!)
                And THE ARMY GOES ROLLING ALONG.

12

Assignments

For soldiers who read the *Army Times* or *Soldiers* magazine for any glimmer of changes to Army personnel policy while waiting for the new regulation updates to arrive in the mail, there is now a new Internet site at *www.perscom.army.mil.* On the enlisted management Web page are everything an inquiring soldier wants to know in real time and up to date. Instead of waiting months to find out if your DA Form 4187, *Personnel Action Request,* for reassignment has gone through, call the IVRS, send an E-mail, use the fax, or, even better, sign on to the Assignment Satisfaction Key, all of which are explained below.

COMMUNICATING WITH PERSCOM
The Army's goal is to get enlisted soldiers more involved in their career management. What was once a paper-intensive and not very responsive personnel system is now, with automation, very responsive to soldiers who care about their next assignment.

The Enlisted Personnel Management Directorate (EPMD) employs five tools to assist soldiers in communicating with their career managers,. These initiatives include an Interactive Voice Response Telephone System (IVRS), expanded e-mail capabilities, high-speed fax machines, mail-grams, and a pocket reference information card that lists telephone numbers, E-mail addresses, and other data valuable to soldiers wanting to help manage their careers.

The cornerstone of the new system is the IVRS. The IVRS is an automated voice response telephone system that provides soldiers with career information 24 hours a day. Soldiers can activate the IVRS by dialing (800) FYI-EPMD or DSN: 221-3763. The 800 number is available only in the continental United States. To use the IVRS system, enter your Social Security number and then follow the menu options that will let you know if you are on assignment or scheduled to attend an Army school. It will also provide topical information on retention, recruiting, drill sergeant, special forces, ranger, compassionate reassignments, Married Army Couples Program, Exceptional Family Member Program, and separations.

EPMD also encourages you to use E-mail to contact your branch. Inquiries concerning the status of personnel actions, future schooling, or assignments are examples of typical information exchanges that can be conducted 24 hours a day. Soldiers can also correspond with their career managers by using fax machines. Soldiers and personnel service centers can save time by faxing communications directly to the desired career branch within EPMD for processing. The EPMD E-mail, fax, and mail addresses are shown below.

ASSIGNMENT SATISFACTION KEY (ASK)
Accessible from the PERSCOM Web site and/or a soldier's Army Knowledge Online (AKO) account, the futuristic vision of soldiers making all their own assignments is slowly becoming a reality. Currently in its infant stage, this innovation provides the soldier with an automated tool to quickly update his or her preferences and contact information via the Internet through their respective AKO account. During the "dream sheet" days you had many assignment locations to choose from but little chance of being assigned to where you asked, unless you were able to correspond with your assignment manager. Today the majority of assignment locations are available to you to select, and those who decline to submit a preference will be assigned according to the needs of the Army. Bottom line, the ASK provides soldiers the capability to post assignment preferences directly onto the Total Army Personnel Database. This system is expected one day to eliminate the paper- and labor-intensive DA Form 4187. The Assignment Selection Key is available through the PERSCOM Web site at *www.perscom.army.mil*. Use your Army Knowledge Online (AKO) account password to gain access, which will ensure that your personal data remains secure.

Participation
You can apply to participate in this new service through PERSCOM's Web site at *www.perscom.army.mil*. Use your Army Knowledge Online (AKO) account password to gain access. Use of AKO will ensure necessary security requirements are met. You may view and update the following information:
• Personal contact information
• Special duty interest
• Assignment preferences
• Assignment location volunteer

Points of Contact
You can contact the Enlisted Personnel Management Directorate in the following ways:

Telephone
Interactive Voice Response System (IVRS)
1-800-FYI-EPMD (CONUS)
1-800-394-3763 (CONUS)
(703) 325-3763 (Commercial)
221-2763 (DSN)

Mail
U.S. Total Army Personnel Command
Attention: (Your branch office symbol. Column 2 in below table)
2461 Eisenhower Avenue
Alexandria, VA 22331

E-mail
Your branch E-mail ID (Column 3 in below table)@*hoffman.army.mil*

Fax
221-XXXX (DSN)
(703) 325-XXXX (commercial)
Your branch fax extension (Column 4 in below table)

ENLISTED ASSIGNMENT CONTACT INFORMATION

Assignment Branch	Office Symbol	E-mail ID	Fax Extension
Infantry	EPK-I	EPINF	4880
Air Defense Artillery	EPK-A	EPADA	4664
Field Artillery	EPK-F	EPFA	4533
Special Forces	EPK-S	EPSF	4510
Armor	EPK-R	EPAR	4683
Engineer	EPL-E	EPENGR	4307
MP	EPL-M	EPMP	4304
MI	EPL-M	EPINTELL	4304
Language	EPL-M	EPLANG	4304
Signal	EPL-S	EPSIG	4306
Aviation	EPL-T	EPAVN	4308
Transportation	EPL-T	EPTRANS	4308
Adjutant General	EPM-A	EPAG	5836
Health Services	EPM-H	EPHS	6402
QM/Chemical	EPM-L	EPQMC	4521
Ordnance	EPM-O	EPORD	6555
CSM/SGM Office	EPZ-E	EPCSMSGM	4694
Retention/Reclass	EPR	TAPCEPR	3565

THE ENLISTED PERSONNEL ASSIGNMENT SYSTEM
The primary goal of the enlisted personnel assignment system is to satisfy the personnel requirements of the Army.

Secondary goals are to:

* Equalize desirable and undesirable assignments by assigning the most eligible soldier from among those of like MOS and grade.
* Equalize hardships of military service.
* Assign soldiers so they will have the greatest opportunities for professional development and advancement.
* Meet soldiers' personal desires.

First-term soldiers with initial enlistments of three years or less will receive only one assignment before expiration term of service (ETS) following basic and skill training. If required to serve in an unaccompanied hardship tour area OCONUS, they will then be given no more than two assignments in different locations. Those with enlistments of more than three but less than four years will receive, following basic and skill training, no more than one CONUS assignment or two OCONUS assignments. Soldiers with enlistments of four or more years, following basic and skill training, will serve no more than two assignments in different locations, regardless of the tour length.

Consistent with Army needs, soldiers will remain as long as possible at their CONUS duty stations. The Army's time-on-station (TOS) requirement for CONUS is 48 months; for OCONUS it is the length of the prescribed tour. Soldiers complete the 48-month TOS/tour requirement unless operational or training necessities are so overriding that they must be reassigned earlier. There is no statutory limitation on the amount of time soldiers may remain overseas, just as there is no statutory limit as to how long a soldier remain at a post. Except for CONUS requirements that are filled from OCONUS returnees who are immediately available, qualified volunteers are considered first for all assignments.

Soldiers may submit a request for reassignment before completion of TOS requirements, but they must complete minimum TOS requirements at their present duty station before movement. When possible, soldiers will remain on station for the maximum number of years possible consistent with Army requirements.

Normally, the Military Personnel Office (MILPO), in coordination with the unit, compares authorized and projected positions with current assigned strength and known or projected gains and losses to determine the requirements for assignments. Requisitions are then prepared for these requirements and submitted to Commanding General, Total Army Personnel Command, in Alexandria, Virginia. On receipt, PERSCOM edits and validates the requisitions. It is the responsibility of the requisitioning unit not to over- or underrequisition and to resolve any discrepancy before submitting the validated requisition for processing. Soldiers become available to be assigned against these requisitions for a variety of reasons. Soldiers who enlist in the Army are available for assign-

Joint Training in Europe

ment on completion of training and award of an MOS. Others are available when they have done one of the following:

- Volunteered for reassignment.
- Completed an overseas tour of duty.
- Completed schooling or training.
- Completed a stabilized tour of duty.
- Completed normal time on station in the continental United States (CONUS) for a given MOS ("turnaround time" varies by MOS).

The Centralized Assignment Procedure III (CAP III) System is used to assign all soldiers except those completing BT and AIT. This automated nomination/assignment procedure compares the requirements recorded on requisitions against selected qualification factors for each soldier. Some of the major qualifications considered are grade, MOS and skill level, area of preference, and special qualification identifier (SQI). Other qualifications considered are the expiration of term of service (ETS), the number of months since last permanent change of station (PCS), the number of months since return from overseas, the soldier's availability month compared with requirement month on the requisition, and any additional skill identifier (ASI). The assignment preferences of the individual and the requirements of the positions receive maximum consideration within the primary goal of filling all of the Army's requirements. The CAP III produces nominations to match the requisition.

Enlisted Personnel Assignment System

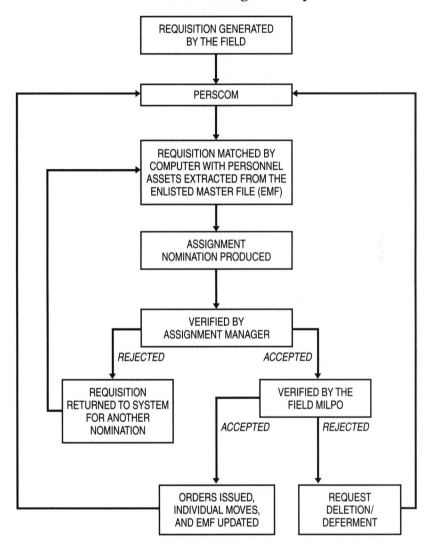

Assignment instructions are transmitted to both the losing and gaining commands or installations by the Automated Digital Network (AUTODIN). The losing commander then verifies the assignment. This step is the key in the process. Because of delays in reporting and errors in the databases, the individuals selected may not qualify for the assignment. When assignment instructions are received by the losing commander's military personnel office, the soldier's qualifications and eligibility are verified. The MILPO interviews the soldier and reviews his or her records.

If the soldier is qualified and the assignment is in keeping with announced Department of the Army policy, the process is finished when the necessary orders for travel are issued. If the soldier does not qualify or cannot qualify in time to meet the requirement, a deletion or deferment request is submitted in accordance with AR 600-8-11.

Homebase and Advance Assignment Program

The Homebase and Advance Assignment Program (HAAP) is governed by AR 614-200-9-1 and AR 600-200, chapter 2, section VIII. Participation in the HAAP is optional. It is open only to noncommissioned officers. A soldier is given a *homebase assignment* when he or she is projected to return to his or her previous permanent duty station after completing a short tour. An *advance assignment* is given when a soldier is projected to be assigned to a duty station other than his or her previous permanent duty station after completing a short tour.

Eligible soldiers are given a homebase or an advance assignment when selected for a dependent-restricted short-tour area. The HAAP minimizes family dislocation and reduces the expenditure of PCS funds.

Compassionate Assignments

AR 614-200 establishes specific policies governing individual requests submitted by soldiers for a PCS or deletion from assignment instructions. A soldier may submit a request for any of the following reasons:

Extreme Family Problems

These are divided into problems that are temporary and can be resolved in one year and those that are not expected to be resolved in one year. Soldiers making compassionate requests are not exempt from PCS moves or temporary duty (TDY) while waiting for resolution.

Sole Surviving Son or Daughter

AR 614-200 S-7 and DA Pam 600-8 apply. The sole surviving son or daughter of a family that has suffered the loss of the father, mother, or one or more sons or daughters in the military service will not be required to serve in combat. Soldiers who become sole surviving sons or daughters after their enlistment may request discharge under AR 635-200. A soldier may waive entitlement to assignment limitations, whether entitlement was based on his or her own application or the request of his or her immediate family.

Assignment of Married Army Couples

AR 614-209 and AR 614-30 apply. Army requirements and readiness goals are paramount when considering personnel for assignment. Married Army couples desiring joint assignment to establish a common household (joint domicile) must request such assignment. The assignment desires of soldiers married to other soldiers are fully considered. Married Army couples must be enrolled in the Total Army Personnel Database (TAPDB) to be considered for joint assignment. Enrollment is a simple process of verifying that two soldiers are married to each other, and having this information transmitted from the servicing Personnel Service Center (PSC) to the TAPDB. A separate transaction is required for each spouse. Once enrolled, both soldiers will be continuously considered for joint assignments. In 1997, approximately 88 percent of those enrolled in the Married Army Couples Program (MACP) were serving in joint domicile assignments.

Army Exceptional Family Member Program AR 608-75
The Exceptional Family Member Program (EFMP) is based on Public Law 94-142, which entitles handicapped children to free education and all medically related services in pursuit of education. The EFMP includes all family members with special medical and educational needs.

Soldiers enroll through their local Army medical treatment facility. The military sponsor and the attending medical or educational specialist complete enrollment forms. When PERSCOM nominates a soldier enrolled in the EFMP for assignment, the assignment manager coordinates with the gaining command to determine if needed medical services are available. When services are not available, PERSCOM considers alternative assignment locations based on existing assignment priorities or sends the soldier in an unaccompanied status.

Assignment of Women Soldiers
Women are authorized to serve in all types of units except those battalion sized or smaller that have a routine mission to engage in direct combat, or that collocate routinely with units assigned a direct combat mission. Female soldiers are assigned in accordance with Direct Combat Probability Coding (DCPC) and are restricted from filling a position with a DCPC of P1 (closed to women). All table of organizational (TOE) elements positions are assigned either a DCPC code of P1 or P2 (open to women). TDA positions are gender neutral.

Exchange Assignments
DA Pam 600-8 and AR 614-200-5-6 apply. For mutual convenience, CONUS-assigned soldiers may request an exchange assignment with a soldier within CONUS; a soldier assigned overseas may request an exchange assignment with a soldier within his or her same overseas command. DA Pam 600-8 contains detailed guidance for preparing and processing requests for an exchange assignment. The *Army Times* publishes lists of soldiers who desire to contact others to arrange for exchange assignments.

Sometimes changes in enlisted assignments are necessary to meet the needs of the Army. When this occurs, PERSCOM offers the enlisted soldier a selection of three locations for a new assignment.

CAREER DEVELOPMENT PROGRAM ASSIGNMENTS

A career development program is a system of intensive management of selected MOSs or CMFs. Career development programs are established to ensure that there are enough highly trained and experienced soldiers to fill positions that require unique or highly technical skills. To develop soldiers with the required proficiency, career fields within each program often require the following:

- Frequent movement from one job to another to gain required experience.
- An above-average frequency of advanced training.
- Lengthy or frequent training periods.
- A combination of any of the above factors.

Unless otherwise stated in AR 614-200, volunteers for a career development program should submit applications on DA Form 4187, using DA Pam 600-8 for detailed application procedures. In applying for career programs and related training, applicants should consider the prerequisites listed in DA Pam 351-4 for the appropriate course of instruction.

Chapter 7 of AR 614-200 contains the minimum requirements (subject to change) for each career program. Attaining the prerequisites does not automatically ensure entry into a career program. The appropriate career management branch selects the best-qualified soldiers for a career program.

Waivers are not granted for remaining service requirements for formal training. Waivers for other eligibility requirements or selection standards are considered unless otherwise stated in AR 614-200. Waivers cannot be implied. Each must be specifically requested. In the application for entry into the program or training requested, the applicant must include the reason for the waiver.

Career development programs include the following:

- Intelligence Career Program.
- Explosive Ordnance Disposal Career Program.
- Technical Escort Career Program.
- Army Bandsman Career Program.

ASSIGNMENT TO SPECIFIC ORGANIZATIONS AND DUTY POSITIONS

AR 614-200 contains specific policies and procedures for nomination, evaluation, selection, and assignment of enlisted soldiers to the following:

- Presidential support activities.
- Observer controller at combat training centers.
- U.S. Military Entrance Processing Command.
- Enlisted aides to general officers.
- Inspector General positions.
- Drill Sergeant Program.
- Assignment as instructors at uniformed service schools.
- Assignment to international and overseas joint headquarters, U.S. Military Missions, Military Assistance Advisory Groups (MAAGs), and Joint U.S. Military Advisory Groups (JUSMAG).

- Assignment to certain Defense and departmental-level organizations and agencies.
- Reserve component or ROTC duty.
- Food inspection specialists.
- Selection and assignment of first sergeants.

OVERSEAS SERVICE

Many Americans work very hard all their lives, and then in their declining years, when they at last have the leisure and money to travel, they see the world. Soldiers not only see the world when they are young, but they also have the unique opportunity to live among foreign peoples for extended periods and learn about their cultures from firsthand experience.

There are two ways that you can approach your first overseas tour. You can go kicking and screaming and spend your time isolated in the American community of some foreign country, never venturing very far outside the cocoon of familiar surroundings, counting the dreary days until you rotate; or you can approach foreign service as a thrilling adventure to be experienced to the fullest, and you can be a goodwill ambassador for the United States of America.

Running afoul of the law in a foreign country can be very dangerous. In countries where a Status of Forces Agreement (SOFA) exists between the U.S. government and the foreign government, soldiers may be tried for offenses under the laws of the country concerned.

Most major overseas commands operate orientation programs for newly arrived personnel in the command. These courses attempt to expose soldiers to the culture in which they will be living in order to lessen the effect of culture shock that some people experience the first time they encounter a foreign society. When you receive overseas assignment instructions, it would be a good idea for you (and your spouse, if you have one) to study the language of the country to which you will be going. Some special assignments require extensive formal language training, but most Army installations do provide some language instruction for soldiers and their dependents who are bound overseas. Learning the rudiments of a foreign language can be fun, and speaking a foreign language is a valuable skill to have once you arrive at your overseas duty station.

Standards of living overseas vary, depending on the country. Germany's standard of living is very high, and your money will not go far there; other countries are beset with substantial economic problems, and the standards of living in those places can sometimes be so low that only the very rich can afford luxuries that are considered common in the United States, and you won't be able to afford them at local prices.

As with everything else, what you get out of your situation is what you make of it. And remember that your overseas tour will not last forever; sooner or later, you must leave to come home. Emotional attachments are very hard to break off, so be warned if you establish any kind of relationship with a foreign man or woman. What usually starts as a casual, fun-filled lark, a pleasant way to pass the time, frequently develops into a serious involvement. If it is not consummated by marriage, its termination can be an emotional trauma that will be painful for both of you. A sad commentary on this subject is the thousands of illegitimate children abandoned by American servicemen in various foreign countries over the years.

Policies

The chief consideration in selecting a soldier for service overseas is that a valid authorization exists for his or her military qualifications. Equitable distribution is made, within a given MOS and grade, of overseas duty assignments, considering both desirable and undesirable locations. All reasonable efforts are made to minimize periods of forced separations and any adverse effects of overseas service encountered by soldiers and their families.

Between overseas tours, with the exception of Hawaii, soldiers are assigned in their sustaining base for at least 12 months on station. Consistent with Army needs, soldiers are retained as long as possible in CONUS. Among individuals who have previous overseas service, those with the earliest date of return from overseas normally will be selected first. Subject to personnel requirements in short-tour areas, soldiers who have completed a normal overseas service tour in a short-tour area will not be assigned to another short-tour area on their next overseas assignment.

Kinds of Overseas Tours

Personnel accompanied or joined by their dependents at government expense must have enough remaining service to serve the tour prescribed for those "with dependents."

Army personnel married to each other and serving in the same overseas area serve tours in accordance with AR 614-30. They must extend or reenlist, if necessary, to have enough time in service to serve the tour prescribed by the table before compliance with orders directing movement.

The "all others" tour is served by soldiers who meet the following criteria:

• Elect to serve overseas without dependents.
• Are serving in an area where dependents are not permitted.
• Do not have dependents (this rule does not apply in areas where personnel who have dependents must serve "with dependents" tours).
• Are divorced or legally separated and pay child support.

Tours are normally the same for all personnel at the same station. Where there are personnel of more than one service, the service having the main interest (normally, the most personnel in the area) develops a recommended tour length that is coordinated with the other services. Tour length may vary within any given country or area, depending on the specific duty station. AR 614-30 lists overseas duty tours for military personnel.

Short-Tour and Long-Tour Eligibility

AR 614-30 chapters 2 and 9 apply. Personnel are assigned to short-tour overseas assignments according to the following priorities:

- Volunteers who have completed a minimum of 12 months' time on station or are not otherwise stabilized.
- Personnel with no previous overseas service.
- Personnel in CONUS who have not previously served in a short-tour area and whose last overseas assignment was a "with dependents" tour; those whose last overseas tour was a "with dependents" tour in a long-tour area and who previously served a short tour; those whose last overseas tour was in a short-tour area and who were in accompanied status; and those who have not previously served in a short-tour area and whose last assignment was an "all others" tour.
- Personnel in Hawaii after completion of a prescribed accompanied tour.
- Personnel in CONUS whose last overseas tour was in a short-tour area and who were in an unaccompanied area.
- Personnel in Hawaii after completion of a prescribed "all others" tour.

Personnel are assigned to long-tour overseas areas according to the following priorities:

- As in the first two conditions listed for short-tour overseas assignments.
- Personnel serving in CONUS whose last overseas tour was "with dependents" in a short-tour area.
- Personnel serving in CONUS whose last overseas tour was "all others" in a short-tour area, "all others" in a long-tour area, and "with dependents" in a long-tour area.
- Personnel in Hawaii after completion of a prescribed "with dependents" tour or an "all others" tour.

Deferments and Deletions

AR 614-30 chapter 6 applies. Because of the possible adverse effect on command operational readiness, granting of deferments for overseas service is strictly controlled and held to an absolute minimum. The need of the service is the major determining factor in granting deferments.

Normally, once an application has been submitted, the soldier will be retained at the home station, pending a final decision. When a soldier requests deferment and it results in his or her having less remaining time in service than the length of the prescribed tour, the individual will continue on the overseas assignment. Unless he or she voluntarily reenlists or extends to be eligible to complete the prescribed tour, the individual must sign a counseling statement, which is a bar to reenlistment. Applications are initiated by the individual concerned on DA Form 4187.

The following conditions normally warrant deferments or deletion from overseas assignment:

- A recent severe psychotic episode involving a spouse or child after a soldier receives assignment instructions.
- The soldier's children being made wards of the court or being placed in an orphanage or a foster home because of family separation. This separation must be because of military service and not because of neglect or misconduct on the part of the soldier.
- Adoption cases in which the home study (deciding whether a child is to be placed) has been completed and a child is scheduled to be placed in the soldier's home within 90 days.
- Illness of a family member (see AR 614-30 for details).
- Terminal illness of a family member where death is anticipated within one year.
- Death of a soldier's spouse or child after receipt of assignment instructions.
- Prolonged hospitalization of more than 90 days when the soldier's presence is deemed essential to resolve associated problems.
- Documented rape of the soldier's spouse or child within 90 days of the scheduled movement date, when the soldier's presence is deemed essential to resolve associated problems.
- Selection to attend the Basic or Advanced NCO Courses or OCS, where attendance will delay overseas travel more than 90 days.
- Enrollment in the Drug and Alcohol Abuse Residential Rehabilitation Treatment Program.
- Pregnancy or related complications exceeding 90 days.

Curtailment of Tours
AR 614-30 chapter 8 applies. Overseas commanders may curtail overseas tours when military requirements so dictate. They may also disapprove curtailment requests.

When curtailments of more than 60 days are considered, commanders must recommend curtailments and request reassignment instructions from PERSCOM as early as possible, not later than 45 days before the departure date. Curtailing a tour must not cause an emergency requisition to fill the vacated position.

Overseas commanders may, at any time, curtail the tour of a soldier who has discredited or embarrassed or may discredit or embarrass the United States or jeopardize the commander's mission. They may also curtail tours when family members are moved to the United States because of criminal activity, a health problem, or death in the immediate family living with the sponsor. In exceptional cases, the commander may waive advance HQDA coordination and attach the soldier to the nearest personnel assistance point for issue of PCS orders. These exceptions are as follows: potential defectors, extreme personal hardship, and expeditious removal of a soldier in the best interests of the service (for example, when a soldier causes an embarrassment to the command in its relationship with a foreign government).

Pregnant soldiers are not curtailed from their overseas tours solely because of pregnancy. If noncombatant evacuation is ordered, however, pregnant soldiers who have reached the seventh month of pregnancy will be curtailed and evacuated. Such a curtailment does not, however, preclude the solder's being reassigned overseas again after completion of the pregnancy and discharge from inpatient status.

Change in Overseas Tour Status

Change of tour requests are normally approved, provided the government has not expended funds for shipment of household goods or movement of dependents, and the gaining command has concurred with the change. Additionally, a soldier may be required to extend or reenlist to meet tour length requirements. Requests are normally not favorably considered if the government has expended funds for shipment of household goods or movement of family members. Exceptions to policy are considered under extenuating circumstances. Army Regulation 55-46, *Travel of Dependents and Accompanied Military and Civilian Personnel to, from, or between Overseas Areas,* the Joint Travel Regulation (JFTR), and AR 614-30, *Overseas Service,* are the applicable regulations.

Consecutive Outside Continental U.S. Tours

Regulatory guidance pertaining to consecutive overseas tour (COTs) is found in AR 614-30 *(Overseas Service),* Chapter 4. Soldiers who volunteer to serve two full consecutive OCONUS tours are authorized government-paid travel for themselves and command-sponsored family members to leave locations equal to the distance to the soldier's home of record. Soldiers may travel greater distances provided they pay the additional travel costs. The leave location is not restricted to CONUS and must normally be between the two tours. The government paid travel is the only benefit associated with a COT; any leave used is chargeable to the soldier.

To be eligible for a COT, soldiers must complete current prescribed tour plus any voluntary extensions and agree to serve another full tour plus leave and travel time between tours. COTs fall into two categories: OCONUS tours that involve a permanent change of station and OCONUS tours that do not involve a PCS.

Concurrent and Deferred Travel

Soldiers being transferred overseas should seek command sponsorship of their family members, as well as concurrent or deferred travel for family members. Sponsorship of soldiers' families is dependent upon the availability of government or economy housing, and, if housing will be available within 60 days, concurrent travel is normally authorized. If housing will not be available until between 61 days and 140 days, deferred travel is normally authorized.

SPONSORSHIP

Every new assignment raises questions and concerns for the soldier and his or her family. The sponsorship program (AR 600-8-8) assists soldiers and their dependents in establishing themselves at a new duty station and guides soldiers while they adjust to their new work environment.

A "sponsor" is an individual designated by name at a gaining organization to assist incoming members and their families in making a smooth transition into the unit and community environment. Sponsors should be a grade equal to or higher than that of the incoming soldier; be the same sex, marital status, and MOS; be familiar with the surrounding area; and not have received assignment instructions.

Sponsors' duties are varied:

- Forward a welcoming letter to the incoming soldier. It should include the sponsor's duty address and telephone number (and home address and home telephone number as well, but this is not specifically required by the regulation).
- Try to provide information requested by incoming soldiers.
- Advise the incoming soldier that he or she will be met at the point of arrival in the area or at the aerial port of debarkation.
- Offer to assist in getting temporary housing (guest house or similar accommodations).
- Accompany the incoming soldier after his or her arrival in the unit while he or she goes through in-processing.
- Acquaint the incoming soldier with the surrounding area and facilities.
- Introduce the incoming soldier to his or her supervisors and immediate chain of command.

Gaining commanders are required to send incoming soldiers welcoming letters. Informality and information sharing are the primary goals of these letters. The welcoming letter and its enclosures should, as a minimum, contain the gaining unit's address and telephone number and information about duty, housing, and living at the new post.

Commanders are also responsible for ensuring that sponsors are provided enough time from their duties to help new soldiers. In addition, commanders arrange transportation so that sponsors can meet new members and their dependents at the point of arrival and bring them back to the unit (overseas only).

The incoming soldier should answer the sponsor's letter immediately and do the following:

- Inform the sponsor of his or her time, date, and point of arrival (including flight numbers). Any changes to the itinerary should be reported to the sponsor immediately.

- Provide the sponsor a unit mailing address and telephone number (commercial or DSN).
- Inform the sponsor of the expected departure date from the losing duty station.
- If desired, provide the sponsor with leave addresses and telephone numbers.

Orientation Program

Commanders and supervisors are responsible for conducting a thorough and timely orientation to start new arrivals off properly. These orientations should make the new soldier feel needed and wanted and instill in him or her the motivation to contribute to the unit's mission.

13

Promotion and Reduction

Nearly all soldiers want to get promoted, but not all do. Many times this is through neglect on their part; sometimes it's through a leader's neglect. On the whole, soldiers control their own destiny.

Soldiers are recommended for promotion only after they develop the skills, knowledge, and behavior to perform the duties and assume the responsibility of the next higher grade. Generally, if soldiers do well in their present grades, they will work well in the next higher grades.

By using standard promotion scoring forms with predetermined promotion point factors, corporals, specialists, and sergeants can measure whether they qualify for promotion. They can set goals to increase their promotion potential. They can then judge their qualifications when compared with those of other soldiers in their MOS. The Army promotes soldiers who are qualified and who will accept Armywide assignments.

Commanders at the grades indicated may promote soldiers, subject to authority and delegation of responsibility by higher commanders.

- *Specialist (SPC) and below.* Unit commanders may advance or promote assigned soldiers to private E-2, private first class, and SPC. When soldiers are fully eligible, promotions to PVT, PFC, and SPC are automatic unless the commander submits DA Form 4187 blocking the promotion no later than the 20th of the preceding month.
- *Sergeant (SGT) and staff sergeant (SSG).* Field-grade commanders lieutenant colonel or higher may promote soldiers attached or assigned or on TDY to their command or installation.
- *Sergeant first class (SFC) and above.* Headquarters, Department of the Army.
- *Hospitalized soldiers.* Commanders of medical facilities may promote hospitalized soldiers to SSG and below.
- *Students.* Commandants and commanders of training installations and activities.
- *Posthumous promotion.* Headquarters, Department of the Army.

PROMOTION OF PRIVATES TO PRIVATE FIRST CLASS

Active Army personnel are advanced to the rank of private E-2 when they have completed six months of active federal service, unless it is stopped by the commander. National Guard and Army Reserve personnel on initial active-duty training are advanced to private E-2 when they complete six months of service from the day of entry, unless it is stopped by the commander. To recognize outstanding performance, local commanders may advance to private E-2 a limited numbers of soldiers who have at least four but less than six months' active service.

Under normal conditions, unit commanders may advance soldiers to private first class who qualify with 12 months' time in service and 4 months' time in grade. To recognize outstanding performance, unit commanders may advance soldiers with a minimum of six months in service and two months' time in grade (which may be waived).

PROMOTION TO SPECIALIST OR CORPORAL

Normally, commanders may advance to specialist or corporal those soldiers who meet the following qualifications:

- Twenty-six months in service.
- Six months' time in grade, waiverable to three months.
- Security clearance appropriate for the MOS in which promoted; advancement may be based on granting an interim security clearance.

To recognize outstanding performance, commanders may advance soldiers on an accelerated basis, providing advancements do not cause more than 20 percent of the total number of assigned specialists and corporals to have less than 24 months' time in service, and providing that soldiers meet the following qualifications:

- Eighteen months in service.
- Three months' time in grade.
- Security clearance required for the MOS in which advanced; may be based on an interim clearance.

PROMOTION TO SERGEANT AND STAFF SERGEANT

Field-grade commanders and Department of the Army both have a hand in promotions to SGT and SSG. The normal sequence from recommendation to promotion to SGT and SSG follows.

1. *The soldier meets requirements.* Time-in-service requirement for attaining eligibility for promotion to SGT is 36 months active federal service for the primary zone and 18 months for the secondary zone. The time-in-grade requirement for attaining eligibility for promotion to SGT is eight months as a CPL/SPC, waiverable to four months for those recommended in the secondary zone. Soldiers in the secondary zone may

appear before a promotion board with 16 months time-in-service and four months time-in-grade as of the first day of the board month.

Time-in-service requirement for attaining eligibility for promotion to SSG is 84 months active federal service for the primary zone and 48 months for the secondary zone. The time-in-grade requirement for attaining eligibility for promotion to SSG is 10 months as a SGT, waiverable to five months for those recommended in the secondary zone. Soldiers in the secondary zone may be boarded with 46 months time-in-service and five months time-in-grade as of the first day of the board month.

Once a soldier reaches primary zone eligibility, the commander must either recommend that he or she appear before a promotion board, or, if a soldier is fully eligible but not recommended, complete the DA Form 3355, *Promotion Worksheet,* with counseling documents and forward them to the promotion authority for final decision. From that point until the soldier is recommended for promotion or is no longer eligible, the unit commander must provide copies of the soldier's performance counseling forms (at least quarterly) to the promotion authority.

Soldiers competing for promotion to SGT or SSG must possess a high school diploma, GED equivalency, or an associate or higher degree. Soldiers competing for promotion to SSG must be graduates of the PLDC before being recommended for promotion.

2. *Soldier's chain of command recommends for promotion.* Soldiers may compete for promotion only in their career progression military occupational specialty (CPMOS), as outlined in AR 611-201. Eligible CPLs/SPCs and SGTs compete Armywide by a three-character MOS, and their relative standing is determined by the points attained on an 800-point system. If a soldier is in the primary zone for promotion and is not selected for appearance before the board, he or she must be counseled in writing about why he or she was not selected to appear.

3. *Administrative points computed (600 points available).* See the table on pages 154–155.

4. *Battalion commander convenes promotion board.* Although AR 600-8-19, *Enlisted Promotions,* states that officers may serve as members of the promotion board with an officer as president, in most cases the board is composed of senior NCOs with the battalion command sergeant major sitting as president. If a command sergeant major is not available, a serving sergeant major may sit as president. Rules for conduct of the promotion board are found in AR 600-8-19.

5. *Board recommends soldier for promotion (150 points available).* See the table on pages 154–155. Based on the soldier's personal appearance, self-confidence, bearing, oral expression and conversational skill,

knowledge of world affairs, awareness of military programs, and knowledge of basic soldiering and attitude, the board awards up to 150 promotion points. (See Stackpole Books' *Soldier's Study Guide* by Walter Jackson on preparing for the promotion board.)

6. *Total promotion points computed (800 total points available).* The minimum score for attaining recommended list status for promotion to SGT is 350 points. The minimum score for attaining recommended list status for promotion to SSG is 450. Upon being recommended for promotion, obtain copies of all source documents used for promotion points (if you're not sure, ask). Soldiers should turn one set in with their initial promotion point worksheet and maintain a second set with a copy of their promotion board proceedings and each DA Form 3355 (initial evaluation and reevaluations). Promotion points cannot be backdated. Soldiers must understand that the Enlisted Distribution and Assignment System (EDAS) generates the promotion points' year/month/date to accurately determine promotions by MOS and grade. EDAS uses the points that are on file at HQDA. Following input to the Total Army Personnel Database (TAPDB) via EDAS input, promotion points are effective for promotion eligibility purposes on the first day of the third month after input.

7. *Education requirements met.* Soldiers must be graduates of the Basic NCO Course (BNCOC) to be promoted to SSG. Soldiers competing for promotion to SGT must be graduates of PLDC before being promoted. Conditional promotions may be made for soldiers who lack the education requirements through no fault of their own. Those soldiers who accept conditional promotions and are subsequently denied enrollment, declared no-shows, become academic failures, or otherwise do not meet graduation requirements will have their promotions revoked and be administratively removed from the promotion list.

8. *DA sets monthly promotion points.* Each month the Department of the Army establishes the total number of soldiers to be promoted based on budgetary and strength constraints. The number of promotions are allocated by primary military occupational speciality (PMOS) within these constraints. Department of the Army promotion cutoff scores are announced monthly. (See the section on cutoff scores in this chapter.)

9. *Soldiers' points meet or exceed DA established points.* After three months on the waiting list, soldiers who meet or exceed the announced cutoff score are promoted if otherwise eligible. Each soldier promoted to SGT must have a minimum of 6 months active federal service remaining at the time of promotion. For promotion to SSG, it must be 12 months.

Congratulations!

WHERE THE POINTS COME FROM
(CHAPTER 3, AR 600-8-19)

Performance Evaluation and Military Training Points	Maximum Allowable	How Achieved	Individual Points
Duty Performance	150	Unit Commander	
a. Competence			30
b. Military Bearing			30
c. Leadership			30
d. Training			30
e. Responsibility and Accountability			30
Weapons Qualification	50	Score ranges from 50 to 14, dependent upon number of targets hit	
Physical Readiness Test	50	Score ranges from 50 to 5, dependent upon APFT score	

Administrative Points

Awards:	100	
Soldier's Medal or higher award		35
Bronze Star Medal (BSM), Purple Heart		30
Defense Meritorious Service, Medal Meritorious Service Medal (MSM)		25
Air Medal, Joint Service Commendation Medal, Army Commendation Medal (ARCOM)		20
Joint Service Achievement Medal, Army Achievement Medal (AAM)		15
Good Conduct Medal, Army Reserve Component Achievement Medal		10
Combat Infantry Badge, Combat Field Medical Badge		15
Expert Infantry Badge, Expert Field Medical Badge, Basic U.S. Army Recruiter Badge (additional badges 5 each), Ranger Tab, Special Forces Tab, Drill Sergeant Identification Badge		10
Parachutist Badge, Air Assault Badge, Parachute Rigger Badge, Divers Badge, Explosive Ordnance Disposal Badge, Pathfinder Badge, Aircraft Crewman Badge, Nuclear Reactor Operator Badge, Awards of higher skill badge count as subsequent awards and will receive points (senior parachutist, master diver, additional recruiting badges), Driver and Mechanic Badge (maximum 5 points), Tomb Guard Identification Badge		5
Soldiers receiving incentive pay for parachute duty: Parachutist		20
Senior		25
Master		30
Campaign Star (Battle Star)		5
Southwest Asia Medal (maximum 12 points)		3
Soldier/NCO of the Quarter—Bde Level		10
Soldier/NCO of the Quarter—Installation/Division		15

WHERE THE POINTS COME FROM *continued*
(CHAPTER 3, AR 600-8-19)

Administrative Points (cont.)	Maximum Allowable	How Achieved	Individual Points
Soldier/NCO of the Year—MACOM			25
Distinguished Honor Graduate			15
Distinguished Leadership Award			10
Commandants List			5
Certificate of achievement awarded by commanders/deputy commanders			5
serving in positions authorized the grade of LTC or higher or any general officer, or CSM at the brigade or higher level (maximum 20)			
Military Education	200		
NCOES courses for resident completion of PLDC and BNCOC			40
Ranger School			32
Special Forces Qualification Course			60
Battalion level or higher training certified by DA Form 87,			4
Certificate of Training, signed by an LTC or above (per week)			
Completion of military correspondence, extension,			1
or nonresident subcourses (per 5 hours)			
Other courses of at least one-week duration (40 hours)			4
Civilian Education	100		
For each semester hour earned of business/trade school/college			1.5
Any soldier completing a degree while on active duty			10
CLEP tests (for each semester hour earned)			1.5
Promotion Board	150		
Personal appearance			25
Oral expression			25
Awareness of world affairs			25
Knowledge of military programs			25
Basic soldiering			25
Soldier's attitude			25
Total Possible Points	**800**		

Keys to Success
Soldiers need to read and be familiar with chapter 3 of AR 600-8-19 and the Monthly Cutoff Score and Junior Enlisted Issues Memorandum (which is available at the battalion Personnel Administration Center [PAC], in the personnel service unit's promotion section, and on PERSCOM On-line [Internet]).

Read the unit bulletin board. The unit is required to post the PERSCOM Enlisted Distribution and Assignment System (EDAS) C10 (promotion eligibility roster) report for all soldiers to review. If it is not current, address the issue with the first sergeant. Soldiers must monitor the EDAS C10 continuously. *This is the most important document a soldier has to refer to after undergoing any type of promotion board or point adjustment action.* If a soldier disagrees with the promotion points and/or promotion points date data reflected on the EDAS C10, he or she must bring it to the attention of the unit chain of command and battalion PAC and be prepared to document all promotion-related requests.

Records Check

Elimination of the paper Military Personnel Records Jacket (MPRJ) is coming one day, and soldiers need to start preparing now to be responsible for maintaining those personnel documents that have a direct impact on their career. Ultimately, the soldier, along with the chain of command, is responsible for the timely processing and accuracy of his or her promotion paperwork and his or her own promotion.

OMPF Online

You may now also review your Official Military Personnel File (OMPF) online by logging on through the Army Portal at *www.us.army.mil* or through the PERSCOM Enlisted Records Evaluation Center Web site at *http://etransserv. erec.army.mil/ompfMain.jsp.* Sign in using your AKO user name and password, then click the "log in" button. Once successfully logged in, the initial screen for OMPF Online will appear. You may now view documents in your OMPF Online.

Recommended List

After completion of all promotion actions during the month, a recommended list is published. It lists all soldiers of the organization who have been selected but not yet promoted. Names are listed by grade and zone in ascending MOS and descending promotion point score order.

Soldiers are promoted from the current recommended list by MOS. Promotions are made on the first calendar day of the month in which they are authorized. Promotion orders may be published with future effective dates.

Soldiers are eligible for promotion on the first day of the second month following date of selection; for example, a soldier recommended in January 2003 becomes eligible for promotion on March 1, 2003.

A soldier's name on the secondary zone list for promotion to sergeant is transferred to the primary zone list on the first day of the month in which he or she completes 33 months of active service. The soldier becomes eligible for promotion in the primary zone on the first day of the month in which he or she completes 36 months' active service.

A soldier's name on the secondary zone list for promotion to staff sergeant is transferred to the primary zone on the first day of the month in which he or she completes 81 months of active service. The soldier becomes eligible for promotion in the primary zone on the first day of the month in which he or she completes 84 months of active service.

Cutoff Scores

When a soldier's number of promotion points is known, many wonder why he or she cannot be promoted immediately if the cutoff is low enough. In the first place, soldiers may be selected for promotion three months before they have the required time-in-service.

Second, reports from the field reflecting the number of soldiers on promotion lists, their number of points, and their zones and MOSs arrive at HQDA about the middle of the month following the month in which the soldier appeared before the promotion board.

At this point, MOS and grade vacancies are computed. The total number of promotions for a particular grade (regardless of MOS) is determined by comparing the number of personnel projected to be in that grade against the number allowed in the Army budget for the month in which promotions are to be made. This projection includes losses, those promoted in and out of the grade, and reductions. Available promotions are distributed to MOSs based on the percentage of fill.

Promotions go to those MOSs with the greatest need first. Secondary zone (waiver) promotions are limited, so they go to MOSs with the greatest need after the primary zone (no waiver) promotions are distributed. At this time—which is one to two months after the soldier appeared before the promotion board—the soldier's number of promotion points comes into the process. For example, if vacancies and budget permit the promotion of 100 soldiers from the primary zone of a particular MOS, a promotion cutoff score is established by going down the scores until the 100 limit is reached. That is, if the top 100 sergeants in an MOS have 716 or more points, the cutoff score would be 716. If the top 100 have 796 or more, the cutoff would be 796.

Reevaluation

A soldier on the current recommended list for six months may request a total reevaluation then and each six months thereafter if he or she is still promotable. A soldier reevaluated is not immediately eligible for promotion based on the new score. The soldier continues to be eligible for promotion based on the promotion point score he or she held immediately before reevaluation. Eligibility under the old score continues until the reevaluated score becomes effective. The new score becomes effective two months from the date of reevaluation because of the two-month reporting time.

After the request for reevaluation is approved, the soldier appears before the organization's next regularly scheduled promotion board. The soldier's promotion list status is then based on the number of points he or she attains. If a soldier remains on the list, his or her original selection date is adjusted to the date on which the promotion authority approves the board report. This gives the soldier a chance to improve his or her total score. However, the soldier also runs the risk of lowering his or her standing by making a poor showing before the board.

Loss of recommended list status through reevaluation does not, however, preclude promotion consideration by future boards. Such consideration is not a vested right. Those being considered to regain recommended list status are subject to the provisions of chapter 3, AR 600-8-19, and the recommendations of their commanders.

Administrative Reevaluations

Soldiers believing they have 20 or more points to add to their promotion score may request an administrative reevaluation of their points by submitting DA Form 4187, *Personnel Action*. With the commander's approval, the promotions clerk will recalculate the promotion point worksheet and increase or decrease, as applicable, the duty performance points and erroneous points. The Personnel Service Branch (PSB) will evaluate the new promotion points and those of the recomputed worksheet. If there is a promotion point increase of 20 points or more, the PSB will enter the new score into the appropriate database.

REDUCTIONS IN GRADE

Commanders at the grades indicated may administratively reduce the grade of assigned soldiers:

- Specialist or corporal and below—company, troop, battery, and separate detachment commanders.
- Sergeant and staff sergeant—field-grade commanders of any organization that is authorized a lieutenant colonel or higher-grade commander. For separate detachments, companies, or battalions, reduction authority is the next senior headquarters within the chain of command authorized a lieutenant colonel or higher-grade commander.

Erroneous Enlistment Grades

Soldiers in higher grades than authorized upon enlistment or reenlistment in the Regular Army or Army Reserve will be reduced to the one to which they are entitled. Authorized grades are prescribed in AR 601-210, AR 140-11, or AR 140-158.

Misconduct

For reductions imposed by court-martial, see the *Manual for Courts-Martial*. Sergeants first class and above cannot be reduced under the provision of Article 15, UCMJ.

Inefficiency

Inefficiency is defined as "demonstration of characteristics which show that the person cannot perform the duties and responsibilities of the grade and MOS" (AR 600-8-19, chapter 7). It may include any act or conduct that shows a lack of abilities and qualities required and expected of a person of that grade and experience. Commanders may consider misconduct, including conviction by civil court, as bearing on efficiency.

A soldier may be reduced under the authority of chapter 7, AR 600-8-19, for long-standing unpaid personal debts that he or she has not made a reasonable attempt to pay.

An assigned soldier who has served in the same unit for at least 90 days may be reduced one grade for inefficiency. The commander starting the reduction action documents the soldier's inefficiency. The documents should establish a pattern of inefficiency rather than identify a specific incident.

The commander reducing a soldier informs him or her, in writing, of the action contemplated and the reasons. The soldier must acknowledge receipt of the letter, by endorsement, and may submit any pertinent matters in rebuttal. Sergeants and above may request to appear before a reduction board. If appearance is declined, it must be done in writing and is considered acceptance of the reduction action. A reduction board, when required, must be convened within 30 days after the individual is notified in writing.

Reduction Boards

When required, reduction boards are convened to determine whether an enlisted soldier's grade should be reduced. This convening authority must ensure that the following conditions exist:

- The board consists of officers and enlisted personnel of mature judgment and senior in grade to the person being considered for reduction.
- For inefficiency cases, at least one member must be thoroughly familiar with the soldier's specialty.
- The board must consist of at least three voting members and will be comprised of both officer and enlisted voting members.
- The board has an officer or senior enlisted member (or both) of the same sex as the soldier being considered for reduction.
- The composition of the board represents the ethnic population of soldiers under its jurisdiction.
- No soldier with direct knowledge of the case is appointed to the board.

A soldier who is to appear before the board will be given at least 15 working days' written notice before the date of the hearing so that the soldier or his or her counsel has time to prepare the case.

The convening authority may approve or disapprove any portion of the recommendation of the board, but his action cannot increase the severity of the board's recommendation. If the convening authority approves a recommended reduction, he or she may direct it. When the board recommends a reduction and the convening authority approves it, the soldier will be reduced without regard to any action taken to appeal the reduction.

The soldier has the right to:

- Decline, in writing, to appear before the board.
- Have a military counsel of his or her own choosing, if reasonably available, or may employ a civilian counsel at own expense, or both.
- Appear in person, with or without counsel, at all open proceedings of the board.
- If the soldier appears before the board without counsel, have the president counsel him or her on the action being contemplated, the effect of such action on his or her future in the Army, and the right to request counsel.
- Challenge (dismiss) any member of the board for cause.
- Request any reasonably available witness whose testimony the soldier believes to be pertinent to the case. When requested, the soldier must tell the nature of the information the witness will provide.
- Submit to the board written affidavits and depositions of witnesses who are unable to appear before the board.
- Employ the provisions of Article 31, UCMJ (prohibition against compulsory self-incrimination), or submit to an examination by the board.
- Have his or her counsel question any witness appearing before the board. Failure of the soldier to exercise his or her rights is not a bar to the board proceedings or its findings and recommendations.

Appeals

Appeals from reduction for misconduct are governed by Article 15, UCMJ; paragraph 135; MCM, and AR 27-10.

Appeals based on reduction for failure to complete training will not be accepted.

Appeals from staff sergeants and below based on reduction for inefficiency or conviction by civil court are allowed. They must be submitted in writing within 30 workdays from the date of reduction. The officer having general court-martial jurisdiction, or the next higher authority, may approve, disapprove, or change the reduction if he or she determines that the reduction was without sufficient basis, should be changed, or was proper. His or her action is final.

ADDITIONAL INFORMATION

The book *Career Progression Guide for Soldiers,* 2nd Edition, by Audie Lewis (Stackpole, 2003), offers greater detail on the promotion process and gives loads of advice on practical means to acquire the necessary promotion points.

To prepare for appearances before promotion boards, CSM (Ret.) Walter Jackson's *Soldier Study Guide,* 4th Edition (Stackpole, 2000), is recommended.

14

Pay and Entitlements

The purpose of this chapter is to explain some basic facts about your Army pay and benefits and provide you a quick reference for questions that may come up in your day-to-day duties.

The soldier who enlists in the Army for the money is in the wrong business. Relatively substantial paychecks do not start coming until a soldier reaches the senior noncommissioned ranks with 20 to 26 years of service.

If pay and benefits were the only inducement to a military career, then we would have no Army. Soldiers reenlist because they like the Army, and when the Army no longer offers young people the challenges and adventure of military life, they will not stay.

PAY AND ALLOWANCES

Military pay consists of basic pay, special and incentive pay, and allowances. Pay is computed on the basis of a 30-day month, and soldiers may elect to be paid once a month (at the end of the month) or twice a month (on the 15th and the 30th of each month).

To change your pay option, contact your local finance and accounting office to execute DA Form 3685, *JUMPS-Army Pay Elections.* Which option you select depends upon how you budget your money. Some soldiers find that they can get along quite well with one lump-sum payment at the end of the month; others prefer to get paid twice a month. Read the pay elections form carefully before filling it out. Submit your options to the finance officer as early in the month as possible to give the finance center enough time to process your request so that your new option will be reflected during the next pay period.

Report discrepancies in your pay immediately. To do so, you must know what you are authorized.

Leave and Earnings Statement (LES)

The LES is a computerized monthly statement of account for each soldier paid. The LES shows all entitlements earned, collections affected, and payments made during the period covered by the statement. In addition, this statement

161

DEFENSE FINANCE AND ACCOUNTING SERVICE MILITARY LEAVE AND EARNINGS STATEMENT

ID	NAME (LAST, FIRST, MI) 1	SOC. SEC. NO. 2	GRADE 3	PAY DATE 4	YRS SVC 5	ETS 6	BRANCH 7	ADSN/DSSN 8	PERIOD COVERED 9

ENTITLEMENTS

TYPE	AMOUNT
10	

DEDUCTIONS

TYPE	AMOUNT
11	

ALLOTMENTS

TYPE	AMOUNT
12	

SUMMARY

+ AMT FWD	13
+ TOT ENT	14
- TOT DED	15
- TOT ALMT	16
= NET AMT	17
- CR FWD	18
= EOM PAY	19

TOTAL 20

| | | | | | | | DIEMS 23 | RET PLAN 24 |

LEAVE

| BF BAL 25 | ERND 26 | USED 27 | CR BAL 28 | ETS BAL 29 | LV LOST 30 | LV PAID 31 | USE/LOSE 32 |

FED TAXES

| WAGE PERIOD 33 | WAGE YTD 34 | M/S 35 | EX 36 | ADD'L TAX 37 | TAX YTD 38 |

FICA TAXES

| WAGE PERIOD 39 | SOC WAGE YTD 40 | SOC TAX YTD 41 | MED WAGE YTD 42 | MED TAX YTD 43 |

STATE TAXES

| ST 44 | WAGE PERIOD 45 | WAGE YTD 46 | M/S 47 | EX 48 | TAX YTD 49 |

PAY DATA

| BAQ TYPE 50 | BAQ DEPN 51 | VHA ZIP 52 | RENT AMT 53 | SHARE 54 | STAT 55 | JFTR 56 | DEPNS 57 | 2D JFTR 58 | BAS TYPE 59 | CHARITY YTD 60 | TPC 61 | PACIDN 62 |

Thrift Savings Plan (TSP)

| BASE PAY RATE 63 | BASE PAY CURRENT 64 | SPEC PAY RATE 65 | SPEC PAY CURRENT 66 | INC PAY RATE 67 | INC PAY CURRENT 68 | BONUS PAY RATE 69 | BONUS PAY CURRENT 70 |
| CURRENTLY NOT USED 71 | TSP YTD DEDUCTIONS 72 | DEFERRED 73 | EXEMPT 74 | CURRENTLY NOT USED 75 |

REMARKS
76

YTD ENTITLE 77   YTD DEDUCT 78

www.dfas.mil

DFAS Form 702, Jan 02

provides the soldier a complete record of transactions that affect his or her leave account for the period of the statement. It also serves as the official leave record.

Changes to the LES

In 2002, the LES changed to reflect a soldier's involvement in the Thrift Savings Plan (TSP). The new blocks are located directly above the "Remarks" area of the LES. The four entitlement categories are Base Pay (blocks 63 and 64 on sample), Special Pay (blocks 65 and 66), Incentive Pay (blocks 67 and 68), and Bonus Pay (blocks 69 and 70). There are two new blocks for each of four entitlement categories. The blocks containing the word "Rate" reflect the percentage rate of the monthly entitlement that the servicemember elects to contribute to TSP. The blocks that contain the word "Current" reflect the dollar amount designated by the servicemember. The "TSP YTD [year-to-date] Deductions" block (72) is simply what a soldier has contributed to date. The "Deferred" block (73) will contain the amount of TSP YTD contributions that are tax deferred. There is a yearly maximum for tax-deferred contributions, and once a soldier reaches the yearly maximum, the system generates a stop transaction and creates a remark with a stop date. The "Exempt" block (74) contains the amount of YTD tax-exempt TSP contributions. Deductions for TSP contributions and loan payments appear in the "Deductions" block (11) of the LES. If a soldier receives a TSP loan payment and any TSP contribution refund, the "Entitlements" block (10) of the LES will denote the amount.

Additionally, two new blocks advise the soldier on his or her retirement status. These blocks are located on the far right side of the document, under the "EOM Pay" block. The "DIEMS" block (date initially entered military service) (23) reflects the date used to establish the soldier's retirement plan. The "RET Plan" block (24) indicates the retirement plan a soldier is under, based on the DIEMS date shown in the preceding block.

Study your LES very carefully. Should you discover any item you believe to be in error or should there be an entry recorded thereon that you do not understand, consult with your local finance office immediately. If, during a routine audit of your pay record, it should be discovered that you have been overpaid at some time in the past, the government will collect what is due.

Online Finance

The Employee/Member Self Service (E/MSS) system at *www.emss.dfas.mil/ emss.htm* allows soldiers to access their pay record and update certain payroll information directly, without having to fill out any paper forms. The E/MSS allows you access to your financial records at either your home or office through the Internet using a personal computer or through an Interactive Voice Response Telephone System (IVRS) using a Touch-Tone telephone. The system allows you to review or make changes to your federal and state tax information, financial allotments, home or correspondence address, savings bonds, and direct deposit or electronic funds transfer (EFT) information without the problems involved with paperwork. When you make a change, the system saves the transaction and sends it to the payroll system the next day for update. This system also allows you to view and print your Leave and Earnings Statement online.

Net Pay Advice (NPA)
An NPA form will be issued at midmonth. All active Army soldiers will receive the NPA, even if they have not elected the midmonth pay option. The NPA will provide midmonth pay data for soldiers who have elected the midmonth pay option. It will provide administrative remarks for all soldiers, regardless of the pay option they have selected.

Collections of Erroneous Payments
Overpayments for two months in a row are collected from the next month's pay. If these payments are two or more months old, collection is delayed to allow time for unit commanders to arrange for prorated collection, if necessary, before computer collection action is initiated.

Normally, the amount deducted for any period will not exceed an amount equal to two-thirds of a soldier's pay. Monthly installments may be increased or decreased to reflect changes in pay.

Soldiers may appeal the validity of a debt, the amount, or the rate of payment. If an enlisted soldier's appeal is denied, the chief of personnel operations, Department of the Army, may consider his or her case for remission or cancellation of the indebtedness.

Advance Payments
An advance of pay is authorized upon permanent change of station to provide a soldier funds for expenses, such as transportation, temporary storage of household goods, packing and shipping costs, and securing new living quarters. Advance payments are limited to no more than one month's advance pay of basic pay less deductions or, if warranted, not more than three months' basic pay less deductions at the old station, en route, or within 60 days after reporting to a new station.

Requests for advance pay from enlisted personnel in pay grades E-1 through E-4 must be approved by their commander, and this approval must be indicated in the *Pay Inquiry Form* (DA Form 2142), together with a statement that the circumstances in the individual's case warrant advancing the amount requested and that advancing a lesser amount would result in hardship to the soldier or his or her family.

The commander's approval for an advance of pay is not required for enlisted personnel in pay grades E-5 through E-9, but advances are not made to senior-grade personnel when it is apparent that the tour of duty (obligated service) will terminate before completion of the scheduled repayment of the advance.

Lump-Sum Payments
A lump-sum payment is made to pay bonuses and accrued leave paid on immediate reenlistments. These payments are made by cash or check through the use of a local payment. Lump-sum payments are always made in even dollar amounts. The maximum amount that may be paid is the gross amount of the enlistment minus the estimate of federal and, when applicable, state taxes. When the computation results in a new amount due in dollars and cents, the amount to be paid may either be the lesser full dollar amount or be rounded to the next higher dollar.

Basic Pay
Basic pay is established by law and is that pay a soldier receives, based on grade and length of service, exclusive of any special or incentive pay or allowances.

Reserve Drill Pay
Reserve drill pay, like basic pay, is established by law. And like basic pay, reserve drill pay is pay a soldier receives based on grade and length of service. Unlike monthly basic pay, however, reserve drill pay is computed and paid for the number of days' service rendered. It is comparable to basic pay.

Basic Allowance for Subsistence (BAS)
Upon entitlement to BAS (separate rations), a soldier's unit commander forwards to the finance officer DA Form 4187, *Personnel Action Request* (see chapter 8, DA Pamphlet 600-8), in duplicate, showing the effective date and hour of entitlement to BAS. When a soldier ceases to be entitled to BAS, the unit commander forwards to the finance officer a DA Form 4187 showing date and hour of termination.

BAS rates for enlisted personnel are as follows:

When on leave or authorized to mess separately	$241.60/month
When rations in-kind are not available	$262.50/month
When assigned to duty under emergency conditions where no messing facilities of the United States are available	$11.21/day

Entitlement to BAS terminates automatically upon permanent change of station (PCS). Care should be taken during in-processing at a new duty station that entitlement is revalidated for personnel authorized separate rations.

Years of Service

Grade	<2	2	3	4	6	8	10	12	14	16	18	20	22	24	26
Commissioned officers															
O-10	0.00	0.00	0.00	0.00	0.00	0.00	0.00	0.00	0.00	0.00	0.00	12,077.70	12,137.10	12,389.40	12,829.20
O-9	0.00	0.00	0.00	0.00	0.00	0.00	0.00	0.00	0.00	0.00	0.00	10,563.60	10,715.70	10,935.60	11,319.60
O-8	7,474.50	7,719.30	7,881.60	7,927.20	8,129.40	8,468.70	8,547.30	8,868.90	8,961.30	9,238.20	9,639.00	10,008.90	10,255.80	10,255.80	10,255.80
O-7	6,210.90	6,499.20	6,633.00	6,739.20	6,930.90	7,120.80	7,340.40	7,559.40	7,779.00	8,468.70	9,051.30	9,051.30	9,051.30	9,051.30	9,051.30
O-6	4,603.20	5,057.10	5,388.90	5,388.90	5,409.60	5,641.20	5,672.10	5,672.00	5,994.60	6,564.30	6,898.80	7,233.30	7,423.50	7,616.10	7,989.90
O-5	3,837.60	4,323.00	4,622.40	4,678.50	4,864.80	4,977.00	5,222.70	5,403.00	5,635.50	5,991.90	6,161.70	6,329.10	6,519.60	6,519.60	6,519.60
O-4	3,311.10	3,832.80	4,088.70	4,145.70	4,383.00	4,637.70	4,954.50	5,201.40	5,372.70	5,471.10	5,528.40	5,528.40	5,528.40	5,528.40	5,528.40
O-3	2,911.20	3,300.30	3,562.20	3,883.50	4,069.50	4,273.50	4,405.80	4,623.30	4,736.10	4,736.10	4,736.10	4,736.10	4,736.10	4,736.10	4,736.10
O-2	2,515.20	2,864.70	3,299.40	3,410.70	3,481.20	3,481.20	3,481.20	3,481.20	3,481.20	3,481.20	3,481.20	3,481.20	3,481.20	3,481.20	3,481.20
O-1	2,183.70	2,272.50	2,746.80	2,746.80	2,746.80	2,746.80	2,746.80	2,746.80	2,746.80	2,746.80	2,746.80	2,746.80	2,746.80	2,746.80	2,746.80
Officers with more than 4 years' active duty as enlisted or warrant officer															
O-3E	0.00	0.00	0.00	3,883.50	4,069.50	4,273.50	4,405.80	4,623.30	4,806.30	4,911.00	5,054.40	5,054.40	5,054.40	5,054.40	5,054.40
O-2E	0.00	0.00	0.00	3,410.70	3,481.20	3,591.90	3,778.80	3,923.40	4,031.10	4,031.10	4,031.10	4,031.10	4,031.10	4,031.10	4,031.10
O-1E	0.00	0.00	0.00	2,746.80	2,933.70	3,042.00	3,152.70	3,261.60	3,410.70	3,410.70	3,410.70	3,410.70	3,410.70	3,410.70	3,410.70
Warrant officers															
W-5	0.00	0.00	0.00	0.00	0.00	0.00	0.00	0.00	0.00	0.00	0.00	5,169.30	5,346.60	5,524.50	5,703.30
W-4	3,008.10	3,236.10	3,329.10	3,420.60	3,578.10	3,733.50	3,891.00	4,044.60	4,203.60	4,356.00	4,512.00	4,664.40	4,822.50	4,978.20	5,137.50
W-3	2,747.10	2,862.00	2,979.30	3,017.70	3,141.00	3,281.70	3,467.40	3,580.50	3,771.90	3,915.60	4,058.40	4,201.50	4,266.30	4,407.00	4,548.00
W-2	2,416.50	2,554.50	2,675.10	2,763.00	2,838.30	2,993.10	3,148.50	3,264.00	3,376.50	3,453.90	3,579.90	3,705.90	3,831.00	3,957.30	3,957.30
W-1	2,133.90	2,308.50	2,425.50	2,501.10	2,662.50	2,782.20	2,888.40	3,006.90	3,085.20	3,203.40	3,320.70	3,409.50	3,409.50	3,409.50	3,409.50
Enlisted members															
E-9	0.00	0.00	0.00	0.00	0.00	0.00	3,564.30	3,645.00	3,747.00	3867.00	3,987.30	4,180.80	4,344.30	4,506.50	4,757.40
E-8	0.00	0.00	0.00	0.00	0.00	2,975.40	3,061.20	3,141.30	3,237.60	3,342.00	3,530.10	3,625.50	3,787.50	3,877.50	4,099.20
E-7	2,068.50	2,257.80	2,343.90	2,428.20	2,516.40	2,667.90	2,753.40	2,838.30	2,990.40	3,066.30	3,138.60	3,182.70	3,331.50	3,427.80	3,671.40
E-6	1,770.60	1,947.60	2,033.70	2,117.10	2,204.10	2,400.90	2,477.40	2,562.30	2,636.70	2,663.10	2,709.60	2,709.60	2,709.60	2,709.60	2,709.60
E-5	1,625.40	1,733.70	1,817.40	1,903.50	2,037.00	2,151.90	2,236.80	2,283.30	2,283.30	2,283.30	2,283.30	2,283.30	2,283.30	2,283.30	2,283.30
E-4	1,502.70	1,579.80	1,665.30	1,749.30	1,824.00	1,824.00	1,824.00	1,824.00	1,824.00	1,824.00	1,824.00	1,824.00	1,824.00	1,824.00	1,824.00
E-3	1,356.90	1,442.10	1,528.80	1,528.80	1,528.80	1,528.80	1,528.80	1,528.80	1,528.80	1,528.80	1,528.80	1,528.80	1,528.80	1,528.80	1,528.80
E-2	1,290.00	1,290.00	1,290.00	1,290.00	1,290.00	1,290.00	1,290.00	1,290.00	1,290.00	1,290.00	1,290.00	1,290.00	1,290.00	1,290.00	1,290.00
E-1	1,150.80	1,150.80	1,150.80	1,150.80	1,150.80	1,150.80	1,150.80	1,150.80	1,150.80	1,150.80	1,150.80	1,150.80	1,150.80	1,150.80	1,150.80

E-1<four months: 1,064.70

RESERVE DRILL PAY (Four Drills) (Effective 1 January 2003)

Years of Service

Grade	<2	2	3	4	6	8	10	12	14	16	18	20	22	24	26
Commissioned officers															
O-10	0.00	0.00	0.00	0.00	0.00	0.00	0.00	0.00	0.00	0.00	0.00	1,610.36	1,618.28	1,651.92	1,710.56
O-9	0.00	0.00	0.00	0.00	0.00	0.00	0.00	0.00	0.00	0.00	0.00	1,408.48	1,428.76	1,458.08	1,509.28
O-8	996.60	1,029.24	1,050.88	1,056.96	1,083.92	1,129.16	1,139.64	1,182.52	1,194.84	1,231.76	1,285.20	1,334.52	1,367.44	1,367.44	1,367.44
O-7	828.12	866.56	884.40	898.56	924.12	949.44	978.72	1,007.92	1,037.20	1,129.16	1,206.84	1,206.84	1,206.84	1,206.84	1,212.92
O-6	613.76	674.28	718.52	718.52	721.28	752.16	756.28	756.28	799.28	875.24	919.84	964.44	989.80	1,015.48	1,065.32
O-5	511.68	576.40	616.32	623.80	648.64	663.60	696.36	720.40	751.40	798.92	843.88	869.28	869.28	869.28	869.28
O-4	441.48	511.04	545.16	552.76	584.40	618.36	660.60	693.52	716.36	729.48	737.12	737.12	737.12	737.12	737.12
O-3	388.16	440.04	474.96	517.80	542.60	569.80	587.44	616.44	631.48	631.48	631.48	631.48	631.48	631.48	631.48
O-2	335.36	381.96	439.92	454.76	464.16	464.16	464.16	464.16	464.16	464.16	464.16	464.16	464.16	464.16	464.16
O-1	291.16	303.00	366.24	366.24	366.24	366.24	366.24	366.24	366.24	366.24	366.24	366.24	366.24	366.24	366.24
Commissioned officers with more than 4 years' active duty as enlisted or warrant officer															
O-3E	0.00	0.00	0.00	0.00	542.60	569.80	587.44	616.44	640.84	654.80	673.92	673.92	673.92	673.92	673.92
O-2E	0.00	0.00	0.00	454.76	464.16	478.92	503.84	523.12	537.48	537.48	537.48	537.48	537.48	537.48	537.48
O-1E	0.00	0.00	0.00	366.24	391.16	405.60	420.36	434.88	454.76	454.76	454.76	454.76	454.76	454.76	454.76
Warrant officers															
W-5	0.00	0.00	0.00	0.00	0.00	0.00	0.00	0.00	0.00	0.00	0.00	689.24	712.88	736.60	760.44
W-4	401.08	431.38	443.88	456.08	477.08	497.80	518.80	539.28	560.48	580.80	601.60	621.92	643.00	663.76	685.00
W-3	366.28	381.60	397.24	402.36	418.80	437.56	462.32	477.40	502.92	522.08	541.12	560.20	568.84	587.60	606.40
W-2	322.20	340.60	356.68	368.40	378.44	399.08	419.80	435.20	450.20	460.52	477.32	494.12	510.80	527.64	527.64
W-1	284.52	307.80	323.40	333.48	355.00	370.96	385.12	400.92	411.36	427.12	442.76	454.60	454.60	454.60	454.60
Enlisted members															
E-9	0.00	0.00	0.00	0.00	0.00	0.00	475.24	486.00	499.60	515.60	531.64	557.44	579.24	600.84	634.32
E-8	0.00	0.00	0.00	0.00	0.00	396.72	408.16	418.84	431.68	445.60	470.68	483.40	505.00	517.00	546.56
E-7	275.80	301.04	312.52	323.76	335.52	355.72	367.12	378.44	398.72	408.84	418.48	424.36	444.20	457.04	489.52
E-6	236.08	259.68	271.16	282.28	293.88	320.12	330.32	341.64	351.56	355.08	361.28	361.28	361.28	361.28	361.28
E-5	216.72	231.16	242.32	253.80	271.60	286.92	298.24	304.44	304.44	304.44	304.44	304.44	304.44	304.44	304.44
E-4	200.36	210.64	222.04	233.24	243.20	243.20	243.20	243.20	243.20	243.20	243.20	243.20	243.20	243.20	243.20
E-3	180.92	192.28	203.84	203.84	203.84	203.84	203.84	203.84	203.84	203.84	203.84	203.84	203.84	203.84	203.84
E-2	172.00	172.00	172.00	172.00	172.00	172.00	172.00	172.00	172.00	172.00	172.00	172.00	172.00	172.00	172.00
E-1>4	153.44	153.44	153.44	153.44	153.44	153.44	153.44	153.44	153.44	153.44	153.44	153.44	153.44	153.44	153.44
E-1<4 months—141.96															

Basic Allowance for Housing (BAH)

The basic allowance for housing combines the two older allowances (BAQ and VHA) into one single payment based on rank, with or without dependents. The new rates are based on housing costs for civilians with comparable income levels in the same area. Under this system, the annual growth in the housing allowance will be indexed in the national average monthly housing cost.

BAH terminates for married personnel when they occupy government quarters or when dependency terminates. Dependency is verified by the local finance and accounting officer. The documentary evidence that must be submitted to substantiate dependence includes the original or certified copy of a marriage certificate, the individual's signed statement (when called to active duty or active duty for training for ninety days or less), birth certificate, or a public church record of marriage issued over the signature of the custodian of the church or public records, and, if applicable, a divorce decree. Entitlements must be recertified upon permanent change of station.

Family Separation Allowance (FSA)

Two separation allowances are payable to eligible personnel to help meet additional family expenses during periods of separation:

- FSA I is paid to a soldier who has dependents and is serving in an overseas location where dependents are not permitted and where government bachelor quarters are not available to help cover living expenses. The amount of this allowance is the same as the BAH that a soldier without dependents would receive.
- FSA II is paid to soldiers with dependents and in any grade who are involuntarily separated from their families because of PCS to a station where dependents are not authorized or because of temporary duty for a continuous period of more than 30 days away from their permanent duty station. It is in the amount of $100 per month.

Station Allowances

A list of areas where station allowances are authorized is in chapter 4, part 3, *DOD Pay Manual,* and chapter 4, part G, volume 1, *Joint Travel Regulations.* These allowances are paid to offset the high cost of living in certain geographical areas (overseas and in the United States). They consist of housing (HOUS) and cost of living allowances (COLA). A temporary lodging allowance (TLA) and interim housing allowance (IHA) may also be paid in certain cases.

Clothing Maintenance Allowance

Clothing maintenance allowance is paid at two different rates:

- Basic, which covers replacement of unique military items that would normally require replacement during the first three years of service.

These exhausted soldiers qualify for additional pay while in a combat zone.

- Standard, which covers the replacement of unique military items after the first three years of service.

Female personnel are also authorized an initial cash allowance established by AR 700-84 for the purchase of undergarments, dress shoes, and stockings.

A soldier receives the clothing maintenance allowance annually, on the last day of the month in which the soldier's anniversary date of enlistment falls.

Civilian Clothing Allowance

When duty assignments require soldiers to wear civilian clothing, they receive lump-sum payments under the following circumstances:

- When both winter and summer civilian clothing ensembles are required.
- When either winter or summer ensembles are required.
- When in a temporary duty (TDY) status from 16 to 30 days.
- When in a TDY status over 30 days.

Enlistment Bonus

The enlistment bonus is an enlistment incentive offered to those enlisting in the Regular Army for duty in a specific MOS. The objective of the bonus is to increase the number of enlistments in MOSs that are critical and have inadequate first-term manning levels. Section A, chapter 9, part 1, of the *DOD Pay Manual* gives basic conditions of entitlement, amount of the bonus, time of payment, and reduction and termination of the award.

Experimental Stress Pay

Experimental stress duty pay is authorized for all Army personnel who, on or after July 1, 1965, participate in thermal stress experiments or experimental pressure chamber duty.

Foreign Duty Pay

All enlisted personnel assigned to an area outside the contiguous 48 states and the District of Columbia where an "accompanied by dependents" tour of duty is not authorized have entitlement to foreign duty or "overseas pay." Chapter 6, part 1, *DOD Pay Manual,* lists the places where foreign duty pay is authorized.

Hardship Duty Pay (HDP)

Hardship duty pay is payable to members entitled to basic pay, at a monthly rate not to exceed $300, while such members are performing specified hardship duty. HDP will be paid to members (a) for performing specific missions, or (b) when assigned to designated locations. Except for certain restrictions, HDP is payable in addition to all other pay and allowances. Hardship duty pay for mission assignment (HDP-M) is payable to members, both officer and enlisted, for performing designated hardship mission. HDP-M is payable at the full monthly rate, without prorating or reduction, for each month during any part of which the member performs a specified mission. Hardship duty pay for location assignment (HDP-L) is payable only to enlisted members when they are assigned to duty in designated locations.

Hostile Fire Pay

Hostile fire pay is paid to soldiers permanently assigned to units performing duty in designated hostile fire areas or to soldiers assigned to temporary duty in such areas. Hostile fire pay is authorized on a monthly basis or one-time basis, depending upon the soldier's period of exposure to enemy fire. While drawing hostile fire pay, soldiers are exempt from federal and state taxes.

Diving Pay

To qualify for special pay for diving duty, a soldier must be a rated diver in accordance with AR 611-75 and be assigned to a table of organization and equipment (TOE) or a table of distribution and allowances (TDA) position of MOS 00B, or to a position that has been designated diving duty by the assistant chief of staff for force development, Department of the Army.

Demolition Pay

A soldier is entitled to receive incentive pay for demolition duty for any month or portion of a month in which he or she was assigned and performed duty in a primary duty assignment.

Flight Pay
Flight pay is authorized for enlisted crew members.

Parachute Pay
Soldiers who have received a designation as a parachutist or parachute rigger or are undergoing training for such designations, and who are required to engage in parachute jumping from an aircraft in aerial flight and actually perform the specified minimum jumps (see Table 2-3-3, *DOD Entitlements Manual*) are authorized parachute duty pay. An additional amount is authorized for parachutists who are assigned to positions requiring high-altitude, low-opening (HALO) jump status.

Special Duty Assignment Pay
Special duty pay is authorized on a graduated scale for enlisted members in designated specialties who are required to perform extremely demanding duties or duties demanding an unusual degree of responsibility. Qualifying jobs include career counselor, recruiter, and drill sergeant.

Selective Reenlistment Bonus (SRB)
The SRB is a retention incentive paid to soldiers in certain selected MOSs who reenlist or voluntarily extend their enlistment for additional obligated service. The objective of the SRB is to increase the number of reenlistments or extensions in critical MOSs that do not have adequate retention levels to man the career force.

The SRB is established in three zones: Zone A consists of those reenlistments falling between 21 months and six years of active service; zones B and C consist of those reenlistments or extensions of enlistments falling between 6 and 14 years of service.

Payments are based on multiples, not to exceed six, of a soldier's monthly basic pay at the time of discharge or release from active duty or the day before the beginning of extension, multiplied by years of additional obligated service.

The SRB is paid by installments. Up to 50 percent of the total bonus may be paid as the first installment, with the remaining portion paid in equal annual amounts over the remainder of the enlistment period.

A list of the MOSs designated for award of SRB and enlistment bonuses is in the DA Circular 611 series, *Announcement of Proficiency Pay/Selective Reenlistment Bonus/Enlistment Bonus/Comparable MOS for Bonus Recipients*. Periodic program changes are announced by Headquarters, Department of the Army.

Temporary Lodging Allowance (TLA)
TLA is the allowance received when arriving at an overseas base that offsets some of the expense of temporary housing and meals. The amount of the TLA depends on variables that include family size, the cost and cooking/dining facilities of quarters, and other allowances the family is receiving.

Temporary Lodging Expense (TLE)
TLE is the allowance received when arriving at a CONUS base that offsets some of the expense of temporary housing and meals. The TLE is up to $110 per day and can last up to 10 days. It applies to stateside base arrivals from both CONUS and OCONUS bases.

THRIFT SAVINGS PLAN (TSP)
The purpose of the TSP is to provide retirement income. It offers soldiers the same type of savings and tax benefits that many private corporations offer their employees under so-called 401(k) plans. Under the plan, soldiers save a portion of their pay in a special retirement account administered by the Federal Retirement Thrift Investment Board. The total amount contributed generally cannot exceed $10,500 for a year, including all or a percentage of any special, incentive, or bonus pay you receive. However, contributions from pay earned in a combat zone do not count against the ceiling.

Participation in the TSP is neither optional nor automatic. You must sign up through your finance office to participate. Soldiers have two "open seasons" per year in which to enroll. (Open seasons are currently May 15 through July 31 and November 15 through January 31.) You contribute to the TSP from your own pay on a pretax basis, and the amount you contribute and the earnings attributable to your contributions belong to you. They are yours to keep even if you do not serve the 20 years ordinarily necessary to receive military retired pay.

While you are a member of the uniformed services, any tax-deferred money withdrawn before the age of $59^{1}/_{2}$ as a result of financial hardship is subject to the IRS 10 percent early withdrawal penalty, as well as regular income tax. With respect to postseparation withdrawals, if you separate from the service during or after the year in which you turn age 55, your withdrawals are not subject to the early withdrawal penalty. If you separate before the year you reach age 55, you can transfer your TSP account to an IRA or other eligible retirement plan (e.g., 401(k) plan, your civilian TSP account) or begin receiving annuity payments without penalty.

ALLOTMENTS
An allotment is a specified amount of money withheld from military pay, normally upon the soldier's authorization, for a specific purpose. Payment is made by government check and mailed to the payee.

Allotments are made by filling out DD Form 2558, *Authorization to Start, Stop, or Change an Allotment for Active Duty or Retired Personnel.* These forms are prepared by the individual's military personnel office, unit personnel office, or finance office, and by Army Emergency Relief and the American Red Cross. Preparation of allotment documents in the finance office, rather than in the personnel office, is intended to eliminate delays of one or more days. When there is a delay near the end of the processing month, the effective date of an allotment may be delayed a full month. Commanders may have DD Form 2558 prepared in the unit personnel office, if it will conserve time and assure that there will be no delays in transmission to the finance office.

Repayment of Army Emergency Relief (AER) Loans. These allotments are authorized in multiples. AER allotments are established for a definite term of not less than three months (although this provision may be waived in certain cases).

Combined Federal Campaign (CFC) Contributions. This allotment is authorized to be in effect one at a time only. CFC allotments are made for a period of 12 months, beginning in January and ending in December. Military personnel who execute the *Payroll Withholding Authorization for Voluntary Charitable Contributions* (a Civil Service form) may do so in lieu of DA Form 1341.

Payment to a Dependent (SPT-V). This kind of allotment is authorized in multiples. This voluntary allotment is paid to a soldier's dependent without regard to whether the soldier is already receiving BAH. In addition, involuntary SPT-V allotments can be administratively established. Normally, the amount of these allotments is not permitted to exceed 80 percent of a soldier's pay. Not more than one SPT-V allotment may be made to the same person.

Payment to a Financial Institution for Credit to a Member's Account (FININ). Only two of these allotments are authorized to be in effect at any one time. FININ allotments are for payment to a financial organization for credit to the allotter's savings, checking, or trust accounts. The FININ allotment may be established for an indefinite term and for any amount the soldier designates, provided he or she has sufficient pay to satisfy the deduction of the allotment.

Payment for Indebtedness to the United States (FED). FED allotments are for the purpose of payment of delinquent federal, state, and local taxes and/or indebtedness to the United States. A separate allotment is required for each debt or overpayment to be repaid.

Payment of Home Loans (HOME). Only one HOME allotment is authorized to be in effect at any one time. This allotment is authorized for repayment of loans for the purchase of a house, mobile home, or house trailer. A HOME allotment is established for an indefinite term and for any amount designated provided the soldier's pay credit is sufficient to satisfy the deduction of the allotment.

Payment of Commercial Life Insurance Premiums (INS). These allotments are authorized in multiples. INS allotments must be made payable to a commercial life insurance firm. INS allotments are not authorized for payment of insurance on the life of a soldier's spouse or children except under a family group contract or for health, accident, or hospitalization insurance. INS allotments are established for an indefinite period and in the amount of the monthly premium, as indicated by the number on DA Form 1341.

Repayment of American Red Cross Loans (REDCR). REDCR allotments are authorized in multiples.

Servicemember's Group Life Insurance (SGLI). Maximum coverage is $200,000, with an automatic deduction of $16 per month for premiums, unless the soldier declines coverage or requests a reduced amount of coverage.

Educational Savings Allotment (EDSAV). This allotment is authorized to allow soldiers entering service after December 13, 1976, (except those who enlisted under the Delayed Entry Program before January 1, 1977) to participate in the Veterans Educational Assistance Program (VEAP). Only one such allotment is authorized. The EDSAV allotment is established with no discontinuance date. The soldier may stop it at any time after one year of participation.

Class X Allotments. A Class X allotment is paid locally and is authorized in emergency circumstances when other classes of allotments are impracticable. This instance applies overseas only. Class X allotments may be ordered by a commander as a standby allotment when adequate provision for the financial support of a soldier's dependents has not been made.

PCS WEIGHT ALLOWANCE (POUNDS)

Pay Grade	With Dependents	Without Dependents
E-9	14,500	12,000
E-8	13,500	11,000
E-7	12,500	10,500
E-6	11,000	8,000
E-5	9,000	7,000
E-4 (over 2 years' service)	8,000	7,000
E-4 (2 years' service or less)	7,000	3,500
E-3	5,000	2,000
E-2, E-1	5,000	1,500

Transportation of Household Goods

Transportation of household goods at government expense is authorized for soldiers in accordance with the table on the previous page. For information on authorized weight limitations for other grades, see *Joint Federal Travel Regulations* (JFTR).

BENEFITS AND ENTITLEMENTS
Government Quarters

Bachelor accommodations for enlisted personnel range from the fairly austere communal living conditions offered junior enlisted personnel in troop units to the small but private and well-appointed quarters offered senior NCOs in bachelor enlisted quarters (BEQ). During the course of an Army career, you will see them all if you do not marry at a young age.

Modern troop billets are dormitory-style facilities with central air conditioning and heating; two-, three-, or four-person rooms; recreational facilities; and convenience facilities. Less than a generation ago, the bulk of the Army's bachelor enlisted personnel were living in one- and two-story wooden World War II barracks that were hot in the summer, cold in the winter, a real effort to keep clean, and generally overcrowded. Older soldiers remember very well living in large troop bays, double-bunked, with only a small wooden footlocker and a metal wall locker to use for the storage of their uniforms and personal clothing.

Family housing—where it is available—ranges in style from detached single-family housing to high-rise apartment-style buildings accommodating scores of families. In some cases, the quarters you are assigned will be in excellent condition and will require little maintenance to keep them that way; others will cause you constant maintenance headaches.

When reporting to some new duty stations, you will find pleasant family housing waiting for you; at other stations, you will have to wait weeks or even months to get any kind of quarters. In some areas, the waiting list for government housing is so long that you might find it necessary to buy or rent off the post. Your family housing officer will be of great assistance to you if you should decide to occupy off-post quarters. Each installation and each major overseas command has a different family housing situation.

Once you attain NCO rank, you may very well find yourself either the senior occupant of a multiple dwelling or responsible for a number of families in a stairwell of such a dwelling. These assignments are necessary, and you should consider them as part of your obligation to the military community. You should discharge them with the same dedication and enthusiasm that you devote to your primary duties, but be prepared for many headaches, and expect that from time to time your patience will be severely tried.

Occupancy of family quarters carries the responsibility for doing "handyman work." The facilities engineer performs all maintenance and repairs other than those that are within the capabilities of the occupants. Emergency work or work beyond your individual capabilities can be obtained by making a service call or submitting a job order request to the installation repair and utilities office. Do not, however, expect the engineers to drop everything and run to your quarters, no matter how severe the emergency.

If you are fortunate enough to be assigned to a single-family dwelling, you will be expected to perform that type of self-help maintenance that is done by any prudent homeowner to conserve funds and preserve the premises, such as minor carpentry, maintenance of hardware (door hinges, and so forth), touch-up and partial interior painting, caulking around doors and windows, repair of screens, repair of simple plumbing malfunctions (minor leaking, defective washers, simple drainage stoppages), and so forth. Accumulate a set of tools that you can use around the house or apartment for this minor maintenance work.

No matter where you live—family quarters or the barracks—you are expected to exercise individual initiative to preserve energy and utilities. Soldiers are among the most flagrant violators of good energy conservation, wasting water and electricity and fuel as if there were no tomorrow. Remind yourself and others to be conservation conscious.

Your quarters will be inspected by someone from the housing office before you are cleared to vacate your quarters. This inspection can be very rigorous. The specific details will be furnished to you by the housing officer. Some people prefer to hire a civilian contractor to do the work for them. You can avoid this unnecessary expense if you and your family take proper care of your quarters while you are living in them. For example, use rugs on the floors, keep the walls clean and in good repair, and keep your appliances clean.

Commissary and Post Exchange Services

The price you pay for a grocery item in the commissary is the same price the government pays for it: If an item is sold to the government for 85 cents, then that is its cost to you. Even the commissary surcharge and tipping do not add as much to the cost of an item as do the standard markups found on similar items in civilian retail outlets.

The commissary surcharge pays for operating supplies, equipment, utilities, facility alterations, and new construction.

The Post Exchange Service was designated the Army and Air Force Exchange Service (AAFES) in 1948. What originally began as an outlet "to supply troops at reasonable prices with articles of ordinary use . . . not supplied by the Government . . . to afford them the means of rational recreation and amusement" has since become a multibillion-dollar enterprise that spans the globe. Many post exchange stores are actually department stores designed for family shoppers, although single soldiers can buy all the necessities of barracks life. Some stores even permit personnel in uniform to be waited on first during certain hours of the day, such as the lunch hour.

Several hundred military exchanges are operated throughout the world by the Department of Defense. (AAFES, headquartered in Dallas and headed by a general officer, operates outlets worldwide.) At a minimum, AAFES customers save the state sales tax, which is not charged.

IDENTIFICATION CARDS

Your DD Form 2A, *U.S. Armed Forces Identification Card* (green, active duty, and reserve duty), is possibly the most important military document you possess. DD Form 1173, *Uniformed Services Identification and Privilege Card,* is equally important to military dependents. These cards identify the bearers as persons who are entitled to the wide range of entitlements, privileges, and benefits authorized for military personnel and their dependents.

DD Form 2A (green) is issued to the following:

- All military personnel on active duty for more than 30 days.
- Members of the Army National Guard and the U.S. Army Reserve.
- Cadets of the U.S. Military Academy.

DD Form 2A (red) is issued to inactive reserves who are not yet entitled to receive retired pay at age 60 and to ROTC college program students in their last two years of training or in receipt of a full service scholarship.

DD Form 2A (retired—blue) is issued to retired personnel of the uniformed services who are entitled to retirement pay. The DD Form 2A (retired) is also issued to persons who retired from ARNG or USAR at age 60 after completing federal service under Section 1331, Title 10, U.S. Code, and personnel permanently retired for physical disability.

All ID cards are the property of the U.S. government. They are not transferable. The individual (or sponsor) to whom the card is issued must turn in cards in the following circumstances:

- Expiration of the card.
- Change in eligibility status (such as change in grade or rank and changes caused by disciplinary action, discharge, death, retirement, reenlistment, age, marriage, or release to inactive duty of the sponsor).
- Replacement by another card.
- Request from competent authority.
- Demand of the installation commander, verifying activity, or issuing activity.
- Recovery of a lost card after a replacement has been issued.
- Request by the installation commander for temporary safekeeping while an individual is taking part in recreation and gymnastic activities.
- Official placement of a sponsor in a deserter status.
- Change in the status of a sponsor if it terminates or modifies the right to any benefit for which the card may be used.

A lost ID card must be reported promptly to military law enforcement authorities or to ID card-issuing authorities. DD Form 1172, *Application for Uniformed Services Identification and Privilege Card,* is used for this purpose. The form also becomes the application for a new card, provided the individual continues to be eligible to receive it. DD Form 1172 must contain a statement of the circumstances of the loss, what was done to recover the card, and the card number, if known.

Any NCO who is performing his or her official duties may confiscate an ID card that is expired, mutilated, used fraudulently, or presented by a person not entitled to use it. Managers and employees of benefit and privilege activities may confiscate any expired or obviously altered ID card or document.

Commissary Cards

Since January 1, 1990, National Guard and reserve soldiers and their families have been required to present their Armed Forces Commissary Privilege Cards to enter and shop in commissaries. They also must show their military or family member ID cards.

Dependent ID Cards

DD Form 1173 is used throughout the Department of Defense to identify persons, other than active-duty or retired military personnel, who are eligible for benefits and privileges offered by the armed forces.

Dependent ID cards are authorized for issue to lawful spouses; unremarried former spouses married to the member or former member for a period of at least 20 years, during which period the member or former member performed at least 20 years of service; children (adopted, legitimized, stepchildren, wards); parents (in special cases); and surviving spouses of active-duty or retired members. See AR 640-3 for specific details.

Generally, DD Forms 1173 are replaced for the same reasons that govern replacement of military ID cards.

To verify initial eligibility for issue of a dependent ID card and entry into the Defense Enrollment Eligibility Reporting System (DEERS), sponsors must be prepared to show marriage certificates, birth certificates, death certificates (in the case of unremarried widows or widowers), or any other documentation prescribed by AR 640-3 required to establish dependency.

Abuse of Privileges

All DD Forms 2, DD Form 1173, and other authorized identification documents issued to Army members and their dependents may be confiscated and overstamped for abuse of privileges in Army facilities. Medical benefits, however, cannot be suspended for these reasons.

Abuse of privileges includes the following:

- Unauthorized resale of commodities bought in Army activities to unauthorized persons, whether or not to make a profit (customary personal gifts are permissible).
- Shoplifting.
- Unauthorized access to activities.
- Misuse of a privilege (such as allowing an unauthorized person to use an otherwise valid ID card to gain access to a facility).
- Issuing dishonored checks in Army facilities.

Penalties for abuse of privileges in an appropriated or nonappropriated fund facility are a warning letter, temporary suspension of privileges, and indefinite suspension of privileges.

LEAVES AND PASSES

Leave

AR 600-8-10 governs leaves and passes. All members of the Army serving on active duty are entitled to leave with pay and allowances at the rate of two and one-half calendar days each month of active duty or active duty for training, including the following:

- Members of the Army serving in active military service, including members of the Army National Guard and the Army Reserve serving on active duty for a period of 30 days or more.
- Members of the Army National Guard and reserve who are serving on initial active duty for training or active duty for training for a period of 30 days or more and for which they are entitled to pay.
- Members of the Army National Guard who are serving on full-time training duty for a period of 30 days or more and for which they are entitled to pay.

The following circumstances do not qualify as periods of earned leave:

- AWOL.
- Confinement as a result of a sentence of court-martial; confinement for more than one day while awaiting court-martial (providing the court-martial results in a conviction).
- When in excess leave.
- Unauthorized absence as a result of detention by civil authorities.
- Absence due to misconduct.

The total accumulation of accrued leave (earned leave) at the end of a fiscal year (September 30) cannot exceed 60 days. Leave accumulated after that date is forfeited. The single exception to this policy applies to personnel who, after January 1, 1968, serve in a designated combat zone, who may accumulate up to 90 days' leave. Leave that begins in one fiscal year and is completed in another is apportioned to the fiscal year in which each portion falls.

Upon discharge and immediate reenlistment, separation at expiration of term of service (ETS), or retirement, soldiers are authorized to settle their leave accounts for a lump-sum cash payment at the rate of one day of basic pay for each day of earned leave, up to 60 days. Public Law 94-212, February 9, 1976, limited settlement for accrued leave during a military career to a maximum of 60 days.

The following types of leave are authorized:

- *Advance leave.* Leave granted before its actual accrual, based on a reasonable expectation that it will be earned by the soldier during the remaining period of active duty.

- *Annual leave.* Leave granted in execution of a command's leave program, chargeable to the soldier's leave account. Also called "ordinary leave," as distinguished from emergency leave and special leave.
- *Convalescent leave.* A period of authorized absence granted to soldiers under medical treatment that is prescribed for recuperation and convalescence for sickness or wounds. Also called "sick leave," convalescent leave is not chargeable.
- *Emergency leave.* Leave granted for a bona fide personal or family emergency requiring the soldier's presence. Emergency leave is chargeable.
- *Environmental and morale leave.* Leave granted in conjunction with an environmental and morale leave program established at overseas installations where adverse environmental conditions exist that offset the full benefit of annual leave programs. This leave is chargeable.
- *Excess leave.* This leave is in excess of accrued and/or advance leave, granted without pay and allowances.
- *Graduation leave.* A period of authorized absence granted, as a delay in reporting to the first permanent duty station, to graduates of the U.S. Military Academy who are appointed as commissioned officers. Not chargeable, providing it is taken within three months of graduation.
- *Leave awaiting orders.* This is an authorized absence, chargeable to accrued leave and in excess of maximum leave accrual, taken while awaiting further orders and disposition in connection with disability separation proceedings under the provisions of AR 635-40.
- *Reenlistment leave.* This leave is granted to enlisted personnel as a result of reenlistment. May be either advance leave or leave accrued or a combination thereof; chargeable against the soldier's leave account.
- *Rest and recuperation (R&R)—extensions of overseas tours.* This is a nonchargeable increment of R&R leave authorized for enlisted soldiers in certain specialties who voluntarily extend their overseas tours. It is authorized in lieu of $50 per month special pay. The tour extension must be for a period of at least 12 months. Options under this program include nonchargeable leaves of 15 or 30 days.
- *Rest and recuperation leave.* This leave is granted in conjunction with rest and recuperation programs established in those areas designated for hostile fire pay, when operational military considerations preclude the full execution of ordinary annual leave programs. R&R leave is chargeable.
- *Special leave.* This is leave accrual that is authorized in excess of 60 days at the end of a fiscal year for soldiers assigned to hostile fire/imminent danger areas or certain deployable ships, mobile units, or other duty.
- *Terminal leave.* This leave is granted in connection with separation, including retirement, upon the request of the individual.

When possible, soldiers should be encouraged to take at least one annual leave period of about 14 consecutive days or longer (paragraph 203b, AR

630-5). Personnel who refuse to take leave when the opportunity is afforded them should be counseled and informed that such refusal may result in the loss of earned leave at a later date.

Leave is requested on part I, DA Form 31, *Request and Authority for Leave.* Requests for leave must be processed through the individual's immediate supervisor, although this step may be waived where supervisory approval or disapproval is inappropriate. This approval authority (generally, the soldier's commanding officer) ascertains that the individual has sufficient leave accrued to cover the entire period of absence requested.

Personnel should be physically present when DA Form 31 is authenticated and when commencing and terminating leave. Commanders may, at their discretion, authorize telephonic confirmation of departure and return.

Pass

A pass is an authorized absence not chargeable as leave, granted for short periods to provide respite from the working environment or for other specific reasons, at the end of which the soldier is actually at his or her place of duty or in the location from which he or she regularly commutes to work. This provision includes both regular and special passes.

Regular passes are granted to deserving military personnel for those periods when they are not required to be physically present with their unit for the performance of assigned duties. Normally, regular passes are valid only during specified off-duty hours, not more than 72 hours, except for public holiday weekends and holiday periods which, by discretion of the president, are extended to the commencement of working hours on the next working day.

Special passes are granted for periods of three or four days (72 to 96 hours) to deserving personnel on special occasions or in special circumstances for the following reasons: as special recognition for exceptional performance of duty, such as soldier of the month or year; to attend spiritual retreats or to observe other major religious events; to alleviate personal problems incident to military service; to vote; or as compensatory time off for long or arduous duty away from the home station or for duty in an isolated location where a normal pass is inadequate.

Passes may not be issued to soldiers so that two or more are effective in succession or used in a series, through reissue immediately after return to duty.

Extension of a pass is authorized provided the total absence does not exceed 72 hours for a regular pass, 72 hours for a special three-day pass, and 96 hours for a special four-day pass. Special passes will not be extended by combination with public holiday periods or other off-duty hours in cases in which the combined total will exceed the maximum limits of a three-day or four-day pass. Passes may not be taken in conjunction with leave, and extensions beyond the authorized maximum are chargeable to leave (AR 600-8-10).

15

Uniforms, Insignia, and Personal Appearance

WEARING THE UNIFORM

Your Army uniform is the outward evidence of your profession and your standing in that profession and a prime indicator of the degree of respect with which you regard your service to the United States of America and the Army. The condition of your uniform and the way you wear it are also a reflection of your own self-respect.

Classification of Service and Utility Field Uniforms

Class A Service Uniform. *For men:* consists of the Army green AG 489 coat and trousers, a short-sleeved or long-sleeved AG 415 shirt with pleated pockets, a black four-in-hand tie (tied in a slip knot with the ends left hanging), and other accessories. *For women:* consists of the appropriate Army green coat and skirt or slacks of the Army green classic uniform; a short-sleeved or long-sleeved AG 415 shirt; a black necktab; and authorized accessories. The Army green maternity uniform (slacks or skirt) is also a Class A service uniform when the tunic is worn.

Class B Service Uniform. *For men:* consists of the same as for the Class A except that the service coat is not worn. The black tie is required when wearing the long-sleeved AG 415 shirt and is optional with the short-sleeved shirt. *For women:* consists of the same as for the Class A except that the service coat and the maternity tunic are not worn. The black necktab is required when wearing the long-sleeved AG 415 shirt and the long-sleeved maternity shirt. It is optional with the short-sleeved version of both shirts.

Class C Uniforms. These are utility, field, and other organizational uniforms, such as the battle dress (BDU), hospital duty, and food service uniforms.

Optional Dress Uniforms. The Army blue uniform, white uniform, blue mess uniform, and white mess uniform are available for optional purchase by enlisted soldiers. The Army blue uniform is issued to soldiers when required as a duty uniform, such as when assigned to the Old Guard at Arlington Cemetery.

Occasions When the Uniform Is Required to Be Worn

The Army uniform is worn by all personnel when on duty unless HDQA has authorized the wearing of civilian clothes. The following general rules apply:

- Installation commanders may prescribe the uniforms to be worn in formations; duty uniforms are generally prescribed by local commanders or heads of agencies, activities, or installations.
- The wearing of combinations of uniform items not prescribed in AR 670-1 is prohibited.
- Uniform items changed in design or material may continue to be worn until wear-out date or unless specifically prohibited by HQDA.

Occasions When the Uniform May Not Be Worn

The wearing of the Army uniform is prohibited for all Army personnel under the following circumstances:

- In connection with the promotion of any political interest or when engaged in off-duty civilian employment.
- Except as authorized by competent authority, when participating in public speeches, interviews, picket lines, marches, rallies, or public demonstrations.
- When wearing the uniform would bring discredit upon the Army.
- When specifically prohibited by Army regulations.

Wearing of Headgear

The Army uniform is not complete unless the proper form of hat, cap, or beret is worn with it. Headgear is worn when outdoors and indoors when under arms.

Soldiers are exempt from wearing headgear to evening social events that occur after retreat. The appropriate headgear is, however, worn when wearing uniforms on all other occasions.

Headgear is not required to be worn when it would interfere with the safe operation of military vehicles. Military headgear is not required to be worn in privately owned or commercial vehicles.

Berets

The black beret is now the Army standard headgear and is worn by those soldiers not currently wearing the green, maroon, or tan beret. Soldiers will wear the beret with the utility and service uniforms in garrison environments only and will wear the patrol cap (formerly called the BDU cap) in the field when authorized to remove their Kevlar helmet. Commanders may authorize the wear of the patrol cap on work details or in other situations when wearing the beret is impractical.

New soldiers receive the black beret at their first permanent duty assignment after the completion of initial entry training or officer/warrant officer basic courses. Soldiers such as the above who are not issued or who do not wear the black beret will wear the patrol cap with utility uniforms and the garrison cap with the service uniforms. Newly assigned soldiers who possess the beret will comply with the installation commander's wear policy. Soldiers who are TDY will wear the headgear prescribed by their parent unit.

For enlisted soldiers, the crest of the unit assigned to is worn centered on the blue Army flash on the black beret. Soldiers wear the beret so that the headband is straight òn the head, one inch above the eyebrows, with the flash over the left eye and the excess material draped over to the right, down to at least the top of the ear, but no lower than the middle of the ear. A dip is formed in the wool, just behind the flash stiffener, and a slight fold is formed to the right front of the beret, next to the flash. Soldiers will tie off the adjusting ribbon into a non-slip knot, cut off the excess adjusting ribbon as close to the knot as possible, and tuck the knot into the edge binding at the back of the beret. The beret is form fitting to the head when worn properly; therefore, soldiers may not wear hairstyles that distort the beret.

The Army green service cap is no longer authorized for wear by officers or enlisted service members. The blue and white service caps remain the prescribed headgear for the blue and white dress and mess dress uniforms.

Uniform Appearance

The word "uniform" as used in this context means "conforming to the same standard or rule." Although absolute uniformity of appearance by all soldiers at all times cannot reasonably be expected as long as armies are composed of so many various individuals, uniformed soldiers should project a military image that leaves no doubt that they live by a common standard.

One important rule of uniformity is that, when worn, items of the uniform should be kept buttoned, zippered, and snapped; metallic devices (such as collar brass insignia) should be kept in proper luster; and shoes should be cleaned and shined. In instances where boots are worn with uniforms, soldiers will not blouse boots any lower than the third eyelet from the top.

Lapels and sleeves of coats and jackets for both male and female personnel should be roll pressed (without creasing). Trousers, slacks, and sleeves of shirts and blouses should be creased.

Care and Maintenance of the Uniform

All solid brass items (belt buckles, belt-buckle tips, collar brass insignia) should be maintained in a high state of luster at all times. These items come coated with a lacquer, and if their surfaces are kept protected and gently rubbed with a soft, clean cloth, they will keep their shine for a long time. But when the lacquer coating becomes scratched, dirt begins to accumulate in the scratches, and the item can be kept shined only by completely removing the lacquer surface.

The safest and most reliable method for removing the coating from brass items is to use Brasso polish applied with thumb and forefinger or a cloth.

Spit-shining does make shoes, boots, and equipment look sharp, but it dries out the leather.

Replace heels on shoes and boots after wear of $7/16$ of an inch or more. To check your footgear, attempt to roll a pencil under the heel.

Pay attention to the removal of stains from your clothing.

Never press dirty clothing, and be careful when pressing clothing that the iron is not too hot. Use a damp cloth between the iron and the fabric when pressing wool items, dampen the surface of cotton clothing before applying the iron, and observe the various fabric settings on the iron when pressing synthetic fabrics.

Frequent cleaning of uniform items increases their longevity and maintains the neat soldierly appearance that the uniform is designed to project. Rotating items of clothing, such as shoes and boots, contributes to their longer life.

Many soldiers, as an economy measure, make minor repairs to their clothing themselves. The best advice to soldiers who want to look sharp is to have their insignia sewn on by a tailor, and save money in some other way.

Fitting of Uniforms

Uniform items purchased in the clothing sales store are fitted (or should be fitted) before they are taken off the premises. Personnel who purchase uniform items through the post exchange or from commercial sources should pay close attention to the proper fit of the items before wearing them.

Your NCO will be able to tell at a glance whether a soldier (male or female) is wearing a properly fitted uniform. Fitting instructions and alterations of uniforms are made in accordance with AR 700-84 and TM 10-227, *Fitting of Army Uniforms and Footwear.*

Clothing Allowance System

Clothing allowances are provided so that each soldier may maintain the initial clothing issue. Monthly clothing allowances provide for the cost of replacement and purchase of new items or the purchase of additional clothing items, not for cleaning, laundering, and pressing. The basic allowance begins on the soldier's 181st day of active duty and is paid each month for the remainder of the first three-year period. The standard allowance begins the day after the soldier completes 36 months on active duty. The clothing allowance accrues monthly and is paid annually during the month of the soldier's basic active service date.

MEN'S ARMY GREEN UNIFORM

The Army green uniform, Class A and Class B variations, may be worn by male personnel when on duty, off duty, or during travel. These uniforms are also acceptable for informal social functions after retreat, unless other uniforms are prescribed by the host.

Men's Class A Uniform

The Army green uniform (Class A) consists of the Army green (AG) shade 489 coat and trousers, worn with either the new long-sleeved or short-sleeved 415 pleated pocket shirt and a black four-in-hand necktie.

The coat should fit with a slight drape in both the front and the back. No pronounced tightness at the waist or flare below the waist is authorized. The length of the coat should extend to below the crotch.

Matching Army green uniform trousers are straight-legged and reach the top of the instep and are cut on a diagonal line to reach a point approximately midway between the top of the heel and the top of the standard shoe in the back. The trousers may have a slight break in the front.

Accessories (Class A)

The U.S. insignia disk is worn on the right lapel collar approximately one inch above the notch. The branch insignia disk is worn on the left lapel collar approximately one inch above the notch. Both are centered on the lapel collar so as to be parallel with the inside of the lapel.

Distinctive unit insignia (unit crests) of the currently assigned unit are worn centered on both shoulder loops (epaulets) of the coat between the outside edge of the shoulder loop button and the seam of the loop.

The current organization shoulder sleeve insignia (patch) is sewn on the left sleeve one-half inch down from the shoulder seam and centered. When the Ranger, Special Forces, or President's Hundred tab is worn, the tab is placed one-half inch below the shoulder seam, and the current organization shoulder patch is then worn one-quarter inch below the bottom of the tab. A shoulder patch for a former wartime organization may be worn on the right sleeve one-half inch below the shoulder seam.

With the Class A Army green uniform, rank insignia is sewn on the sleeve halfway between the elbow and the shoulder seam of the coat.

When awarded, sew-on service stripes (hash marks) are placed four inches above the bottom of the left sleeve and centered on the sleeve. Overseas bars (Hershey bars) are placed four inches above the bottom of the right sleeve.

The nameplate is worn on the right breast pocket of the coat, centered between the top of the button and the top of the pocket.

Unit awards, such as the Distinguished Unit Award, Presidential Unit Award, and so forth, are worn one-eighth inch above the right breast pocket.

Individual decorations and service ribbons are worn one-eighth inch above the left breast pocket of the coat. When combat and special skill badges are worn, they are centered one-quarter inch above the ribbons. When more than one badge is worn above the ribbons, the badges are stacked one-half inch apart and may be aligned to the left to present a better appearance.

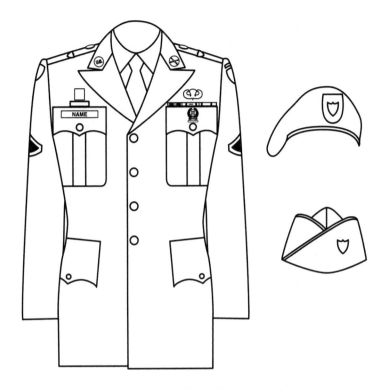

Class A Uniform for Men

Marksmanship badges are worn on the left breast pocket flap one-eighth inch below the top seam of the pocket. If more than one badge is worn, they are spaced one inch apart and centered in relation to the bottom edge of the ribbons and the pocket button. When special skill badges, e.g., driver's badge, are worn on the pocket flap, they are placed to the right of the marksmanship badges.

The Army black beret, organizational berets, and drill sergeant hats are authorized for wear with the Class A and Class B uniforms. The green garrison cap is only authorized if the soldier's organization has not switched to the black beret.

Men's Army Green Dress Uniform

The men's Army green dress uniform consists of the Army green coat and trousers, with a commercially purchased long-sleeved white shirt and black bow tie. The dress uniform is restricted to formal social functions, private or official, and transit to and from such functions. It cannot be worn for duty or travel. Boots, berets, or organizational items, such as brassards or MP accessories, are not used with the green dress uniform.

Men's Class B Uniform

The men's Class B uniform merely omits the coat. It consists of the long-sleeved or short-sleeved AG 415 shirt and AG 489 trousers with black web belt and brass buckle. The black four-in-hand necktie must be worn with the long-sleeved shirt and is optional for the short-sleeved shirt.

Since October 1, 1999, male soldiers have had to own and wear the new short-sleeved and long-sleeved AG 415 shirts with pleated pockets. They are required to have one long-sleeved and two short-sleeved shirts.

Individual awards and decorations are authorized to be worn on the Class B uniform shirts. Their placement is as on the coat. Check AR 670-1 for additional details.

Shoulder mark rank insignia is worn on the Class B uniform shirt for all NCOs and on the shirt collars for non-NCO enlisted grades.

WOMEN'S ARMY GREEN UNIFORM

The women's Army green uniform, Class A and Class B variations, may be worn by female personnel when on duty, off duty, or during travel. These uniforms are also acceptable for informal social functions after retreat, unless other uniforms are prescribed by the host.

Women's Class A Uniform

The women's Class A uniform consists of the Army green coat and either the Army green skirt or slacks, a new AG 415 short-sleeved or long-sleeved tuck-in shirt, and a black wraparound necktab with hook and pile fastener. The long- and short-sleeved AG 415 overblouse is now an optional purchase item. Shirts without princess pleats are no longer authorized.

The women's coat is a hip-length, single-breasted coat with four buttons and button-down shoulder loops. The Army green classic skirt has a waistband and side zipper closure. The skirt length cannot be more than one inch above or two inches below the crease in the back of the knee. The matching green classic slacks have undergone a change. Since October 1, 1999, women wear the new AG 489 green slacks, which have belt loops and are worn with a one-inch black web belt and matching brass buckle. The belt must be worn so that the tipped end is to the woman's right, which is opposite of the men's belt.

Accessories (Class A)

Specifications for wear of the organizational shoulder sleeve insignia (patch), unit crests, rank insignia, service stripes, overseas bars, and regimental crests are the same for the women's Class A uniform as they are for the men's Class A uniform described above. There are, however, some differences.

The U.S. insignia disk is centered on the right collar of the coat approximately five-eighths inch up from the notch, with the center line of the insignia parallel to the inside edge of the lapel. The branch insignia disk is centered in the same manner on the left collar.

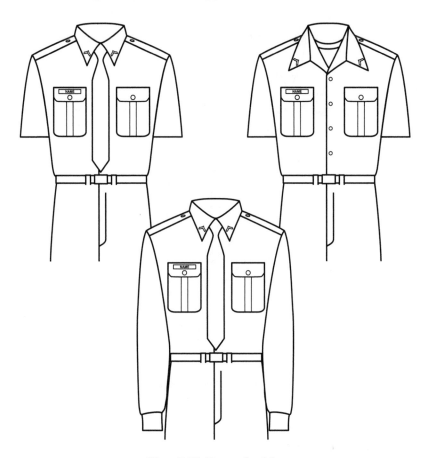

Class B Uniforms for Men

The key to the alignment of accessories on the women's Class A uniform is the placement of the plastic nameplate. The nameplate can be adjusted to conform to individual figure differences. The nameplate is centered horizontally on the right side between one and two inches above the top button of the coat. Individual and service ribbons are aligned on the left side parallel to the bottom edge of the nameplate. Other badges are aligned on the nameplate or the ribbons in the same manner as on the men's Class A uniform.

The Army black beret cap, service cap, organizational berets, and drill sergeant hats are authorized for wear with the Class A and Class B uniforms. The garrison cap is only authorized for wear if the soldier's organization has not switched to the black beret. The garrison cap is worn with the front vertical crease of the cap centered on the forehead in a straight line with the nose. No hair should show on the forehead below the front bottom edge of the cap, which should be situated approximately one inch above the eyebrows.

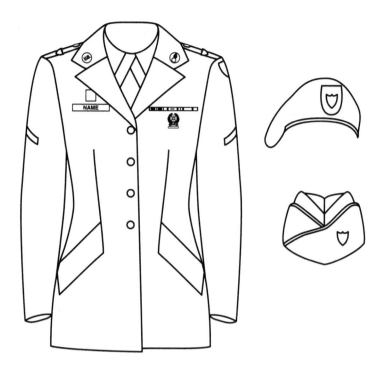

Class A Uniform for Women

Women's Army Green Dress Uniform

The women's Army green dress uniform consists of the Army green coat and skirt or slacks, with a commercially purchased long-sleeved white shirt. The Army black necktab is worn. The dress uniform is restricted to formal social functions, private or official, and transit to and from such functions. It cannot be worn for duty or travel. Boots, berets, or organizational items, such as brassards or MP accessories, are not used with the women's green dress uniform.

Women's Class B Uniforms

The women's Class B uniform merely omits the coat. It consists of the long-sleeved or short-sleeved AG 415 shirt, which is worn with either the new AG 489 slacks, black web belt, and brass buckle or the AG 489 classic skirt. The black necktab must be worn with the long-sleeved shirt and is optional for the short-sleeved shirt.

Female soldiers are required to have one long-sleeved and two short-sleeved shirts and two pairs of slacks by October 2003.

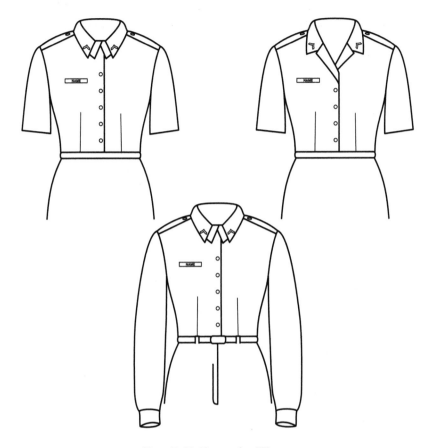

Class B Uniforms for Women

Individual awards and decorations are authorized to be worn on the Class B uniform shirts. Their placement is as on the coat. Check AR 670-1 for additional details.

Shoulder mark rank insignia is worn on the Class B uniform shirt for all NCOs and on the shirt collars for non-NCO enlisted grades.

Green Maternity Uniform
The pregnant soldier has been provided with a special uniform. Accessories, insignia, awards, badges, and accoutrements for the maternity uniforms follow the same regulations as those for the servicewomen's Class A, Class B, and green dress uniforms.

WORK AND DUTY UNIFORMS

Temperate and Enhanced Hot Weather Battle Dress Uniforms (EHWBDU)
This uniform is authorized for year-round on-duty wear by all personnel when prescribed by the commander. The EHWBDU replaced the hot weather battle dress uniform.

Desert Battle Dress Uniform (DBDU)
The DBDU may be worn only when prescribed by the commander. The wear of the DBDU at public functions other than homecoming parades and activities directly related to the celebration of the return of soldiers from an operational area is not authorized without an exception from the major command.

Cold Weather Uniform
The OG 108 cold weather uniform is designed for year-round wear by all personnel when issued as organizational clothing and prescribed by the commander. It is not authorized for travel or wear off military installations except in transit. Components of this uniform may be worn with utility and other organization uniforms as part of a cold weather ensemble when issued and prescribed by the commander.

Hospital Duty Uniform (Male)
This year-round duty uniform for all male soldiers in the Army Medical Specialist Corps and those in medical, dental, or veterinary MOSs is worn in medical healthcare facilities as prescribed by the medical commander. The commander may authorize the wear of this uniform in a civilian community when in support of civilian activities.

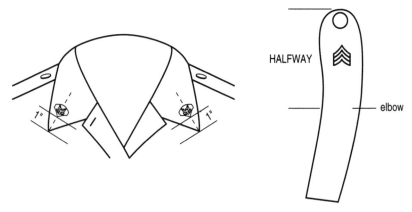

Polished Pin-on Insignia   **Sew-on Insignia of Grade**
of Grade on Collars

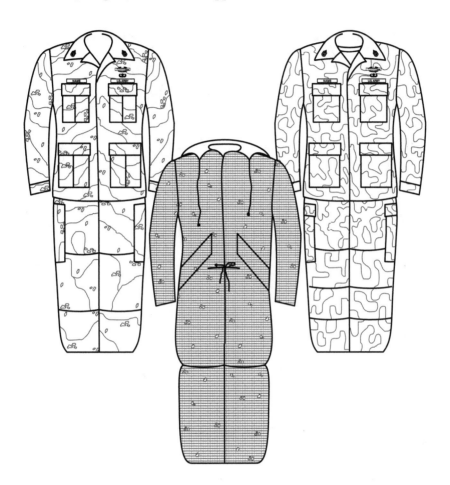

**Desert BDU, Night Desert Coverall,
Temperate and Enhanced Hot Weather BDU**

Hospital Duty and Maternity Uniform
This authorized year-round uniform is worn by Army Medical Specialist Corps personnel and enlisted women with medical, dental, or veterinary MOSs.

Flight Uniform
This uniform is authorized for year-round wear when on duty in a flying or standby-awaiting-flight status. Commanders may direct exceptions to wear policy.

Hospital Duty Uniforms

Combat Vehicle Crewman (CVC) Uniform

The CVC is a year-round duty uniform for combat vehicle crewmen when on duty or as directed by the commander. This uniform is not for travel.

Maternity Work Uniform

This uniform is authorized for year-round on-duty wear by pregnant soldiers. It is not intended as a travel uniform, but it may be worn in transit between the individual's quarters and duty station.

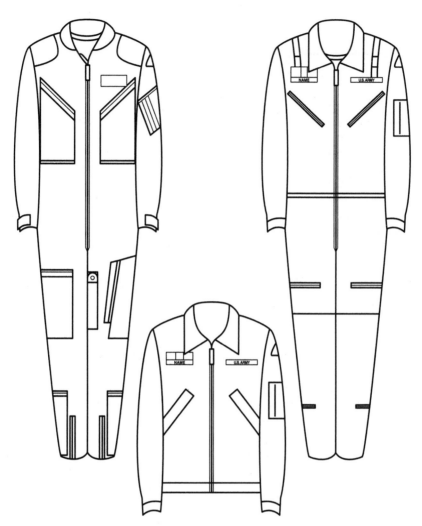

Flight Uniform and Combat Vehicle Crewman Uniform

OPTIONAL UNIFORMS

Army Blue Uniform (Male and Female)

This uniform is authorized for optional wear by enlisted personnel. Although primarily a uniform for social functions of a general or official nature before or after retreat, it may be worn on duty if prescribed by the commander.

Other Authorized Uniforms
- Army white uniform for both male and female soldiers.
- Army blue mess uniform.
- Army white mess uniform.

OUTERWEAR
A unisex cardigan sweater (optional) replaces the individual male and female black army cardigan and may be worn buttoned or unbuttoned indoors, but must be buttoned outdoors. The old sweaters can no longer be worn.

A black double-breasted and belted all-weather coat replaced the unbelted black all-weather coat.

DISTINCTIVE UNIFORM ITEMS
The following uniform items are distinctive and should not be sold to or worn by unauthorized personnel: all Army headgear, badges, decorations, service medals, awards, tabs, service ribbons, appurtenances, and insignia of any design or color that have been adopted by the Department of the Army.

Headgear
The following items of headgear are authorized for Army personnel:

Item	Female Version*
Beret, black (Army)	Beret, black (Army)
Beret, green (Special Forces)	
Beret, maroon (Airborne)	
Beret, tan (Ranger)	
Cap, cold weather (AG 344)	
Cap, cold weather, utility	
Cap, food handler's, white, paper	
Cap, garrison, green (AG 489)	Cap, garrison (AG 489)
Cap, hot weather	
Cap, service, blue	Hat, service, blue
Cap, service, white	Hat, service, white
Hat, camouflage, desert	
Hat, drill sergeant	Hat, drill sergeant

*These are distinctively female items. Other items of headgear listed may be worn by female soldiers, as prescribed in AR 670-1.

Combat Leader's Identification
The Combat Leader's Identification insignia is a green cloth loop, one and five-eighths inches wide, worn in the middle of both shoulder loops of the Army green and cold weather coats. Personnel cease to wear them when reassigned

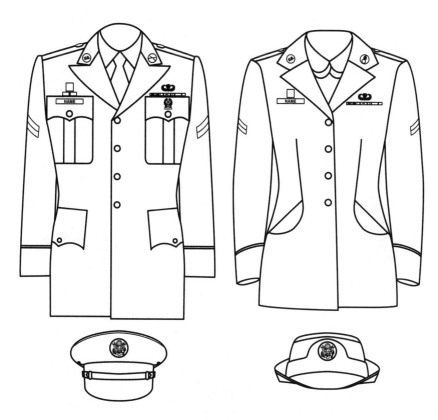

Army Blue Uniform

from a command position or from an organization where these insignia are authorized to be worn.

The specific leaders in units authorized to wear the Combat Leader's Identification insignia are these: commanders, deputy commanders, platoon leaders, command sergeants major, first sergeants, platoon sergeants, section leaders (when designated in TOE), squad leaders and tank commanders, and rifle squad fire team leaders.

Unit Insignia and Heraldic Items

Distinctive unit insignia (DUI) are made of metal or metal and enamel and are usually based on elements of the design of the coat of arms or historic badge approved for a specific unit. Sometimes erroneously referred to as "unit crests," DUI are subject to the approval of the Institute of Heraldry, U.S. Army, and, like shoulder sleeve insignia, are authorized for wear on the uniform as a means of promoting esprit de corps.

Adjutant General's Corps   Air Defense Artillery   Armor

Branch Immaterial   Aviation   Cavalry

Chaplain Assistant   Chemical Corps   Civil Affairs

Corps of Engineers   Field Artillery   Finance

Enlisted Insignia of Branch

DECORATIONS, SERVICE MEDALS, AND BADGES

U.S. ARMY AND DEPARTMENT OF DEFENSE MILITARY DECORATIONS

Medal of Honor (Army)

**Distinguished Service
Cross (Army)**

**Defense Distinguished
Service Medal**

**Distinguished Service
Medal (Army)**

Silver Star

**Defense Superior
Service Medal**

Legion of Merit

**Distinguished Flying
Cross**

**Soldier's Medal
(Army)**

Bronze Star Medal

Purple Heart

**Defense
Meritorious Service
Medal**

**Meritorious Service
Medal**

Air Medal

**Joint Service
Commendation
Medal**

**Army
Commendation
Medal**

**Joint Service
Achievement
Medal**

**Army
Achievement
Medal**

**Prisoner of War
Medal**

**Good Conduct
Medal (Army)**

**Army Reserve
Components
Achievement
Medal**

**National Defense
Service Medal**

**Antarctica
Service Medal**

**Armed Forces
Expeditionary
Medal**

**Vietnam
Service Medal**

**Southwest Asia
Service Medal**

**Kosovo
Campaign Medal**

**Armed Forces
Service Medal**

**Humanitarian
Service Medal**

**Military
Outstanding
Volunteer
Service Medal**

**Armed Forces
Reserve Medal**

U.S. ARMY SERVICE AND TRAINING RIBBONS

**NCO
Professional
Development
Ribbon**

**Army
Service Ribbon**

**Overseas
Service Ribbon
(Army)**

**Army Reserve
Components
Overseas
Training Ribbon**

NON-U.S. SERVICE MEDALS

**United Nations
Medal**

**NATO
Medal**

**Multinational
Force and Observers
Medal**

**Republic of
Vietnam Campaign
Medal**

**Kuwait
Liberation Medal
(Kingdom of
Saudi Arabia)**

**Kuwait
Liberation Medal
(Government of
Kuwait)**

U.S. ARMY AND DEPARTMENT OF DEFENSE
UNIT AWARDS

**Presidential Unit
Citation (Army)**

**Joint
Meritorious Unit
Award**

**Valorous Unit
Award**

**Meritorious Unit
Commendation
(Army)**

**Army
Superior Unit
Award**

U.S. ARMY BADGES AND TABS

Combat and Special Skill Badges

**Combat Infantryman Badge
1st Award**

**Combat Medical Badge
1st Award**

**Combat Infantryman Badge
2nd Award**

**Combat Medical Badge
2nd Award**

**Combat Infantryman Badge
3rd Award**

**Combat Medical Badge
3rd Award**

Expert Infantryman Badge

Expert Field Medical Badge

Master Astronaut Badge

Basic Astronaut Badge

Senior Astronaut Badge

Master Aviator Badge

Basic Aviator Badge

Senior Aviator Badge

Basic Flight Surgeon Badge

Master Flight Surgeon Badge

Senior Flight Surgeon Badge

Basic Aircraft Crewman Badge

Master Aircraft Crewman Badge

Senior Aircraft Crewman Badge

**Master Parachutist
Badge**

**Basic Parachutist
Badge**

**Senior Parachutist
Badge**

**Combat Parachutist
Badge (1 Jump)**

**Combat Parachutist
Badge (2 Jumps)**

**Combat Parachutist
Badge (3 Jumps)**

**Combat Parachutist
Badge (4 Jumps)**

**Combat Parachutist
Badge (5 Jumps)**

Air Assault Badge

Glider Badge

Pathfinder Badge

Special Forces Tab
(Metal Replica)

Ranger Tab
(Metal Replica)

Salvage Diver
Badge

Second Class Diver
Badge

First Class Diver
Badge

Master Diver
Badge

Scuba Diver
Badge

Master Explosive
Ordnance Disposal Badge

Basic Explosive
Ordnance Disposal Badge

Senior Explosive
Ordnance Disposal Badge

**Nuclear Reactor Operator
Badge (Basic)**

**Nuclear Reactor Operator
Badge (Second Class)**

**Nuclear Reactor Operator
Badge (First Class)**

**Nuclear Reactor Operator
Badge (Shift Supervisor)**

**Parachute Rigger
Badge**

**Driver and Mechanic
Badge**

Marksmanship Badges

Marksman

Sharpshooter

Expert

Identification Badges

Presidential Service

Vice-Presidential Service

Secretary of Defense

Joint Chiefs of Staff

Army Staff

**Guard,
Tomb of the Unknown Soldier**

Drill Sergeant

**U.S. Army Recruiter
(Active Army)**

**U.S. Army Recruiter
(Army National Guard)**

**U.S. Army Recruiter
(U.S. Army Reserve)**

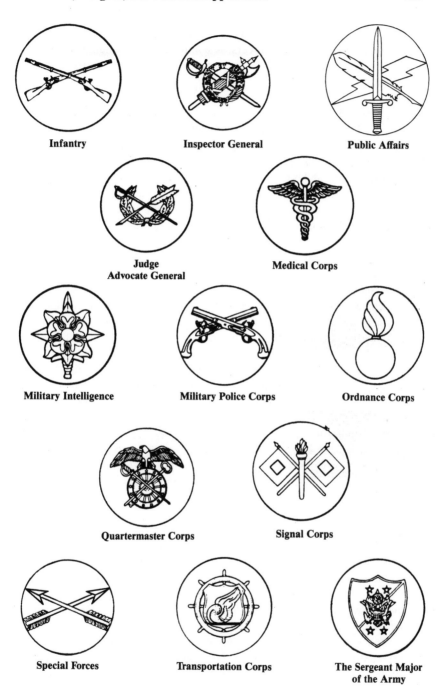

Infantry   Inspector General   Public Affairs

Judge Advocate General   Medical Corps

Military Intelligence   Military Police Corps   Ordnance Corps

Quartermaster Corps   Signal Corps

Special Forces   Transportation Corps   The Sergeant Major of the Army

Enlisted Insignia of Branch

When authorized, these insignia are worn by all assigned personnel of an organization, except general officers. A complete set of insignia consists of three pieces: one for each shoulder loop and one for headgear (garrison, utility, cold weather caps, or berets).

Regimental Insignia

Regimental DUI are worn by all personnel affiliated with a regiment. The "crest" of the affiliated regiment is worn centered and one-eighth inch above the pocket seam or one-half inch above unit and foreign awards, if worn, on the Army green, white, and blue uniforms. The DUI worn on the shoulder loops of the Army green, white, and blue (enlisted men only) coats and jackets is always the unit of assignment. If assigned and affiliated to the same regiment, then all three crests are the same.

Distinctive Items—Infantry

Infantry personnel are authorized to wear the following distinctive items:
- A shoulder cord of infantry blue formed by a series of interlocking square knots around a center cord. The cord is worn on the right shoulder of the Army green, blue, and white uniform coats and shirts, passed under the arm and through the shoulder loop, and secured to the button on the shoulder loop.
- A plastic infantry blue disk, one and one-quarter inches in diameter, is worn by enlisted personnel of the infantry, secured beneath the branch of the service and the U.S. insignia, with a one-eighth-inch border around the insignia. It is authorized to be worn on the Army green, blue, and white uniforms.
- An insignia disk of infantry blue plastic, one and three-quarter inches in diameter, is worn secured beneath the insignia on the service cap. Criteria for wear are the same as those for the infantry blue insignia disk.

Organizational Flash

This shield-shaped embroidered patch with a semicircular bottom approximately two and one-quarter inches long and one and seven-eighths inches wide is worn centered on the stiffener of the beret by personnel authorized to wear one of the organizational berets (Ranger, Special Forces, and Airborne).

Airborne Background Trimming

Background trimming is authorized for wear with the parachutist or air assault badge. When authorized, such background will be worn by all personnel of an airborne-designated organization who have been awarded one of the parachute badges or by personnel in an organization designated air assault who have been awarded the air assault badge.

Airborne Insignia

This white parachute and glider in a blue disk with a red border, approximately two and one-quarter inches in diameter, is worn by all personnel on jump status or by parachute-qualified personnel in special nonairborne duty (recruiting personnel or instructors). Enlisted personnel wear the insignia designed with the glider facing forward when it is worn centered on the left curtain of the garrison cap, one inch from the front crease.

PERSONAL APPEARANCE

A vital ingredient of the Army's strength and military effectiveness is the pride and discipline that soldiers bring to their service. It is the responsibility of noncommissioned officers to ensure that the military personnel under their supervision present a neat and soldierly appearance. It is the duty of each individual soldier to always take pride in his or her appearance.

Standards for All

Dreadlocks are prohibited. Hair color must look natural on the soldier. No tinted or colored contacts are permitted. Fingernails must be neatly trimmed: males to the tip of the finger; females $1/4"$ from the tip.

Standards for Men

Many hairstyles are acceptable in the Army. The hair must be neatly groomed, and the length and bulk of the hair cannot be excessive or present a ragged, unkempt, or extreme appearance. Hair should present a tapered appearance and, when combed, should not fall over the ears or eyebrows or touch the collar. Block cuts are permitted in moderate degree, but in all cases the bulk and length of hair cannot interfere with the normal wear of headgear or protective mask. Men may shave their heads bald; they may not wear nail polish.

A soldier's face should be clean shaven, except that Army regulations do permit mustaches. No portion of a mustache is permitted to cover the upper lip line or extend beyond the crease of the upper and lower lips. Handlebar mustaches, goatees, and beards are not authorized. Where beard growth is prescribed by appropriate medical authority, as is sometimes necessary in the treatment of different types of skin disorders, the length required for medical treatment should be specified: "A neatly trimmed beard is authorized. The length will not exceed one-quarter inch," for example. If you have such a medical condition, be sure to keep your exemption slip handy at all times when in uniform.

Standards for Women

The principle that soldiers should always maintain a neat and well-groomed personal appearance applies equally to men and to women, though the specific grooming standard for each reflects the traditional differences in appearance between the sexes.

Hair must be neatly groomed. The length and bulk of the hair should not be excessive or present a ragged, unkempt, or extreme appearance. Women may wear braids and cornrows. Hair should not fall over the eyebrows or extend below the bottom edge of the collar. Hairstyles cannot interfere with the proper wearing of military headgear or protective masks.

Cosmetics should be applied conservatively and in good taste. Two-tone or multitone manicures and nail designs are prohibited. Prohibited nail polish colors include bright fire engine red, khaki or camouflage, purple, gold, blue, and black.

Wearing of Civilian Jewelry

The wearing of a personal wristwatch, identification wrist bracelet, and no more than two rings is authorized with the Army uniform as long as they are not prohibited for safety reasons and the style is conservative and in good taste. The wearing of a purely religious medal on a chain around the neck is authorized, provided that neither the medal nor the chain is exposed.

No jewelry, watch chains, or similar civilian items, including pens or pencils, should be allowed to appear exposed on the uniform. Exceptions are that a conservative tie tack or tie clasp may be worn with the black four-in-hand necktie, and a pen or pencil may appear exposed on the hospital duty and food service uniforms.

Soldiers in and out of uniform are prohibited from displaying pierced body parts while on military installations worldwide—except for women with pierced ears. Women may wear screw-on or post-type earrings with the service, dress, or mess uniforms. Earrings may not be worn with Class C utility uniforms (utility, field, or organization, including hospital duty and food service uniforms). Earrings must be small in diameter, six millimeters or one-quarter inch; gold, silver, or white pearl; unadorned; and spherical. They must fit snugly against the ear and must be worn as a matched pair with only one in each earlobe.

One electronic device is authorized for wear on the uniform in official duties. It must be black in color and measure not more than 4" x 2" x 1". Items that do not comply must be carried elsewhere.

Wearing of Civilian Clothing

Civilian clothing is authorized for wear off-duty unless the wear is prohibited by the installation commander within CONUS or the major command overseas. When on duty in civilian clothes, soldiers must conform to the appearance standards of AR 670-1, unless specifically authorized for mission requirements.

Security Badges

Security identification badges are worn in restricted areas as prescribed by local commanders. They are usually laminated plastic identification badges worn suspended from clips. They should never be worn outside the secure area for which they authorize an individual access. To prevent the possibility of losing them, some personnel suspend them from a chain worn around the neck and, when in public, under their outer garments.

REFERENCES

AR 600-8-22, *Military Awards.*
AR 670-1, *Uniform and Insignia.*
AR 700-84, *Issue and Sale of Personal Clothing.*
FM 3-21-15 [21-15] *Care and Use of Individual Clothing and Equipment.*

16

Awards and Decorations

The Army's awards and decorations program provides tangible recognition for acts of valor, exceptional service or achievement, special skills or qualifications, and acts of heroism not involving actual combat. It is the responsibility of any soldier having personal knowledge of an act, an achievement, or a service believed to warrant the award of a decoration to submit a formal recommendation for consideration.

Under this criterion, it is possible that a private may recommend a captain for a decoration, but usually the system works the other way. The only consideration that should be used is this one: Does the person's act or service warrant an award?

PRECEDENCE

Decorations, the Good Conduct Medal, and service medals are ranked in the following order of precedence when worn or displayed:

U.S. military decorations
U.S. unit awards
U.S. nonmilitary decorations
POW Medal
Good Conduct Medal
Army Reserve Components Achievement Medal
U.S. service medals and training ribbons
U.S. Merchant Marine awards
Foreign military decorations (excluding service medals and ribbons)
Foreign unit awards
Non-U.S. service awards

U.S. military decorations, the Good Conduct Medal, and U.S. service medals are ranked in the following order of precedence when worn or displayed:

Medal of Honor
Distinguished Service Cross
Defense Distinguished Service Medal
Distinguished Service Medal

Silver Star
Defense Superior Service Medal
Legion of Merit
Distinguished Flying Cross
Soldier's Medal
Bronze Star Medal
Purple Heart
Defense Meritorious Service Medal
Meritorious Service Medal
Air Medal
Joint Service Commendation Medal
Army Commendation Medal
Joint Service Achievement Medal
Army Achievement Medal
Prisoner of War Medal
Good Conduct Medal
Army Reserve Components Achievement Medal
State awards for Army National Guard soldiers

U.S. unit awards:
Presidential Unit Citation
Joint Meritorious Unit Award
Valorous Unit Award
Meritorious Unit Commendation
Army Superior Unit Award

U.S. service medals:
Army of Occupation Medal
National Defense Service Medal
Antarctica Service Medal
Armed Forces Expeditionary Medal
Vietnam Service Medal
Southwest Asia Service Medal
Kosovo Campaign Medal
Global War on Terrorism Expeditionary Medal
Global War on Terrorism Service Medal
Armed Forces Service Medal
Humanitarian Service Medal
Military Outstanding Volunteer Service Medal
Armed Forces Reserve Medal
NCO Professional Development Ribbon
Army Service Ribbon
Overseas Service Ribbon
Army Reserve Components Overseas Training Ribbon

Non-U.S. service medals:
   United Nations Medal(s)[1]
   NATO Medal
   Multinational Force and Observers Medal
   Republic of Vietnam Campaign Medal
   Kuwait Liberation Medal (kingdom of Saudi Arabia)
   Kuwait Liberation Medal (government of Kuwait)

As we went to press in mid-2003, the president issued an executive order authorizing the Department of Defense to create two new military medals for service in the global war against terrorism. The first one is the *Global War on Terrorism Expeditionary Medal.* This medal will recognize servicemembers who participate in an expedition to combat terrorism on or after September 11, 2001. This medal is initially limited to those who deploy as part of Operation Enduring Freedom/Iraqi Freedom.

The second medal is the *Global War on Terrorism Service Medal.* It will recognize service in military operations to combat terrorism on or after September 11, 2001. This is limited to Operation Noble Eagle and to those servicemembers who provide support to Operation Enduring Freedom/Iraqi Freedom from outside the area of eligibility designated for the Global War on Terrorism Expeditionary Medal.

---

[1]Servicemembers may wear only one United Nations Medal. It may be the U. N. Medal or the medal and ribbon of the first U. N. operation in which they participated.

WEARING OF MEDALS AND RIBBONS

All individual U.S. decorations and service medals (full-size medals, miniature medals, and ribbons) are worn above the left breast pocket or centered on the left side of the coat or jacket of the prescribed uniform (with the exception of the Medal of Honor, which may be worn suspended around the neck). Decorations are worn with the highest displayed above and to the wearer's right of the others.

Full-size decorations and service medals may be worn on the Army blue, white, and green uniform when worn for social functions or when directed. They are worn in order of precedence from the wearer's right to left, in one or more lines, without overlapping within a line, with one-eighth-inch space between lines. No line should contain fewer medals than the one above it. The Medal of Honor is worn with the neckband ribbon around the neck, outside the shirt collar and inside the coat collar, with the medal hanging over the necktie.

Miniature decorations and service medals are authorized for wear on the mess and evening mess uniforms only. They may be worn side by side or overlapped, but the overlap should not exceed 50 percent and should be equal for all. There are no miniature medals authorized for the Medal of Honor.

Service ribbons are worn in the order of precedence from the wearer's right to left in one or more lines either without a space between rows or with a one-eighth-inch space. No row should contain more than four service ribbons. Male and female personnel are authorized to wear them on the Army green, white, and blue uniforms.

Retired personnel and former soldiers may wear either full-size or miniature medals on appropriate civilian clothing on Veterans Day, Memorial Day, and Armed Forces Day and at formal occasions of ceremony and social functions of a military nature.

U.S. Army Badges and Tabs

Badges are of three types:
- Combat and special skill badges
- Marksmanship badges and tabs
- Identification badges

Badges are awarded in recognition of attaining a high standard of proficiency in certain military skills. There is no established precedence with badges as there is with decorations and service medals or ribbons. Subdued combat and special skill badges and the Ranger and Special Forces tabs are authorized on field uniforms.

Appurtenances

Appurtenances are devices affixed to service or suspension ribbons or worn in place of medals or ribbons. They are worn to denote additional awards, participation in a specific event, or other distinguished characteristics of the award.

Ribbons Representing
Decorations and Service Medals

	1		2	
3		4		5
6		7		8
9		10		11

1. Medal of Honor
2. Distinguished Service Cross
3. Distinguished Service Medal
4. Silver Star
5. Legion of Merit
6. Distinguished Flying Cross

7. Soldier's Medal
8. Bronze Star Medal
9. Purple Heart
10. Meritorious Service Medal
11. Air Medal

These include oak leaf clusters, numerals, V device, clasps, service stars and arrowheads as well as service ribbons, miniature medals and lapel buttons.

Unauthorized Wearing of Decorations and Badges
Federal law prescribes stiff penalties for the unauthorized wearing of U.S. decorations, badges, appurtenances, and unit awards:

> Whoever knowingly wears . . . any decoration or medal authorized by Congress for the Armed Forces of the United States or any of the service medals or badges awarded to the members of such forces, or the ribbon, button, or rosette of any such badge, decoration or medal, or any colorable imitation thereof, except when authorized under regulations made pursuant to law, shall be fined not more than $250 or imprisoned not more than six months, or both.
>
> —62 Stat. 732, 25 June 1948, as amended 18 U.S.C. 704

The U.S. Code (18 U.S.C. 703) further prescribes:

> Whoever, within the jurisdiction of the United States, with intent to deceive or mislead, wears any naval, military, police, or other official uniform, decoration, or regalia of any foreign state, nation, or government with which the United States is at peace, or anything so nearly resembling the same as to be calculated to deceive, shall be fined not more than $250 or imprisoned not more than six months or both.

17

Military Justice

A fact of military life is that, despite the availability of information on the subject and the effort of commanders to keep their soldiers informed, many individuals simply do not know very much about the military justice system. Specific provisions pertaining to administration of the military justice system are in the *Manual for Courts-Martial* and AR 27-10, *Military Justice.*

NONJUDICIAL PUNISHMENT
Article 15 of the Uniform Code of Military Justice (UCMJ) provides commanding officers the authority and procedures to impose disciplinary punishments for minor offenses without a court-martial. Punishment without court-martial is called "nonjudicial" punishment. Such punishments may be in addition to or in lieu of admonition or reprimand. Unless the accused is embarked on a ship, Article 15 punishment may not be imposed if the accused demands trial by court-martial.

Punishments authorized under Article 15 are less severe than court-martial punishments. Unlike a special or general court-martial, Article 15 is not considered a federal conviction for a criminal offense. Article 15 is intended to provide a swift, efficient, and relatively easy method for punishing those committing minor offenses, for maintaining discipline, and for deterring future offenses. Under Article 15, commanders have wide latitude in punishments that may be imposed, ranging from oral reprimand to reduction in pay grades, fines, restriction, extra duty, or a combination of these.

It is a mistake to disregard the effect of an Article 15 on a soldier's career, although those received in the junior enlisted grades can generally be overcome. The original copy of DA Form 2617, *Record of Proceedings under Article 15, UCMJ,* may be filed either in the official military personnel file performance portion of the permanent record or in the restricted portion. Records of Article 15 punishments can be used in a wide variety of personnel decisions and can lead to an involuntary administrative discharge.

Under Article 15 proceedings, legal rules of evidence do not apply, and providing defense counsel at the hearing is not mandatory. Nevertheless, the accused does have protection against arbitrary use of Article 15. In addition to the right to demand trial in lieu of Article 15 punishment, the accused has the right to consult with counsel to decide whether to accept the punishment; if the accused accepts Article 15 and considers the punishment too harsh, he or she may appeal it. Other rights include the right to remain silent, to fully present his or her case in the presence of the imposing commander, to call witnesses, to present evidence, to be accompanied by a spokesperson, to request an open hearing, and to examine available evidence.

In order to find the soldier guilty, the commander must be convinced beyond a reasonable doubt that the soldier committed the offense. The maximum punishment depends on the rank of the commander imposing punishment and the rank of the soldier being punished.

Purposes of Nonjudicial Punishment
Nonjudicial punishment may be imposed in appropriate cases for the following purposes:
- To correct, educate, and reform offenders who have shown that they cannot benefit by less stringent measures.
- To preserve, in appropriate cases, an offender's record of service from unnecessary stigmatization by record of court-martial conviction.
- To further military efficiency by disposing of minor offenses in a manner requiring less time and personnel than trial by court-martial.

Generally, the term *minor offenses* includes misconduct not involving any greater degree of criminality than is involved in the average offense tried by summary court-martial.

Nonpunitive measures usually deal with misconduct resulting from simple neglect, forgetfulness, laziness, inattention to instructions, sloppy habits, immaturity, difficulty in adjusting to disciplined military life, and similar deficiencies. These measures are primarily tools for teaching proper standards of conduct and performance and do not constitute punishment. Included are denial of pass or other privileges, counseling, administrative reduction in grade, extra training, bar to reenlistment, and MOS reclassification. Certain commanders have the authority, apart from any under Article 15, to reduce enlisted persons administratively for inefficiency or other reasons. *Nonpunitive measures and nonjudicial punishment should not be confused.*

A written admonition or reprimand should contain a statement indicating that it has been imposed merely as an administrative measure and not as punishment under Article 15. Conversely, admonitions and reprimands that are imposed as punishment under Article 15 should be clearly stated to have been imposed as punishment under that article.

MAXIMUM PUNISHMENTS
FOR ENLISTED MEMBERS UNDER ARTICLE 15*

*Note: The maximum punishment imposable by any commander under summarized proceedings cannot exceed extra duty for 14 days, restriction for 14 days, oral reprimand, or any combination thereof.

Punishment	Imposed by Company Grade Officers	Imposed by Field Grade or General Officers
Admonition/Reprimand	Yes	Yes
and		
Extra Duties[1]	14 days	45 days
and		
Restriction	14 days	60 days
or		
Correctional Custody[2]		
(PV1, PV2, PFC)	7 days	30 days
or		
Restricted Diet Confinement		
(PV1, PV2, PFC attached		
or embarked on a vessel)	3 days	3 days
and		
Reduction		
(PV1, PV2, PFC, SPC, CPL)	One grade	One grade or more
(SGT, SSG)		One grade in peacetime[3]
and		
Forfeiture[4]	7 days' pay	Half of 1 month's pay for 2 months

---

[1]Combinations of extra duties and restriction cannot exceed the maximum allowed for extra duty.

[2]Subject to limitations imposed by superior authority and presence of adequate facilities. If punishment includes reduction to private first class or below, reduction must be unsuspended.

[3]Only if imposed by a field grade commander of a unit authorized to have a commander who is a lieutenant colonel or higher.

[4]Amount of forfeiture is computed at the reduced grade, even if suspended, if reduction is part of punishment.

Commanding officers also have the authority to impose restraints or restrictions on a soldier for administrative purposes, such as to ensure the soldier's presence within the command. This authority exists apart from the authority to impose restriction as nonjudicial punishment. These nonpunitive measures may also include, subject to any applicable regulation, administrative withholding of privileges.

Extra training or instruction is one of the most effective nonpunitive measures available to a commander. It is used when a soldier's duty performance has been substandard or deficient. For example, a soldier who fails to maintain proper attire may be required to attend classes on the wearing of the uniform and stand inspection until the deficiency is corrected.

Summarized Proceedings

Summarized proceedings under Article 15 may be used if, after a preliminary inquiry, a commander determines that the punishment for an offense should not exceed extra duty or restriction for 14 days; oral reprimand or admonition; or any combination of these punishments. The record of these proceedings is made on DA Form 2627-1. Generally, summarized proceedings are conducted like proceedings for more serious cases prosecuted under nonjudicial punishment, except that the individual normally is allowed 24 hours to decide whether to demand trial by court-martial and to gather matters in defense, extenuation, and/or mitigation. Because of the limited nature of the punishments imposed under these proceedings, the soldier has no right to consult with legally qualified counsel nor the right to a spokesperson.

Nature of Punishments

Nonjudicial punishments include the following actions:

Admonition and Reprimand. An admonition or reprimand may be imposed in lieu of or combined with Article 15 punishments.

Restriction. The severity of this type of restraint is dependent upon its duration and geographical limits specified when the punishment is imposed. A soldier undergoing restriction may be required to report to a designated place at specified times if it is considered reasonably necessary to ensure that the punishment is being properly executed.

Extra Duties. This involves the performance of duties in addition to those normally assigned to the person undergoing the punishment. Extra duties may include fatigue duties. In general, extra duties that would demean his or her position as a noncommissioned officer may not be assigned a corporal or above.

Reduction in Grade. This form involves the following considerations:
* Promotion authority. The grade from which a soldier is reduced must be within the promotion authority of the imposing commander or the officer to whom authority to punish under Article 15 has been delegated.

- Lateral appointments or reductions of corporal to specialist are not authorized. An NCO may be reduced to a lower pay grade, provided the lower grade is authorized in his or her primary MOS.
- Date of rank. When a soldier is reduced in grade as a result of unsuspended reduction, the date of rank in the grade to which reduced is the date the punishment of reduction was imposed.
- Entitlement to pay. When a soldier is restored to a higher pay grade because of a suspension or when a reduction is mitigated to a forfeiture, entitlement to pay at the higher grade is effective on the date of the suspension or mitigation.
- Senior noncommissioned officers. Sergeants first class and above may not be reduced under the authority of Article 15.

Forfeiture of Pay. Pay refers to basic pay of the individual plus any foreign duty pay. Forfeitures imposed by a company-grade commander may not be applied for more than one month, while those imposed by a field-grade commander may not be applied for more than two months. The maximum forfeiture of pay to which a soldier is subject during a given month, because of one or more actions under Article 15, is one-half of his or her pay per month. Article 15 forfeitures cannot deprive a soldier of more than two-thirds of his or her pay per month.

Combination and Apportionment

No two or more punishments involving deprivation of liberty may be combined in the same nonjudicial punishment to run either consecutively or concurrently, but other punishments may be combined. Restriction and extra duty may be combined in any manner to run for a period not in excess of the maximum duration imposable for extra duty by the imposing commander.

Suspension, Mitigation, Remission, and Setting Aside

Suspension. The purpose of suspending punishment is to grant a deserving soldier a probational period during which the individual may show that he or she deserves a remission of the suspended portion of his or her nonjudicial punishment. If, because of further misconduct within this period, it is determined that remission of the suspended punishment is not warranted, the suspension may be vacated and the suspended portion of the punishment executed.

Mitigation. Often there are factors other than the facts and circumstances of the offense that show that the accused should receive a light punishment. Examples include lack of past criminal record, good duty performance, and family hardship.

Remission. Remission can cancel any portion of the unexecuted punishment. Remission is appropriate under the same circumstances as mitigation.

FORFEITURES OF PAY AUTHORIZED UNDER ARTICLE 15

Maximum monthly authorized forfeitures of pay under Article 15, UCMJ, may be computed using the applicable formula below:

1. Upon enlisted persons:

$$\frac{(\text{monthly basic pay}^{1,2} + \text{foreign pay}^{1,3})}{2} = \begin{array}{l}\text{maximum forfeiture per month}\\\text{if imposed by major or above}\end{array}$$

$$\frac{(\text{monthly basic pay}^{1,2} + \text{foreign pay}^{1,3}) \times 7}{30} = \begin{array}{l}\text{maximum forfeiture if imposed}\\\text{by captain or below}\end{array}$$

2. Upon commissioned and warrant officers when imposed by an officer with general court-martial jurisdiction or by a general officer in command:

$$\frac{(\text{monthly basic pay}^{2})}{2} = \begin{array}{l}\text{maximum authorized forfeiture}\\\text{per month}\end{array}$$

---

[1] Amount of forfeiture is computed at the reduced grade, even if suspended, if reduction is part of the punishment imposed.
[2] At the time punishment is imposed.
[3] If applicable.

Setting Aside and Restoration. Under this action, the punishment or any part or amount thereof, whether executed or unexecuted, is set aside, and any property, privileges, or rights affected by the portion of the punishment set aside are restored. The basis for this action is ordinarily a determination that, under all the circumstances of the case, the punishment has resulted in a clear injustice.

Notification and Explanation of Rights

The imposing commander must ensure that the soldier is notified of the intention to dispose of the matter under Article 15. The imposing commander may delegate notification authority to another officer, warrant officer, or NCO (sergeant first class and above), providing that person outranks the person being notified. If an NCO is selected, that person should normally be the unit first sergeant or another NCO who is the senior enlisted person in the command in which the accused is serving.

The soldier must be given a "reasonable time" to consult with counsel, including time off from duty, if necessary, to decide whether to demand trial. The amount of time granted is normally 48 hours.

Before deciding to demand trial, the accused is not entitled to be informed of the type or amount of punishment he or she will receive if nonjudicial punishment is imposed. The imposing commander will inform the soldier of the maximum punishment allowable under Article 15 and the maximum allowable for the offense if the case proceeds to a trial by court-martial and conviction for the offense.

Right to Demand Trial

The demand for trial may be made at any time before imposition of punishment. The soldier will be told that if trial is demanded, it could be by summary, special, or general court-martial. The soldier will also be told that he or she may object to trial by summary court-martial and that at a special or general court-martial he or she would be entitled to be represented by qualified military counsel or by civilian counsel obtained at the soldier's expense.

Appeals

Only one appeal is permitted under Article 15 proceedings. An appeal not made within a "reasonable time" may be rejected as untimely by the superior authority. The definition of what constitutes a "reasonable time" varies according to the situation. Generally, an appeal, including all documentary matters, submitted more than five calendar days (including weekends and holidays) after punishment is imposed will be presumed to be untimely. If, at the time of imposition of punishment, the soldier indicates a desire not to appeal, the superior authority may reject a subsequent election to appeal, even if it is made within the five-day period.

Appeals are made on DA Form 2627 or DA Form 2627-1 and forwarded through the imposing commander or successor-in-command to the superior authority. The superior must act on the appeal unless otherwise directed by competent authority. A soldier is not required to state the reasons for the appeal, but he or she may present evidence or arguments proving innocence or why the sentence should be mitigated or suspended. Unless an appeal is voluntarily withdrawn, it must be forwarded to the appropriate superior authority. A timely appeal does not terminate because a soldier is discharged from the service but must be processed to completion.

Announcement of Punishment

The punishment may be announced at the next unit formation after punishment is imposed or, if appealed, after the decision. It also may be posted on the unit bulletin board. The purpose of announcing the results is to avert the perception of unfairness of punishment and to deter similar misconduct by others.

Records of Punishment
DA Forms 2627 are prepared in an original and five copies. What happens to those copies, especially the original, is of the utmost importance to soldiers who receive punishment under nonjudicial proceedings.

Original. For enlisted soldiers, the original copy is forwarded to the U.S. Army Enlisted Records and Evaluation Center, Indianapolis, Indiana. The decision on where in the punished soldier's Official Military Personnel File (OMPF) this copy will be placed is made by the imposing commander at the time punishment is imposed and is final. The imposing commander will decide whether it is to be filed in the performance fiche or the restricted fiche of the individual's OMPF.

Other Copies. For those Articles 15 filed in the performance fiche of the OMPF, copy one is placed in the permanent section of the Military Personnel Records Jacket (MPRJ) unless the original is transferred from the performance to the restricted fiche, at which time it is destroyed. Otherwise, it is kept in the unit personnel files and destroyed two years from the date of punishment or on the soldier's transfer, whichever occurs first. Copies two through four are used variously as prescribed by AR 27-10, depending on whether forfeiture of pay is involved and whether the punished soldier appeals. Copy five is given to the individual.

COURTS-MARTIAL

Courts-martial are the agencies through which Army magistrates try personnel accused of violations of the punitive articles of the UCMJ. These are Articles 77 through 134 of the UCMJ and are designed to provide punishment of three broad groups of crimes and offenses:

- Crimes common to both the military and civilian law, such as murder, rape, sodomy, arson, burglary, larceny, and fraud against the United States.
- Crimes and offenses peculiar to the military services, such as desertion, disobedience, misbehavior before the enemy, and sleeping on post.
- General offenses that are prosecuted under Article 134, the General Article, which covers "all disorders and neglects to the prejudice of good order and discipline in the armed forces, all conduct of a nature to bring discredit upon the armed forces, and crimes and offenses not capital."

During peacetime, courts-martial may impose sentences ranging from simple forfeiture of pay to confinement and forfeiture of all pay and allowances to death. (See appendix 12 of *Manual for Courts-Martial* for the Maximum Punishment Chart.) During time of war, a general court-martial may impose any penalty authorized by law, including death.

Who May Prefer Charges

Charges are initiated by anyone bringing to the attention of the military authorities information concerning an offense suspected to have been committed by a
person subject to the UCMJ. This information may be received from anyone,
whether subject to the UCMJ or not.

Action by Immediate Commander

Upon receipt of information that an offense has been committed, the commander exercising immediate jurisdiction over the accused under Article 15, UCMJ,
must make a preliminary inquiry into the charges in order to permit an intelligent disposition of them.

Based on the outcome of the preliminary inquiry, a commander may decide
that all or some of the charges do not warrant further action, and those charges
may be dismissed. The commander may also decide, based on the preliminary
investigation, that the offenses committed warrant punishment under Article 15,
UCMJ, or he or she may refer more serious charges to higher authority for trial
by court-martial.

Effective Dates of Sentences

Whenever a sentence includes a forfeiture of pay or allowances in addition to
confinement, the forfeiture applies to pay or allowances becoming due on or
after the date the sentence is approved by the convening authority.

Confinement included in a sentence begins to run from the date of sentenc-
ing by the court-martial. Reductions are effective on the date the sentence is
approved. All other sentences of courts-martial are effective on the date they are
ordered executed.

REFERENCES

AR 27-10, *Military Justice,* 1989.
FM 1-04.1 [27-1], *Legal Guide for Commanders,* 1987.
FM 1-04.14 [27-14], *Legal Guide for Soldiers,* 1986.
Manual for Courts-Martial, 1984.
Servicemember's Legal Guide, 4th Edition, by Lt. Col. Jonathan P. Tomes,
U.S. Army, Ret. (Mechanicsburg, Pa.: Stackpole Books, 2001).

18

Personal Affairs

Soldiers often allow their personal needs to pile up under more pressing professional matters. Doing so can be costly to you, and especially to your loved ones.

Consider, for example, that neglecting to get life insurance and a last will and testament can cause surviving family members to be left out in the cold, financially and otherwise. Consider, too, that medical bills for unforeseen illnesses and injuries can devastate your financial future. What can you do about portions of major bills disallowed by Tricare or Delta Dental? Do you really understand your family's medical and dental benefits, and how and under what circumstances Tricare supplements are strongly recommended?

What happens, for example, when you go to work in a new job in Europe or elsewhere overseas and your spouse and children remain behind in local quarters? Do your family members have what they need to achieve a decent quality of life and standard of living in their new environment? Where can they turn for help when problems arise?

What if, for some reason beyond your control and ability to rectify, your end-of-month Leave and Earnings Statement reads "No Pay Due" and you must pay rent and meet other living expenses? Who can help fully or partially defray necessary payments to landlords, banks, and other creditors until your pay is sorted out?

Are your personal affairs in order? To what extent? Do you keep records? Where are they? Who else knows where your vital records are kept? Does your spouse or significant other know important account numbers and first and supplemental points of contact? You must make the effort to consider and take charge of your personal affairs. It is your responsibility to plan for your personal needs and those of your family. Remember that deployability includes personal readiness.

Keep your chain of command informed on personal issues. Your superiors don't want to involve themselves in your life; however, it is much easier for your leaders to assist you prior to the explosion, rather than trying to pick up the pieces afterward. Remember, helping you with your problems is one of the things they get paid to do. If they can't help, they will surely be able to point you in the right direction.

AGENCIES AND PEOPLE THAT CAN HELP

Army Community Services

Army Community Services (ACS) is an official Department of the Army organization established to provide information, aid, guidance, and referral services to military personnel and their families. ACS activities are monitored by the Army Adjutant General.

The ACS provides a wide variety of services, including the following:
- Referrals for handicapped dependents.
- Family counseling services.
- Financial planning services.
- Lending services to provide bedding, linens, and housewares to military families until they can get settled at a new post.
- Volunteer services providing transportation to dependents when required.
- Child abuse information and referral.
- An emergency food locker from which needy families may draw supplies.

Army Emergency Relief

Army Emergency Relief (AER) operates as a part of the Army Community Services. AER provides badly needed financial assistance to soldiers and their dependents. A local AER officer can authorize interest-free cash loans. Large loans must be approved by Headquarters, AER.

AER loans may be approved for the following purposes:
- Defray living expenses because of nonreceipt of military pay.
- Provide money to help defray emergency travel expenses.
- Help pay rents, security deposits, and utilities.
- Help pay essential privately owned vehicle (POV) expenses.
- Pay funeral expenses above and beyond those allowed by the government.
- Pay grants to the widows and orphans of deceased soldiers, in some cases.
- Provide cash to buy food when it is not available from the ACS food locker.
- Provide money to replace lost funds.

Soldiers must apply for AER loans through their unit commanders by filling out DA Form 1103, *Application for AER Financial Assistance.* The soldier must document his or her expenses or financial situation, and an allotment must be executed before the AER will disburse any money.

Each year, AER disburses millions of dollars to help soldiers and their families. The only source for these funds is cash donations by Army members solicited annually during Armywide fund-raising drives.

Guide for Obtaining Information and Assistance

	YOUR CHAIN OF COMMAND	PERSONNEL NCO OR OFFICER	REENLISTMENT NCO	JUDGE ADVOCATE	INSPECTOR GENERAL	FINANCE OFFICER	CHAPLAIN	HOUSING OFFICER	TRANSPORTATION OFFICER	AMERICAN RED CROSS	ARMY COMMUNITY SERVICES	ARMY EMERGENCY RELIEF	EDUCATION OFFICER/ADVISOR
Appeals	1	2		2	2		2						
Assignment, reassignment, MOS, and proficiency pay	1	1				2							
Reenlistment	1		1										
Personnel matters: promotion, reduction, discharge, retirement / Veterans' benefits	1	1	2	2									
Complaints (requests for assistance)	1	2	2	2	2	2	2	2	2	2	2	2	
Debts and civilian creditors	1	1		2		2	2				2		
Dependents' schools	1	1											2
Family and religious affairs	1	2					1			2	2		
Travel of dependents, shipment of POV and household goods	1	2				2			1		2		
Medical service (individual and dependents)	1	1											
Pay, allowances, and incentive pay	1	2				1							
Leaves and passes	1	2											
Insurance, all types (SGLI and commercial)	1	1				2							
Legal assistance, including U.S. and foreign law, wills, and powers of attorney	1			1									
Military education	1	2	2										
Nonmilitary education	1	2											2
PX, commissary, QM sales store	1				2								
Government quarters, off-post housing	1	2						1					
Registration/operation of privately owned vehicle (POV), registration of firearms	1												
Entry into U.S., passport, visa, naturalization, immigration, birth certificate (children born in foreign country)	1	2		1							2		
Home conditions and emergency leave	1	2					2			2	2	2	
Emergency financial assistance	1	2					1			2	2	2	
Postal service	1												
Drug and alcohol rehabilitation program	1						2				1		

1. Primary source
2. Other sources as appropriate

Army Family Action Plan

Today, more than half the active Army force is married. The Army now pays considerable attention to soldiers' families. The Army Family Action Plan (AFAP) is part of Army Community Services. It includes four major themes: relocation, medical, family support and role identity, and education and youth. The specific areas in which AFAP can help include:

- Army family team building.
- Community life programs.
- Employment assistance (spouse).
- Exceptional family member programs.
- English as a second language.
- Financial assistance.
- Family advocacy.
- Operation Ready—family support during deployment.
- New parent support.
- Community outreach.
- Relocation assistance.

Legal Assistance

A legal assistance officer can advise you on such matters as a will, power of attorney, divorce and separation actions, estates, tax problems, and other civil matters. The legal assistance officer can also provide you with a "legal checkup," which is designed to identify any potential legal problems you may have.

This officer is not normally permitted to represent you in civil court or to give you advice in matters of a criminal nature. Neither may he or she advise you about court-martial investigations or charges (a military counsel appointed by the judge advocate will assist you in such cases). If your problem requires the services of a civilian lawyer, the legal assistance officer can refer you, through cooperating bar associations, to civilian legal advisers or legal aid bureaus.

The *Serviceman's Legal Guide, 3rd Edition,* published by Stackpole Books, provides comprehensive information on what soldiers and their families need to know about the law.

Chaplains

Chaplains are available to help soldiers, family members, and civilians with any type of concern they may have, be it spiritual, work related, or otherwise. Chaplains can help in areas ranging from marriage and family counseling to stress management and suicide prevention. Soldiers seeking counseling don't necessarily have to be churchgoers to use the chaplains to help them through the rough times. Lastly, Army chaplain regulations state that any communications to a chaplain acting as a spiritual adviser must be kept in confidence and cannot be told to anyone else without permission.

LIFE INSURANCE

It is beyond the scope of this book to discuss all the things to look for when you are shopping for life insurance. What kind of policy to get and how much insurance you may need depends strictly on your individual or family situation. You are particularly insurable if you are still relatively young and you have school-age children who depend on you. Shop around. There are numerous good individual and group insurance plans available; there are some pretty bad ones available as well (and plenty of unscrupulous insurance agents willing to take your money from you).

While you are on active duty, you have Servicemen's Group Life Insurance (SGLI), which offers coverages up to a maximum of $200,000, for very low premiums. The maximum you will pay per month is $18, and that entitles you to $200,000 worth of coverage. And when you leave the service, your SGLI is convertible to Veterans Group Life Insurance (VGLI).

MEDICAL INSURANCE—TRICARE

Army healthcare beneficiaries—you and your family—should take a long-term view toward medical and dental health. Eat foods that contribute to a longer life. Exercise regularly for the same reason. Rest properly. Brush and floss after meals. Get periodic physical and dental examinations. Follow the advice of doctors, dentists, and other Army health and medical care providers. Stay healthy to limit the effects of illness or disease. Beware of unsafe acts and unsafe conditions to avoid injury. When a person is ill or injured, nothing matters more than recovery.

When an active-duty soldier becomes sick or gets hurt, the Army direct-care medical system provides care at no cost. In fact, AR 40-3, *Medical, Dental and Veterinary Care,* prohibits active-duty soldiers, including active-duty reserve component soldiers, from seeking and obtaining medical and dental care from civilian sources without prior authorization from the local Army medical treatment facility commander. So, while soldiers are on active duty, they do not need medical and dental insurance. But Army family members do—and they have it provided by the Civilian Health and Medical Program of the Uniformed Services (CHAMPUS), or Tricare, and the Dependent Dental Plan, which is offered through Tricare.

Tricare

Tricare is a healthcare program for members of the uniformed services and their families, and survivors and retired members and their families. Tricare brings together the healthcare resources of each of the military services and supplements them with networks of civilian healthcare professionals to provide better access and high-quality service while maintaining the capability to support military operations. There are 12 Tricare regions in the United States, each with an assigned lead agent who is responsible for the military health services system in that region.

ACTIVE-DUTY FAMILY MEMBERS

	Tricare Prime E-1 through E-4	Tricare Prime E-5 and above	Tricare Extra	Tricare Standard
Annual Deductible	None	None	$150 individual/ $300 family for E-5 and above; $50/$100 for E-4 and below	$150 individual/ $300 family for E-5 and above; $50/$100 for E-4 and below
Civilian Outpatient Visit	None	None	20% of negotiated fee	20% of allowable charge
Civilian Inpatient Admission	None	None	Greater of $25 or $11.90/day	Greater of $25 or $11.90/day
Civilian Inpatient Mental Health	None	None	$20/day	$20/day

Under Tricare, family members have two basic choices for seeking medical care: (1) the Enrolled Choice (Tricare Prime) and (2) the Non-Enrolled Choice (Tricare Extra/Tricare Standard). Active-duty members must enroll in Tricare Prime and thus are not eligible for the Non-Enrolled Choice.

Choice 1. Enrolled Choice (Tricare Prime) provides the most comprehensive healthcare benefits to the patient at the lowest cost. Tricare Prime guarantees priority access to care at a military treatment facility or, where available, an off-post, civilian, contracted doctor's office.

All active-duty military members must enroll in this choice and must use military facilities. Family members must also enroll to use this option. Those who select the Enrolled Choice will be assigned to a primary care manager (PCM). This is the healthcare provider you will see first for all your medical needs. If necessary, your PCM will refer you to specialty medical care, when needed. There are no enrollment fees for active-duty families in Tricare Prime.

Choice 2. The Non-Enrolled Choice (Tricare Extra/Tricare Standard) allows family members to seek medical care from any physician of their choice in the civilian community. The Non-Enrolled Choice is a more costly option than the Enrolled Choice. This choice incorporates two programs (Tricare Extra and Tricare Standard). Medical expenses are covered under these programs when family members are not enrolled in Tricare Prime. A single deductible covers the use of either program.

Active enrollment and preauthorization are not required for your family to use the Non-Enrolled Choice, but a nonavailability statement must be obtained for civilian inpatient care. See your local health benefits adviser for more information.

What Will Tricare Cost?
The chart on the previous page provides examples of cost shares for families using Tricare. Health benefits advisers at military treatment facilities or representatives at Tricare Service Centers can assist you and your family in obtaining the medical care and services you need.

If you have questions about your military healthcare benefits under Tricare, there are many places to get answers. A *Member Handbook* may be obtained by visiting or calling your local Tricare Service Center or by calling the health benefits adviser at your nearest military hospital or clinic. Each medical facility has a health benefits adviser, Managed Care Office, or Tricare Service Center. This should be your first contact for information. Additionally, listed below are telephone numbers for each region, where you can call and get information about Tricare and your healthcare benefits.

Region 1	Maine, New Hampshire, Vermont, Massachusetts, Connecticut, Rhode Island, Delaware, Maryland, New Jersey, New York, Pennsylvania, District of Columbia, northern Virginia, and northeast corner of West Virginia	**(888) 999-5195**
Region 2	North Carolina and most of Virginia	**(800) 931-9501**
Region 3	South Carolina, Georgia, and Florida excluding Panhandle	**(800) 444-5445**
Region 4	Florida Panhandle, Alabama, Mississippi, Tennessee, and eastern third of Louisiana	**(800) 444-5445**
Region 5	Michigan, Wisconsin, Illinois, Indiana, Ohio, Kentucky, and West Virginia excluding the northeast corner	**(800) 941-4501**
Region 6	Oklahoma, Arkansas, western two-thirds of Louisiana, Texas excluding the southwest corner	**(800) 406-2832**
Region 7	New Mexico, Arizona excluding Yuma, Nevada, and southwest corner of Texas including El Paso	**(888) 874-9378**

Region 8	Colorado, Utah, Wyoming, Montana, Idaho excluding northern Idaho, North Dakota, South Dakota, Nebraska, Kansas, Minnesota, Iowa, and Missouri	**(888) 874-9378**
Region 9	Southern California and Yuma, Arizona	**(800) 242-6788**
Region 10	Northern California	**(800) 242-6788**
Region 11	Washington, Oregon, and northern Idaho	**(800) 404-4506**
Europe	Europe, Africa, Middle East, Azores, Iceland	**(888) 777-8343**
Latin America	Panama, Canada, Central America, South America	**(888) 777-8343**
Pacific	Alaska, Hawaii	**(800) 242-6788**

TRICARE DENTAL PROGRAM (TDP)

Active duty soldiers receive all dental care, at no cost, from military dental treatment facilities and are, therefore, ineligible for the Tricare Dental Program. The TDP is a voluntary dental plan open to families of all active duty, selected reserve, and Individual Ready Reserve soldiers ordered to active duty for more than 30 consecutive days.

Sponsors must have at least 12 months remaining on their service commitments at the time of enrollment. After completing the initial 12-month enrollment period, they may continue in the TDP on a month-to-month basis.

Soldiers failing to pay premiums or disenrolling before completing the 12-month "lock-in" are responsible for payment of all remaining premiums. Unless disenrolling for a valid reason, soldiers are prohibited from reentering in the program for 12 months.

Soldiers may disenroll from the TDP before completion of the mandatory 12-month enrollment for the following reasons: when a sponsor or family member loses Defense Enrollment Eligibility Reporting System (DEERS) eligibility; when TDP enrolled members relocate outside the CONUS service area; or when an active duty member transfers with enrolled family members to a duty station where space-available dental care for the enrolled members is readily available at the local Uniformed Service dental treatment facility.

United Concordia Companies, Inc. administers and underwrites the TDP. For further information, call Tricare Dental Program, United Concordia Companies, Inc. (UCCI) at (800) 866-8499 (For enrollment information call (888) 622-2256. See also the UCCI Web site at *www.ucci.com.*

LONG TERM CARE

The Federal Long Term Care Insurance Program is an important new benefit for members of the Army family, including retirees and qualified relatives. It is insurance that helps pay for care to help you perform daily activities if you had an ongoing illness or disability. It also includes the kind of care you would need if you had a severe cognitive problem such as Alzheimer's disease. Care includes help with eating, bathing, dressing, transferring from a bed to a chair, toileting, continence, etc. This type of care isn't received in a hospital and isn't intended to cure you. Rather than acute care, it is chronic care that you might need for the rest of your life. It can be received in your own home or, at a nursing home or other long term care facility.

If you are younger than 40 and healthy when you retire you might find that the Federal Long Term Care Insurance Program is not the best deal, and that you can obtain comparable coverage at a lower monthly premium from one of the large companies that offer long term care insurance. Check the premiums calculator offered by the Office of Personnel Management on the Internet at *www.opm.gov/insure/ltc/index.htm#premiums* for more information. To qualify, you must answer more questions about your health and habits than regular military personnel.

FAMILY CARE PLAN

The wrong time for you, either as a dual military or single parent, to begin planning who will take care of your children is when you find yourself on a short notice deployment to somewhere. AR 600-20, *Army Command Policy,* stipulates that every single-parent soldier, dual-military parent, and single and dual-military pregnant soldier must develop a Family Care Plan. The plan, DA Form 5305, as a minimum includes proof that a guardian has agreed to care for dependent children under the age of 18. Powers of Attorney for medical care, guardianship, and the authorization to start or stop financial support should be in the packet, and the children should have military ID cards. Lastly, the regulation requires a letter of instruction to the guardian/escort. This letter should contain specific instructions needed for the guardian to ensure the care of the dependents.

Although not required for the packet, birth certificates, social security cards, shot records, other medical or insurance cards, medication dosages for the child if necessary, and lists of family member addresses and phone numbers in case of emergency should be kept in a central location (an accordion-style organizer or file cabinet special drawer is suitable) and labeled to make it easy for the guardian to find documents fast. You might also want to contact financial institutions, children's doctors, schools, and daycare providers prior to deployment, so there won't be questions when your guardian comes to sign your children out of school to take them to the doctor.

YOUR WILL

The importance of having a will cannot be overemphasized. You may not consider that you "own" very much, but not having a will could cause many legal complications after your death. If you were to die without a will—*intestate*—your estate would be distributed according to the descent and distribution laws of your state of legal residence or, in the case of real property located in another state, the laws of that state.

If you are married, both you and your spouse should have wills, even if each will makes the same distribution of property and assets. It is particularly important to have a will if you have minor children so that their interests can be protected through a guardianship of your choice in the event both you and your spouse die.

Once you have made your will, review it periodically to keep it up to date. As circumstances change, you may want to update it to be sure that it still expresses your desires about the distribution of your property and assets.

Keep your will in a safe place. The safest place to keep it (and other important papers) is in a safe-deposit box at your bank. It is not a bad idea to send a copy of your will together with a statement as to the location of the original to the principal beneficiary or the person named in the will as the executor.

PERSONAL AFFAIRS RECORDS

The simplest way to keep your survivors informed about arrangements you have made for them is to prepare a record of your personal affairs. As a minimum, be sure that they know the location of the following:

- Your birth certificate and those of all members of your immediate family.
- Your marriage certificate.
- Divorce papers or previous spouse's death certificate, if applicable.
- Your life insurance policies.

If you put the original of your will and other key documents in a safe-deposit box, be sure that your spouse or executor has access to it. If you die and no one has access to the box, a court order must be obtained to open it.

A personal affairs record is a necessity for the married soldier, because it serves as a vital source of information for his or her family.

A personal affairs record can be detailed, but make sure it includes at least the following:

- Insurance policy numbers and their amounts. Include automobile and homeowner's policies.
- Previous years' tax records.
- Copies of titles and bills of sale.
- Information on bank accounts.
- A list of all pay allotments.
- Information regarding any veterans' benefits to which you may be entitled.

If you are married, be sure that someone in your family knows how to pay your household bills, when they are due, and where to find them.

MILITARY RECORDS

Keep a file of all records about your military service. Keep copies of orders, discharge certificate, awards, citations, letters of appreciation and commendation, medical and dental records, Leave and Earnings Statements, and other information about your military history, even old NCOERs. Information is frequently needed throughout your active service career and afterward when you apply for certain benefits.

Emergency Data

Your DD Form 93, *Record of Emergency Data,* must be accurate and up-to-date at all times. This record tells your MILPO where your next of kin can be located immediately. It gives the name of the person you want to receive your pay if you are missing in action, as well as other information of benefit to your dependents.

POWER OF ATTORNEY

A power of attorney is a legal document by which you give another person the power to act as your agent, either for some particular purpose or for the transaction of your business in general.

In the wrong hands, a power of attorney can ruin you because the agent who holds such a power has, within the limits granted by it, full authority to deal with your property without consulting you. Grant it only to someone you can trust, and only when you must.

You may never need a power of attorney, or if you do need one, it may be required only to perform certain acts and no others—a limited or special power of attorney. Always consult a legal assistance officer or a lawyer before assigning a power of attorney, and cancel it as soon as it is no longer required.

BANK ACCOUNTS

If you are married, you and your spouse should decide who manages the accounts. Make them joint accounts so that if anything happens to you, your family will have ready access to funds.

Current regulations require soldiers to have guaranteed direct deposit to a financial institution. With a guaranteed direct deposit from the U.S. Army Finance Center, you do not have to bother with anything but picking up your Leave and Earnings Statement on payday.

HOUSING

Military families often must rent local housing while waiting for government quarters to become available. If you find yourself in that situation, you might want to consider renting an apartment on a month-by-month basis. Should you sign a lease for a specified period of time and then have to break it because a set of quarters unexpectedly becomes available, you have to forfeit your deposit (usually an amount equal to a month's rent).

Renting an apartment gives single soldiers a degree of independence and privacy not available in the barracks, and for this reason, many soldiers want to move off post.

Whether a single soldier can move off post depends on the following:

- Your post commander's policy. It is also up to the commanding officer of your unit. Some commanders are liberal in granting this privilege; it depends on your unit's mission. Commanders of headquarters units can be more liberal than those of tactical or combat support units.
- The amount and quality of troop housing available. Some small, specialized units have trouble finding adequate troop housing, especially at overcrowded installations in metropolitan areas. Where sufficient troop housing is available, however, commanders normally fill the billets up first before allowing lower-ranking single personnel to move off post.
- Nonabuse of the privilege. Your commander will revoke permission to live off post as soon as you start coming to work late, running up debts, or causing disturbances among the local population.

Be sure that you can afford to live off post. Your military pay combined with your housing and substance allowances may be enough, depending on the geographical area, but just enough and no more. If supporting yourself in an apartment leaves you flat broke at the end of the month, you are better off living in the barracks.

Some soldiers find it a good idea to team up with two or three friends and rent a place by splitting all the costs. This is an excellent idea if your companions can be trusted to pay their share, take care of the communal areas, and respect your privacy and personal property.

PERSONAL PROPERTY

Joint ownership of property can have certain advantages in establishing an automatic and known passage of ownership upon the death of one owner and can also have certain disadvantages. Inquire into federal and state laws regarding ownership of family property, and take actions that put your estate in the most favorable ownership positions.

In the event of your death, your immediate personal effects will be forwarded at government expense to the person entitled to their custody. This does not give the recipient legal title to them, but they should be retained for disposition under the law.

If you own real estate in your name and it is not paid for, show on your personal affairs record whether there is a mortgage or a deed of trust against it, along with the name of the person or organization to whom you are indebted. Also include information about property taxes and insurance.

Transfer of automobile ownership is sometimes complicated because of varying state laws. Remember that joint titling may make you or your spouse subject to personal property taxes. Active-duty personnel are generally exempt from payment of personal property taxes, so adding your spouse's name to an automobile title can cost you a lot of money.

INCOME TAXES

Military pay in general is subject to income tax. You do not pay tax on subsistence, quarters, and uniform allowances. Dislocation allowance, special duty pay, and hardship pay are, however, taxable.

Any nonmilitary earnings, including the pay received while employed during off-duty hours and the income of any of your dependents, are taxable. Military pay is excluded from federal income tax for service in any area that the President of the United States designates by executive order to be a combat zone.

The Soldiers' and Sailors' Civil Relief Act provides that a state in which a soldier is stationed but that is not the servicemember's legal residence cannot tax service pay. Legal residence is established at enlistment or thereafter when a soldier executes DD Form 2058, *State of Legal Residence Certificate.*

The following states do not withhold income tax from the pay of military personnel: Alaska, Florida, Nevada, New Hampshire, South Dakota, Tennessee, Texas, Washington, and Wyoming. Soldiers claiming legal residence in foreign countries or U.S. territories are also exempt from paying state income taxes. Appendix K, "State Tax Withholding," to AR 37-104-3 contains specific information relative to each state for which withholding tax applies.

Appendix 1

Chain of Command

It is to your benefit to know your chain of command. Listed here are the personnel normally found in the formal chain of command. Check with your first sergeant to fill in the names. The number of personnel and the terminology for the positions within the chain vary in some Army units.

CHAIN OF COMMAND

Commander in Chief	President of the United States
Secretary of Defense	_____
Secretary of the Army	_____
Chairman of the Joint Chiefs of Staff	_____
Chief of Staff, Army	_____
MACOM Commander	_____
Corps Commander	_____
Post/Division/Command Commander	_____
Brigade/Group Commander	_____
Battalion Commander	_____
Company Commander	_____
Platoon Leader	_____
Squad Leader	_____

The NCO support channel complements and parallels the chain of command and provides a structure for the day-to-day activities of the Army.

NCO SUPPORT CHANNEL

Sergeant Major of the Army   _____

MACOM Command Sergeant Major   _____

Corps Command Sergeant Major   _____

Post/Division/Command Command
Sergeant Major   _____

Brigade/Group Command Sergeant Major   _____

Battalion Command Sergeant Major   _____

First Sergeant   _____

Platoon Sergeant   _____

Squad Leader   _____

Appendix 2

Acronyms

AAFES	Army and Air Force Exchange Service
AAR	after action report
ABCMR	Army Board for the Correction of Military Records
ACAP	Army Career and Alumni Program
ACE	American Council on Education
ACES	Army Continuing Education System
ACS	Army Community Services
ACTPEP	American College Testing Proficiency Examination Program
ADA	air defense artillery
ADAPCP	Alcohol and Drug Abuse Prevention and Control Program
AEA	assignment eligibility and availability
AEC	Army Education Center
AEN	Army Employment Network
AER	Army Emergency Relief
AFAP	Army Family Action Plan
AFQT	Armed Forces Qualification Test
AG	Adjutant General
AI	assignment instruction
AIDS	acquired immunodeficiency syndrome
AIPD	Army Institute for Professional Development
AIT	advanced individual training
ALC	Army Learning Center
AMD	Army Medical Department
AMOS	additional military occupational specialty
ANCOC	Advanced Noncommissioned Officer Course
AP/CPB	Annenberg Project and Center for Public Broadcasting
APFT	Army Physical Fitness Test
APOD	aerial port of debarkation
APOE	aerial port of embarkation
AR	Army Regulation
ARC	American Red Cross
ARTEP	Army Training And Evaluation Program

ASK	Assignment satisfaction key
ASEP	Advanced Skills Education Program
ASI	additional skill identifier
ATACMS	Army Tactical Missile System
AUSA	Association of the U.S. Army
AUTODIN	Automated Digital Network
AWOL	absent without leave
BAH	basic allowance for housing
BAQ	basic allowance for quarters
BASD	basic active service date
BCT	basic combat training
BDFS	bachelor's degree for soldiers
BDU	battle dress uniform
BEQ	bachelor's enlisted quarters
BESD	basic enlisted service date
BNCOC	Basic Noncommissioned Officer Course
BSEP	Basic Skills Education Program
BT	basic training
CAP III	Centralized Assignment Procedure III System
CE	Commander's Evaluation
CFC	Combined Federal Campaign
CFP	contingency force pool
CHAMPUS	Civilian Health and Medical Program of the Uniformed Services
CID(C)	Criminal Investigation Division (Command)
CLEP	College Level Examination Program
CMF	career management field
COHORT	Cohesion, Operational Readiness, and Training
COLA	cost-of-living allowance
CONAP	Continental United States Area of Preference
CONUS	continental United States
CPMOS	career progression military occupational specialty
CQ	charge of quarters
CS	combat support
CSM	command sergeant major
CSS	combat service support
CTT	Common Task Training
CVC	combat vehicle crewman
DA	Department of the Army
DANTES	Defense Activity for Nontraditional Education Support
DBDU	desert battle dress uniform
DEERS	Defense Enrollment Eligibility Reporting System
DEROS	date of estimated return from overseas

DMOS	duty military occupational specialty
DOD	Department of Defense
DODDS	Department of Defense Dependents Schools
DOE	Department of Education
DOR	date of rank
DRF	Deployment Ready Force
DROS	date returned from overseas
DSST	Defense Subject Standardized Tests
DUI	distinctive unit insignia
DVA	Department of Veterans Affairs
EAD	entry on active duty
EANGUS	Enlisted Association of the National Guard of the United States
EDAS	Enlisted Distribution and Assignment System
EHWBDU	enhanced hot weather battle dress uniform
EMF	enlisted master file
EML	environmental and morale leave
ENTNAC	Entrance National Agency Check
EO	equal opportunity
EOD	explosive ordnance disposal
EPMD	Enlisted Personnel Management Directorate
EPMS	Enlisted Personnel Management System
EPW	enemy prisoner of war
ETS	expiration of term of service; enlisted training system
FAO	Finance and Accounting Office
FAST	Functional Academic Skills Training
FIST	fire support team
FM	field manual
FORSCOM	U.S. Army Forces Command
FSA	family separation allowance
FTX	field training exercise
GCM	general court-martial
GCMCA	General Court-Martial Convening Authority
GED	General Educational Development
GRE	Graduate Record Examination
HAAP	Homebase and Advance Assignment Program
HALO	high-altitude, low-opening (parachute jumps)
HBA	health benefits adviser
HIV	human immunodeficiency virus
HMMWV	high-mobility multipurposed wheeled vehicle
HOR	home of record
HQDA	Headquarters, Department of the Army
HSCP	High School Completion Program

IBCT	Interim Brigade Combat Team
IET	Initial Entry Training
IFV	infantry fighting vehicle
IG	Inspector General
IHA	interim housing allowance
ISR	Individual Soldier's Report
ITEP	Individual Training Program
ITT	intertheater transfer
IVRS	Interactive Voice Response Telephone System
JAC	Job Assistance Center
JAG	Judge Advocate General
JSEP	Job Skills Education Program
JTR	Joint Travel Regulations
JUMPS	Joint Uniform Military Pay Schedule
KFOR	Kosovo Force
LES	Leave and Earnings Statement
LOD	line of duty
MAC	Military Airlift Command
MACP	Married Army Couples Program
MACOM	Major Army Command
MEDDAC	Medical Department Activity
METL	Mission Essential Task List
MFT	master fitness trainer
MILES	Multiple Integrated Laser Identification System
MILPO	Military Personnel Office
MLRS	Multiple Launched Rocket System
MOOTW	military operations other than war
MOS	military occupational specialty
MPRJ	military personnel records jacket
MP	military police
MSC	Medical Service Corps
MTOE	Modified Table of Organization and Equipment
NAC	National Agency Check
NATO	North Atlantic Treaty Organization
NBC	nuclear, biological, and chemical
NCOA	Noncommissioned Officer Academy; Noncommissioned Officers Association
NCOER	Noncommissioned Officer Evaluation Report
NCOES	Noncommissioned Officer Education System
NMS	New Manning System
OCONUS	outside continental United States
OCS	Officer Candidate School
ODCSPER	Office of the Deputy Chief of Staff for Personnel
OJE	on-the-job experience

OJT	on-the-job training
OMPF	Official Military Personnel File
OP	operating procedures
OSUT	One-Station Unit Training
PAC	Personnel Administration Center
PCS	permanent change of station
PERSCOM	Total Army Personnel Command
PLDC	Primary Leadership Development Course
PMCS	preventive maintenance checks and services
PMOS	primary military occupational specialty
POR	preparation of replacements for overseas movement
POV	privately owned vehicle
PPG	Priority Placement Group
PSC	Personnel Service Center
PSNCO	personnel staff noncommissioned officer
PT	physical training
PX	post exchange
QM	Quartermaster
RE Code	Reenlistment Code
ROTC	Reserve Officers' Training Corps
R&R	rest and recuperation
SAT	Scholastic Achievement Test
SB	special branches
SD	special duty
SDNCO	staff duty noncommissioned officer
SF	Special Forces
SFC	sergeant first class
SFOR	Stabilization Force
SGLI	Servicemen's Group Life Insurance
SIDPERS	Standard Installation/Division Personnel Reporting System
SL	skill level
SMOS	secondary military occupational specialty
SOC	Servicemembers Opportunity Colleges
SOCAD	Servicemembers Opportunity Colleges Army Degree
SOFA	status of forces agreement
SOP	standard operating procedures
SQI	special qualification identifier
SRB	selective reenlistment bonus
SSB	special separation bonus
SSN	Social Security Number
TA	tuition assistance
TAO	tuition assistance officer
TAPDB	Total Army Personnel Database
TC	Transportation Corps

TCO	test control officer
TDA	Table of Distribution and Allowances
TDP	Tricare Dental Program
TDY	temporary duty
TE	technical escort
TEC	training extension course
TIG	time in grade
TIS	time in service
TLA	temporary lodging allowance
TLE	temporary lodging entitlement
TOE	Table of Organization and Equipment
TRADOC	U.S. Army Training and Doctrine Command
TSO	test scoring officer
TSP	Thrift Savings Program
UCMJ	Uniform Code of Military Justice
USAEREC	U.S. Army Enlisted Records and Evaluation Center
USAR	U.S. Army Reserve
USASMA	U.S. Army Sergeants Major Academy
USASSC	U.S. Army Soldier Support Center
USATC	U.S. Army Training Center
USMA	U.S. Military Academy
USMAPS	U.S. Military Academy Preparatory School
VA	Veterans Administration
VEAP	Veterans Educational Assistance Program
VHA	variable housing allowance
VSI	Voluntary Separation Incentive

Index

STACKPOLE BOOKS

Military Professional Reference Library

Professional Reading Library